True stories

Helen Garner was born in Geelong in 1942. Her award-winning books include novels, stories, screenplays and works of non-fiction. *The First Stone*, her first work of non-fiction, became an instant bestseller.

Books by Helen Garner

FICTION
Monkey Grip (1977)
Honour and Other People's Children (1980)
The Children's Bach (1984)
Postcards from Surfers (1985)
Cosmo Cosmolino (1992)
The Spare Room (2008)

NON-FICTION
The First Stone (1995)
True Stories (1996)
The Feel of Steel (2001)
Joe Cinque's Consolation (2004)

FILM SCRIPTS
The Last Days of Chez Nous (1992)
Two Friends (1992)

True stories

Helen Garner

TEXT PUBLISHING MELBOURNE AUSTRALIA

The Text Publishing Company Pty Ltd
Swann House
22 William Street Melbourne Victoria 3000
Copyright © Helen Garner 1996
www.textpublishing.com.au

First published 1996 by The Text Publishing Company
This edition published 2008

Printed and bound in Australia by Griffin Press
Design by Susan Miller
Typeset by Midland Typesetters Australia

National Library of Australia
Cataloguing-in-Publication data:

Garner, Helen, 1942–

True stories : selected non-fiction / Helen Garner.

ISBN: 9781921351846 (pbk.)

Short stories.
Australian essays—20th century.
Australia—Social life and customs.

823.3

'A Scrapbook, an Album' first appeared in *Sisters*, ed. Drusilla Modjeska, HarperCollins, 1993, and is reproduced with the permission of the publisher. 'Three Acres, More or Less' first appeared in *Gone Bush*, ed. Roger McDonald, Transworld, 1990. 'Cypresses and Spires' first appeared as the introduction to *The Last Days of Chez Nous & Two Friends*, McPhee Gribble, 1992. Other pieces in this book, some of them in a different form, first appeared in the *Age*, *Digger*, *Eureka Street*, *Independent Monthly*, *National Times*, *Scripsi*, *Sydney Morning Herald*, *Sydney Papers*, *Sunday Age*, *Time*, *Times on Sunday*, and *Vashti's Voice*.

Contents

To Michael Davie

The Art of the Dumb Question

MY WORKING LIFE has been a series of sideways slides, of adaptations rather than ambitions. It seems to me that I have never actually been trained to do anything—except by one person. When I was nine my parents took me out of Ocean Grove State School, on the south coast of Victoria, and put me into the fifth grade of The Hermitage, an Anglican girls' school in Geelong. There I had a ferocious teacher called Mrs Dunkley. She was thin, with short black hair and hands that trembled. She wore heels and a black suit with a nipped-in waist. She mocked me for my broad accent and my slowness at mental arithmetic. I was so frightened of her that I taught myself to count on my fingers under the desk at lightning speed (a skill I still possess). My mother says I used to scream out Mrs Dunkley's name in my sleep. But Mrs Dunkley also taught grammar and syntax. She drew up meticulous columns on the board and taught us parts of speech, parsing, analysis. She was the person who put into my head a delight in the way English works, and into my hands the tools for the job.

I left school and never saw her again. Naturally, she died. Ten years ago I had a dream about her. In the dream I walked along the verandah off which the Hermitage staffroom opened, and looked in through the glass of the big French doors. I saw Mrs Dunkley moving across the room as if under water—but instead of her grim black forties suit, she was dressed in a glorious soft buckskin jacket of many colours. As she moved, colour streamed off her into the air in ribbons and garlands, so that she drew along behind her a dense, smudged rainbow-trail. It's only now, writing this, that I make the connection between Mrs Dunkley and my favourite character in all fiction, namely the Fairy Blackstick in Thackeray's *The Rose and the Ring*, who came to the christening of a certain baby princess and said, over the cradle, 'As for this little lady, the best thing I can wish for her is a *little misfortune*.'

In the mid-sixties, when I crawled out of Melbourne University with a hangover and a very mediocre honours degree in English and French, any dingbat with letters after her name could get a job as a high school teacher. You didn't even need a Dip. Ed., they were so desperate. One summer morning I bowled up to the Education Department in Treasury Place and presented my meagre qualifications to the lady on the front desk. She gave them a cursory glance, and pointed to a large map of Victoria which hung on the wall behind her. 'What do you want?' she said wearily, 'Werribee or Wycheproof?' All I knew about Wycheproof, in north-western Victoria, was that the railway line ran down the middle of the main street. I chose Werribee, thus forfeiting my chance to live and work in the Mallee, the region my father comes from.

My enjoyable but less than brilliant career in teaching lasted, on and off, for about seven years, and ended in ignominy, as one of the stories in this book relates. To this day chalkies of both sexes approach me with a grin in public places and say, 'You owe me a day's pay. I went out on strike for you in 1973.' It was a great stir, and I'm happy about the support but, after wasting a lot of perfectly good time in regret and martyrdom, I was obliged to acknowledge that getting the sack was the best thing that could have happened to me. It forced me to start writing for a living.

I worked for—or, more correctly, I 'was part of the collective that produced'—the counter-culture magazine the *Digger* for a couple of years in the early seventies. Then I caught hepatitis.

I went home and got into bed and stayed there, expertly cared for by my housemates, for weeks. I read *War and Peace*. Somebody brought me the stories of the Russian writer Isaac Babel. When I read, in Lionel Trilling's introduction, that Babel's work had got him offside with the Soviet authorities because 'it hinted that one might live in doubt, that one might live by means of a question', I put down the book and howled.

Maybe it was just the gloom that goes with hepatitis—but more likely it was because till that moment I had never admitted to myself how ill at ease I was, writing for a paper like the *Digger*. (Only one story I wrote for it has made it into this collection.) Things I wrote then felt false to me. I was bluffing. I secretly knew myself to be hopelessly bourgeois.

I was also greatly taken by Babel's statement that 'there is no iron that can enter the human heart with such stupefying effect as a full stop placed at exactly the right point'. This of course was Mrs Dunkley's territory, though I failed to realise it at the time, and though she would not have expressed herself so stylishly. Years later I was reminded that I ought to keep a lid on my passion for punctuation when I bragged to my friend Tim Winton that I had just written 'a two-hundred-word paragraph consisting of a single syntactically perfect sentence'. He scorched me with a surfer's stare and said, 'I couldn't care *less* about that sort of shit.'

When I got over the hep, I rode my bike down to Silver Top in Rathdowne Street and applied for a taxi licence. But before I could do the test, a communist friend pointed out to me the existence of the Supporting Mother's Benefit and my eligibility for it, as a separated mother of a small child. I applied for one of these instead, and got it. I still regret that I never drove a taxi.

This was the period now loosely referred to as 'the seventies'. *The group* was paramount. In certain circles a person could offend by being 'too articulate'. But along with all the absorbing collective stuff—dancing and love affairs and communal house-holds and consciousness-raising groups and women's liberation newspapers and Pram Factory shows and demos and dropping acid and mucking around all summer at the Fitzroy Baths with the kids—I got a fair bit of solitary reading done. At government expense, and don't think I'm not grateful, I launched into Proust, lying on my bed all day by the open window with my head propped on two big pillows and one small hard one, the weighty volume resting upright on my chest.

One day, struggling with a Shakespeare sonnet, I got bogged down in its syntax, and took it across the hall to a bass player who had a science degree he wasn't using. He laid his guitar on the bed and said, 'OK. Let's see if we can work it out.' We dismantled the sonnet and pieced it back together. The pleasure of this process was so intense as to be almost excruciating: it felt more illicit than sex. Neither of us ever mentioned it again. More typical of my chosen life at the time was the response I got from a boyfriend when he was sick in bed and, thinking to alleviate his boredom (or my own, now I come to think of it), I said to him, 'Hey—how about we discuss the nature of good and evil?'

'Steady on, Hel!' he said, shrinking back against the pillows.

So I opened my sewing box and mended his shirt instead, while he watched me fondly and played a little tune on his harmonica. In my diary I wrote a song. It went like this.

> My charming boy's got a rip in his jacket
> I'd take out my needle and thread and attack it
> If I wasn't hip to this particular racket…

In those days there weren't many rackets I was hip to, for all the talk. I couldn't even spot my own.

I don't remember ever *planning* to write a novel. There's nothing like having studied literature at university to make you despise your own timid attempts to tell a story on paper—or even to describe people and houses, or write down dialogue. For years you turn on yourself the blowtorch of your tertiary critical training. You die of shame at the thought of showing anyone what you've written. Somebody somewhere says, though, that 'the urge *to preserve* is the basis of all art'. Unaware of this thought, you keep a diary. You keep it not only because it gratifies your urge to sling words around every day with impunity, but because without it you will lose your life: its detail will leak away into the sand and be gone forever.

Then one day it occurs to you that you can see a *shape* to the diary, a curious sort of bulge or curve in the order of events. You try to ignore this, but it keeps coming to mind. One morning you put the Spirex exercise books in a plastic bag and hop on your bike. You dink your daughter to school and, instead of turning round and going home, where a band will later be practising in the front room and the egg cartons tacked to the wall will fail to muffle the roar of the speakers, you pedal on through Carlton and down to the domed Reading Room of the State Library in the city. You sit down under one of those green-shaded lamps, and turn back to the day in the diary where you think you can see a possible starting-point: an end of wool poking out of the tangled skein. 'Without hope and without despair,' as Isak Dinesen says, you begin.

At first you simply transcribe. Then you cut out the boring bits and try to make leaps and leave gaps. Then you start to trim and sharpen the dialogue. Soon you find you are enjoying yourself. You can't wait to get there each morning. You make yourself stop at one o'clock and ride home, because if you do more than three hours at a stretch you're scared you'll have a heart attack from the excitement. It takes just over a year. Then you retire to your bedroom and you type it. The thunder of your second-hand Olivetti drowns out the band. For the first time in your life you don't care if you've got a boyfriend or not. You know nothing about lay-out, and produce a horrible-looking manuscript on cheap quarto paper, single-spaced, with mingy margins. But it's *fat*. It's got a title. Your name is on the front of it. *You wrote it*. So this is what it's all been for. What is it, though? Have you got the gall to call it a novel?

A year later, *Monkey Grip* was in the shops. But between the day I signed the contract and the day the book appeared, I circulated the manuscript round the households, in an attempt at candour, since the book's dozen characters were all versions of actual people. And here's the weird bit. Not a single one complained. I'm not saying they all *liked* it. But no one objected. The only person who went out of his way to contact me with a comment on his (very small) appearance in the book was a roadie who phoned me one afternoon, excited and happy, to thank me for putting him in. 'It's one little bit of my life,' he said, 'that hasn't been lost.'

Becoming self-consciously 'a writer' after the surprise success of *Monkey Grip*, I tried to apply what I thought of as 'fictional techniques' to the mess of my experience. I got lost in the attempt and, like many writers, produced a second book which was poorer in spirit than its artless predecessor. The more I tried to disguise real people as 'characters', the more furious they got with me for writing about them at all. This second book of fiction, *Honour & Other People's Children*, in its clumsy and premature attempts to shape painful experience into 'stories', caused wounds in certain people which have not healed.

The question of writers' 'use' of 'real' events and people in their books is not new. It has always caused vexation and it always will. It's the nature of a writer to exhibit what Nadine Gordimer calls 'a monstrous detachment'. Writers, she says in the introduction to her stories, have 'powers of observation heightened beyond the normal...The tension between standing apart and being fully involved: that is what makes a writer'.

I used to think that if I examined my motivation as ruthlessly as I could, I would be able to do better than just write fiction which was a 'settling of accounts' with people. I thought I'd be ethically in the clear as long as I wrote 'in good faith'—that is, if I laid myself on the line as well, applied to myself the same degree of analysis and revelation that I did to the other people concerned. I still happen to think this attitude is legitimate, as far as it goes—but it's based on an assumption of consciousness in the novelist which is over-optimistic to the point of being grandiose.

I realise, specially since I published *Cosmo Cosmolino*, in 1992, that in fiction, when you get down into the muck of life—marriage and sex and God and death and old, old friendships—you are working blind. You think you're seeing what you're doing, but you're seeing only darkly. You may start from the 'real'—but in fiction you soon forget which bits are 'true' and which bits you made up. You get so engaged with the technical problems of making a story work that the connection between its characters and what exists outside the book becomes less and less visible to you, and of less and less interest. It can be years before you see with real clarity (if you ever do) what urges you were gripped by when you were writing that book. Often, what you thought you had a handle on turns out to have had a handle on *you*.

In non-fiction you don't have the freedom—ethical, aesthetic, or temporal—to go in that deep. Non-fiction isn't easier than fiction, but for the most part it's broader and shallower. In non-fiction, the writer's contract with the reader is different. Someone reading a novel wants you to create a new world, parallel perhaps to the 'real' one, in which the reader can immerse himself for the duration. But a reader of non-fiction counts on you to remain faithful to the same 'real' world that both reader and writer physically inhabit. As a non-fiction writer you have, as well, an implicit contract with your material and with the people you are writing about: you have to figure out an honourable balance between tact and honesty. You are accountable for the pain you can cause through misrepresentation: you have a responsibility to the 'facts' as you can discover them, and an obligation to make it clear when you have *not* been able to discover them. Fiction's links with the 'real' are more complex and tenuous. But they can still get a writer into all sorts of personal trouble. I didn't know this in 1980 when *Honour* got me into hot water, but I notice now how soon afterwards it was that I started busily doing journalism—really throwing myself into it. It may have been firstly to earn a living—but it was surely also for the relief: instead of feeling an irksome obligation to make things up, in journalism I was not allowed to.

When I hunted out the stories that make up this book, I was amazed at the sheer quantity of non-fiction I've written over the last twenty-five years. You forget how hard you have to work, to make a freelance living. Also, there's a kind of snobbery that makes you forget everything you've done except the books. They stand up in the landscape behind you, visible at a distance and clearly marked with dates, while the non-fiction and the journalism lie flat, forming a dense, prickly undergrowth. All right—I accept that theatre and film reviews, though they put food on the table for years, don't belong between covers—but how could I have forgotten writing about Mr Tiarapu? The marmalade display at the Royal Melbourne Show? The purchase of the violet jacket? Deadlines give you time for only a minimal amount of polish and perfecting. Like the doctors of the Penrith story in this book, you have to keep moving—on, on, on.

When I first started publishing regular feature articles, a newspaper man came up to me at a party and said genially, 'I like your journalism, Helen—but you should write more. You should write *faster*.' A publisher's editor standing nearby overheard this. I saw his mouth drop open. The journalist moved on and the editor said to me in a voice faint with horror, 'That was *awful*. It was like hearing the *devil* talking.'

But in the early eighties the *Age* had a wonderful editor, an Englishman called Michael Davie. He had a black-and-white photo of Samuel Beckett pinned to his office wall. I respected his judgement, loved his dry, elegant sparkle, and was always just a little bit scared of him. When I did my first feature for him, he sent me a bottle of champagne. He offered me *a retainer*. He was funny and sophisticated and he thought writing mattered. He didn't stay long in Australia, but he was the first editor I worked for who lent dignity to the job of writing features for a daily newspaper.

After he went back to London, I made an appointment with his successor, for I was labouring under the delusion that, since I was in a very minor way on his payroll, I ought out of courtesy to present myself in person. The new editor lost no time in letting me know that he was not in the business of 'massaging writers' egos'. *Crrrrunch*. Things were back to normal. Thus ended my formal relationship with the *Age*.

It is very squashing to come to feature journalism from a publishing house, where one's work is treated with respect. These days, with newspapers and magazines, I am crabby enough to demand and get proofs, but back then I was still at the mercy of the sub-editors and their brutally applied house style. I have never to my knowledge actually seen a sub, but their harsh pencils (or whatever they use) have punctured many a balloon of my modest rhetoric. I once wrote a piece for the *Age* in which I rhapsodised about looking out the window of an interviewee's kitchen in an outer suburb and seeing 'miles and miles of golden grass'. This appeared on Saturday morning as 'kilometres and kilometres of golden grass'.

Further into the eighties I worked for the *National Times* and the *Times on Sunday*, which were based in Sydney. Sunday became the worst day of the week. Their typesetters were slaphappy and their subs not merely deflating—they delighted to slash and burn. Between them they could mangle the meaning out of the simplest sentence. 'Operatic' became 'operative'. 'Hedonistic' turned into 'pessimistic', 'rhetorical' into 'theoretical'. A friend of mine who also wrote for them phoned me one Sunday morning. 'Have you seen what they've done to my story?' he said in a choking voice. 'I've just smashed the toaster with a hammer.'

Journalism is a tonic for narcissists like me. It gets you out of the house—literally, but also in the sense that it blasts you out of your immediate personal situation and into direct contact with strangers. The more of it I try to write, the deeper grows my respect for the great interviewers. I used to think a lot of Joan Didion, but when I reread *Slouching towards Bethlehem*, lately, I found it rigid with mannerisms, with *style*. I'm thinking rather of writers like Janet Malcolm (*The Silent Woman*, most recently), the Englishman Tony Parker (*Life after Life*, interviews with twelve murderers), Norman Mailer of *The Executioner's Song*—and the French documentary maker Claude Lanzmann (*Shoah, Tsahal*).

Lanzmann has a humility before his material which is exemplary and rare. He never shirt-fronts, or tries to get people on the back foot—but he is persistent, gently stubborn. He is the king of the apparently dumb question, the simple, unaggressive gambit that releases a flow of talk from a person not accustomed to self-expression. 'Do you like tonks?' he says sweetly in his comical accent, to a member of an elite Israeli tank corps. A Jew, he picks up a flicker of stifled emotion in an old Nazi who is blankly justifying his role in the death camps; Lanzmann has the quiet nerve to ask, 'Why are you sad?' He is prepared to leave the surface of his work porous. There is no one in the world less eager than he is to have the last word. I admire him more than I can say.

Interviewing is not what people imagine. Before you try

it, you think it must be like pulling teeth. You approach each interview fearing that you will not get enough. But what you learn is that you must humble yourself before the other. You have to let go of your anxious desire to control and direct the encounter. You have to live for a while in the uncertainty of not knowing where it's heading. You don't lead. You learn to follow. And then you are amazed at what people are prepared to tell you.

People will always tell you more than you need to know and more than they want you to know. This is not only because you are alert to their body language as well as their speech. I think it's because most ordinary people can't really believe that anyone else is interested in them. In your average casual conversation, the listener is only just restraining himself from butting in with 'Well, I—'. As an interviewer you have to discipline your narcissism. You have to train yourself to shut up about what *you* did and saw and felt. You learn by practice to listen properly and genuinely, to follow with respect the wandering path of the other's thoughts. After a while this stops being an effort. You notice that your concentration span is getting longer—longer than you ever thought it could become. Fewer and fewer things bore you. Curiosity is a muscle. Patience is a muscle. What begins as a necessary exercise gradually becomes natural. And then immense landscapes open out in front of you. A woman who spoke to me when I was researching the Penrith story in this book kept cutting herself off mid-sentence and saying, 'But this must be boring.' After the fifth time she said this, I heard myself say—*and mean*—words that I had never dreamt would pass my lips: 'Listen. I am one of the least boreable people you are ever likely to meet.'

A risk is that you over-identify with your subject. Often it can take days to disentangle yourself. Sometimes, years later, you are still waking up at three in the morning in a sweat over someone else's troubles. Other strange processes can intrude.

Once, months after I'd done a long interview with a woman I'll call X, I arranged to meet her in a cafe so she could check her quotes. I walked in on time. She wasn't there. There was only a total stranger at a table against the wall. I hesitated at the door. The stranger waved to me. I stared at her. 'Helen,' she said, puzzled, 'it's me—X.'

I was mortified. I realised I had completely transformed her appearance as I wrote up our conversation. When she checked the quotes and found them accurate I was giddy with relief. Perhaps what's really odd is that this so rarely happens. Clearly it's the beginning of the process of creating a *character*—a habit that slithers over the border from fiction, the land where you are always disguising people and trying to cover your tracks.

Writing fiction is lonelier than doing journalism. Journalism feeds your extraversion, while a novel demands years on your own in a room with the door shut. When in 1992 I hung out for three days with notebook and pencil at the city morgue, I was strangely happy. I felt sociable, accepted, content. I never wanted to go home. I mentioned to one of my sisters how much I was enjoying turning up at the lab on the dot of nine each morning, and exchanging casual greetings with the technicians. 'Hi, Helen!' they'd say, glancing up from their corpses. 'Hi, Jodie! Hi, Kevin!' I'd answer. My sister regarded me for a moment with narrow eyes. 'What *you* need,' she said dryly, 'is a *job*.'

A job! I haven't had what you could call a job for over twenty years. I remember how enviously, in Paris in 1978, I witnessed one morning through the *guichet* the astonishing spectacle of bank employees arriving at work and doing a leisurely tour of the office to *shake hands* with every single one of their colleagues. I remember my first job, at Griffiths' bookshop in Geelong in the early sixties, when Australians still had manners, how one greeted the two brothers who owned the shop: 'Morning, Mr Jack, morning, Mr Bob'; and how at half past five when the working day was done we all said to each other, seriously, 'Goodnight'. I remember a kind old bloke called Mr Winstanley who, if some scallywag neglected to return his formal greeting, would turn away murmuring ironically, '*Silence was the stern reply.*'

Most poignantly of all, though, when I get fed up with working alone, I remember Victorian high school staffrooms of the sixties and seventies: the rigid hierarchy with its irritations, but also the chiacking, the squabbles, the timely advice from some old stager with a fag drooping off his lip. The awful decorated tea mugs, the solemnity of a new fiancée describing her 'sheets and towels in autumn tonings'. The rough teasing, the flirting, the ping-pong games, the laboured jokes about longing for Friday and whether one was 'happy in the service'. The sudden hush when the principal walked into the room. The groans at the sound of the bell, the quoting of what the kids had said, their howlers; the seething about the unfair timetable. And the line of silent, companionable admirers, along the top-floor windows, watching the Greek and Italian boys playing soccer, down in the rainy yard.

I used to have a fantasy (if I ever thought of the future at all) that one day I would be able to live on fiction. It was only a matter of time, I thought. Meanwhile, journalism would feed me and my daughter, and fill the gaps—but then I found, and am still finding, how well journalism suits me. 'Ideas' for non-fiction come flapping over the horizon from editors, or seeping out of the ground right under my feet. One will always present itself to save me, just as I'm about to sit down before the abyss of thinking about a novel. There is always some public ritual I'd like to gape at, a place I long to loiter in (a crematorium, a hospital) to which the only passport is a reporter's notebook—and where I might stumble on material whose meaning journalism will not exhaust.

But there is also the other sort of notebook, the one where

you scribble down the tiny things that sprout persistently in the cracks between non-fiction stories. I file them under 'Notes: aimless'.

the proximity of rivers
cicadas: columns of sound
a man called Terry Treasure
their feeble personalities can make no impression on the
*   impassive house*
she relishes obstructions
the cheerful orphan
'black with sin as I am'—Chekhov
a man trying to stuff a huge, dun-coloured eiderdown into a
*   locker at Spencer Street station*
landscape of childhood: worn out from being looked at
champions practising
the gift of tears
'sparkling jewels and opulent mantles'
the language of furniture
Melbourne girls with their great brown crinkly capes of hair

I open the folder and see with a secret thrill these strange notations. Why did I keep them? What did I plan to do with these lost things? They have detached themselves long ago from their origins in 'reality', and floated free. But I recognise them—I know what they're for. They are the hints and tremors of fiction, and that is where, one day, I will make the place where they belong.

PROLOGUE

Mr Tiarapu

Mr Tiarapu

ONE SUMMÉR I went to Sydney to visit my friend in hospital. He had just had a brain tumour removed and was lying, on a very blustery day, in a ward with flapping blinds and no air-conditioning. My friend was recovering well, considering. He was quite shaven, and half his head was bandaged.

When I arrived he was propped against his pillows, eating oysters out of a flat grey cardboard box. He offered me one and said, 'Pity you didn't arrive ten minutes earlier. Because do you know who gave me these oysters? Patrick White. I was hoping you'd arrive before he left; but another friend of mine came instead, and when I introduced them she looked terribly excited and said, "Not *the* Patrick White?" and he said, "No. *A* Patrick White".'

We ate the oysters. When we had finished them, my friend said, 'But I would like to introduce you to the bloke in the next bed. Because he's from Tahiti, and lives in Noumea, and he can't speak English—perhaps you could talk French with him.' He sat up with his bandaged head and called to the man, who appeared to be asleep. 'Eh, M'sieu.'

The man turned his body slowly towards us. He was a very tall man with a big head, perhaps forty-five years old, and evidently in pain: his brown islander skin was greyish and his cheeks were hollow. My friend, in his carefully enunciated fourth-form French, explained that I was someone who spoke French better than he did. The Tahitian put out his hand and took hold of mine.

'*Enchanté, madame,*' he said.

We exchanged courtesies and platitudes about our experiences among the French.

'*Les Français sont des racistes, des hypocrites,*' he said. 'They speak to you politely, then they massacre you behind your back.'

He told me that he lived in Noumea, and that he had a wife and six children at home. He did not know what the matter was with him, except that he was unable to walk, and had not been able to for some months. He said that he had been taken to hospital in Noumea for this unexplained weakness of the legs, and that suddenly hospital officials had told him he was to be sent to Sydney 'to have some tests done'. Since his arrival at the Royal Prince Alfred Hospital, he had not understood anything that had happened to him, nor anything that had been said to him, until he had been moved into the bed beside my friend with the opened head. 'Your friend,' he said, looking earnestly at me, 'is a very very nice person.'

I asked him if he would like me to stay till the doctors came, and try to interpret for him. He said he would like this very much, but that I was not to put myself out if I had something else to do. He said that he had not been given time, in Noumea, to see his wife and children before they had bundled him on to the plane. He said that he would like to write to his wife to tell her that he was all right and where he was and that he was waiting for tests to be done. He said he had not been able to write before, because he had not been able to ask for paper.

I asked a nurse for paper and a pad was procured, also an envelope and a biro. He sat up as far as he could and leaned on a magazine and wrote, in a large formal hand, a long letter. While he wrote, I talked with my friend. It was very hot indeed and, because there was a nurses' strike on, the nurses who wanted to strike but who did not wish to leave their seriously ill patients unattended were working dressed in ordinary street clothes instead of uniforms. This gave them a less brisk, less intimidating appearance, but it did not help the Tahitian man with his language problem. One of the nurses said to me, 'They arrive at the hospital from Noumea in plane loads.'

I asked when the doctors would be coming round, and the nurse said they would be there any minute. The man, whose name was Mr Tiarapu, finished his letter and addressed the envelope and stuck it down and then lay there with it against his chest, as if not sure what to do next. He looked from side to side.

I said, 'Would you like me to take it downstairs and post it for you?'

He said he would like that, if it were not too much trouble.

Two doctors entered the ward. They were very young men, younger than I was, and one of them was Australian and the other was Thai. They came to the end of Mr Tiarapu's bed shyly, as if they and not I were visiting. They looked at the chart attached to the foot of the bed.

I said, 'I can speak French, and wondered if I could explain to Mr Tiarapu what is the matter with him, because he doesn't know.'

The doctors looked at each other like two schoolboys, each waiting for the other to speak. The Thai said, 'Well, we are going to do some more tests.'

I said, 'Can you perhaps tell him more than that, because he must be very anxious, not knowing what is the matter with him.'

The Australian said, 'Does he want to ask us any questions in particular that you could translate?'

I translated this for Mr Tiarapu who was lying with his big head held up in a strained position, as if trying to understand by sheer effort of will.

He said, 'I would like to know if I will be able to walk again. It is my legs, it is awful, not to be able to walk. Will you ask the doctors why I can't walk, and whether they can do anything about it?'

The doctors, speaking in duo, said that there was a blockage in the spine somewhere, and that the tests they would do were to determine the possibilities of a cure. 'If it is only a blockage,' said one of them, looking slightly helpless, 'tell him he will be able to walk again if he does the exercises we will give him. If he does the exercises, he can only improve, if all he has is a blockage.'

I translated this. Mr Tiarapu looked much less anxious. He did not seem to want to make further inquiries, and the doctors said they would come back at a certain time the next day and that they would appreciate it if I could be there to interpret again. I said I would be there.

Mr Tiarapu took my hand and thanked me. He looked at me in a way that made me feel very bad, and sad, as if I were a kind of lifeline. I would have liked to kiss his cheek, but I was afraid of overstepping some line of protocol that might exist between white and black, or well and ill.

I said goodbye to my friend, and to Mr Tiarapu, and picked up the cardboard box with the oyster shells in it and dropped it in the rubbish bin on my way out of the ward. I took Mr Tiarapu's letter across the road in the gritty wind and into the post office, and got them to put the right stamps on it, and posted it.

Next morning, I returned to the hospital. The weather had not broken. When I walked into the ward I saw that Mr Tiarapu's appearance had undergone a shocking change. His face was no longer brown at all; the colour had left it, his cheeks had sunk right in, and he seemed to find it difficult to open his eyes. But he saw me and took my hand and held it.

I said, 'You look tired. Didn't you sleep well?' I did not know whether to call him *vous* or *tu* so I said *vous*.

'Not very,' he said. 'I was thinking of my wife, and I was worried.'

Before the doctors came on their round, the door at the end of the ward burst open and two cheerful nurses entered. They approached Mr Tiarapu's bed and seized his chart. 'Yes, this is the one,' said one of the nurses. She directed a powerful, jolly smile right into Mr Tiarapu's face. 'We're moving you today!' she announced. 'Different ward!' She grabbed a corner of Mr Tiarapu's blue cotton blanket.

Mr Tiarapu's face was grey now with fear.

I said, 'He doesn't understand what you are saying. He doesn't understand any English at all.'

'Oh,' said the nurse, stepping back.

At this moment the two doctors came into the ward. They said good morning to all concerned. Mr Tiarapu gazed from my face to theirs, waiting.

'Can you explain to him why he is being moved?' I said. 'Because he has only just got used to being here and talking to the bloke in the next bed.'

The doctors looked at each other. One of them said, after a short pause, 'We have to move him to another ward to do tests.'

I translated to Mr Tiarapu that he was going to another ward in order to have more tests. This information did not cause the look on his face to alter.

'Which ward?' I asked the doctors.

'Oncology,' said one of them, and he looked me right in the eyes with an expression at once blank and challenging. He said oncology. He did not say cancer. And I was not absolutely certain, not one hundred percent certain, that oncology did mean cancer. And I couldn't ask because Mr Tiarapu was holding my hand and staring at me and the doctors with his grey face, and the French word for cancer is so similar to the

English that it would have been impossible to disguise it.

'Do you want me to explain what you mean?' I said to the doctors.

They looked embarrassed, moved their feet on the spongy lino, and glanced at each other. 'If you like,' said one of them.

'But do you think I *should?*' I said.

They both shrugged, not because they didn't care but because they were very young, and because they probably didn't know any more than I did whether he was going to live or die. The longer we talked and gestured like this, without my translating anything, the clearer it became to Mr Tiarapu that there was something someone didn't want him to know. The responsibility for the transmission of information had been shifted squarely on to me, and I was not adequate.

I said to Mr Tiarapu, 'They are moving you to a different ward because they have to do the tests, and they're still not sure what is wrong with you, and they can't do the tests here.'

Mr Tiarapu nodded, and lay back down.

I said to the doctors, 'Don't you have interpreters here? Because I have to go back to Melbourne tonight. I can't stay any longer.'

'Oh, yes, I think so,' said one of the doctors. 'There's supposed to be a woman somewhere round, but she's renowned for her lack of tact.'

The nurses got Mr Tiarapu ready for the move. I stood between his bed and that of my friend, who had been watching this without speaking. When Mr Tiarapu was on the trolley and it was time to go, he took my hand again and said, 'You have been very, very kind to me. I will always remember your kindness.'

My friend also said goodbye, and Mr Tiarapu was wheeled away.

1980

PART ONE

A Scrapbook, an Album

The Schoolteacher

IT'S HAPPENED TO me half a dozen times, lately. I'm coming home through the Edinburgh Gardens, or along Brunswick Street at dusk, and I see them a block in front of me, ambling along, shoving each other, heading towards me, their legs a moving thicket—heavy kids, eight of them, maybe ten. I keep walking, but I keep my eyes on them, and my feet wait for the sign to take off.

The kids are not sharpies. They are Greeks and Italians, all boys, all wearing green or maroon cardigans with a double black stripe round the chest, Levis or Wranglers that fit just right, showing a bit of sock and reddish shoes with big heels. I move across to the outside of the footpath to let them pass without a confrontation. They spread out a little, taking the courtesy as a right. They're close enough now in the almost-dark for me to see their faces. And it's all right, because the front one is Chris from Fitzroy High and he says, 'Hello, miss!' and the others are kids who have grinned and nodded at me a hundred times in the yard at school.

I'd already been teaching at Melbourne's Fitzroy High for a year when, in 1972, I moved into a house right opposite the school. Some teachers, the kind who think if the kids know your first name they've got something on you, told me I would find things difficult if I didn't separate my work from the rest of my life. It was the only house I could find. But I've never been sorry.

The evening I moved in, I was standing at the front gate wondering if I was too lazy to clean up the yard. Two boys from my old second-form class strolled past and stopped for a talk. Jim, a wiry, clever boy considered by most teachers to be lazy, was known as the King, and treated respectfully by people with social acumen. Spiro was one of those boys who are men at fifteen. There were twelve children in his family. I had seen him in the park with some of the smaller children: he was perfectly at ease with them, unabashed to be holding a child in his arms. He had a trick of looking at you through half-closed eyes, with his head tilted back. His courtesy was instinctive. He rarely came to school, and ignored the uniform rule, so was disliked by the administration, but he could not be fazed. Teachers' tirades simply flowed around him.

'You movin' in here, miss?' asked Jim.

'Yes.'

'Why, miss? It's a dump.'

I looked at the house. Its paint was peeling, there were holes in the roof, the garden was full of weeds. It *was* a dump, if you lived in one of those scrubbed shining cottages in Woodhead Street, kept that way by women in black scarves who speak no English and rest in the evenings on chairs on the verandahs, impassively surveying the street.

'Well…I like it, I guess,' I replied, feeling a little apologetic. We stood in companionable silence in the evening air. Jim whistled calmly through his teeth. Spiro examined the neglected garden.

'What are you gonna plant, miss?'

'Flowers, and some trees.'

'*Flowers?* Miss, you don't need flowers. You need tomatoes, and lettuces and *beans*.'

We considered this advice. They prepared to stroll on.

'One thing you can be sure of, miss,' said Jim with his ironic, cordial smile. 'Nothing will be stolen from your house.'

We said goodnight. The vegetables were never planted, but nor was anything ever stolen.

I had taught migrants before, but Fitzroy High is one of those legendary inner-suburban schools which can no longer be properly described as Australian. In none of the classes I took were there more than four kids with Australian names. A blond head was a surprise. The administration battled to assimilate these kids into a recognisable mould. In a hundred subtle ways they were defeated. The first official handout of the year included an instruction to teachers about pumpkin seeds. We were told it was a Mediterranean custom to eat them, and that they were not permitted in the school. The reason given was that the shells made a mess. As far as I could see they were no more messy than Cheezels.

Most of the girls had pierced ears and had worn gold earrings since they were babies. The line was that plain gold sleepers were the only ear decorations allowed. At the time when it was fashionable to wear a zillion coloured plastic bangles up your arm, teachers strove hopelessly to prevent this display of gaiety. The girls went on wearing them, and pulled their sleeves down when they saw a senior mistress coming. One of the older women teachers whispered to a hushed staff meeting that girls who were virgins did not wear the bangles: the number of bangles a girl wore indicated exactly how far from virginity she was. 'And after all,' the teacher added, 'one of the things we must teach them is *good taste*.'

There were weekly segregated assemblies. I don't know what they told the boys, but at one girls' assembly I actually heard the senior mistress say, 'As *girls* we must be modest, quiet, hardworking and well-groomed at all times.' One woman teacher had a habit of saying, 'Girls, if you stood up straight and got your hair out of your eyes, you could really make something of yourselves.'

What astonished me, the product of a provincial girls' school, was the stubbornness of the kids' resistance to these rules. They didn't organise or protest. They defied. If the pressure got too much for them, they stayed away. And yet they hated to be suspended. One boy was suspended for a week, and every day I'd see him leaning against my front fence, staring wistfully at the school where his mates were tight-roping their way dangerously through the day.

In the three other schools I'd taught at, I'd been an authoritarian, a 'good disciplinarian'. It wasn't only political or educational thinking that changed my attitude at Fitzroy High. It was the kids themselves. I suppose I fell in love with the whole nine hundred of them. In other schools, I'd known kids who were 'trouble-makers' or 'over-achievers', or 'responsible' or 'anti-social'. But somehow the kids at Fitzroy cut right through those categories.

To begin with, they made me *laugh*. I can't remember ever knowing such exuberant, merry kids. Every class had more than its share of natural clowns. The plays they invented were full of hilarious delight. In a second-form class I had for a year, two Italian boys called Claudio and Joseph used to present weekly plays so excruciatingly funny that we lay across the desks aching and wiping our eyes. The plays were always about a waiter and a diner in a restaurant—an ancient comic relationship. A kid called Ilya wrote wonderful, magical stories; he could write fairy tales his grandparents had told him in Yugoslavia, or stories about going to a soccer match and not realising till he stood up at the end that he'd been sitting on a piece of chewing gum. Lemonia could break your heart with a story about a lost fountain pen, and Dora with an account of her dreams. Their English may have been rocky, but there was a pure, delicate humour lying bone-deep in them that nothing could corrupt.

Not only did they make me laugh—they looked out for me, came to see me at my house, played with my daughter, shared their food with me, brought me their family photos and pieces of wedding cake. They took care to include me in jokes and games. Looking back on it now, I don't know for sure which came first—my decision to make my classroom as free as I could, or their open friendliness to me.

The second year I was there, somehow we started spending as much time out of the school as in. In the warm weather we went to the baths and the park. Having no money, we walked everywhere, in great squads: to the museum, to Melbourne University, the Fitzroy Gardens, along the Merri Creek, to the Carlton theatre, the cemetery, St Patrick's Cathedral.

They combined a sophisticated ability to handle their immediate area with astonishing ignorance of how this area fitted into the city as a whole. From our upstairs classroom most form one and two kids weren't sure in which direction the city lay. Some had never been closer to the city than Johnston Street, the boundary of their suburb but barely a kilometre from Bourke Street. On the other hand a few (boys, of course) sold papers in the city and brought back tales of drunks, working for bosses, swimming at the newsboys' club. At the end of one school year we took a day trip to a beach on the Mornington Peninsula, an hour's drive to the south-east of Melbourne. Most of them had never heard of it. It seemed like the end of the earth to them.

The more time I spent with them, the clearer it became that I was on their side of the fence. I still don't understand how it happened. I got certain insights when the senior mistress told me to stop wearing jeans to school (I did for a while, then changed my mind). On our long walks, and times in the park and at the baths, I got to know the kids pretty well. If a kid's rubbing sunburn oil on your back, or if you're putting a bandaid on her blister, the talk is likely to be frank. Some of them started to call me Helen, but old habits die hard, and they'd address me like this: 'Helen, I'm going down for the lunches, miss.' A couple of times I was even called 'Mum' (this happens to a lot of teachers)—always by boys, for some reason. They were always mortified by this slip.

On the long walks they worked hard at teaching me to read the Greek signs in Smith Street. The Clifton Hill kids took me to meet their sixth-grade teacher when we walked past their old school. We got good at ignoring each other's roles and, when it was appropriate, ignoring each other. They were very easy to be with. Once we spent an afternoon mucking round down the Merri Creek. One of the boys, an Australian called Johnny, stayed with me for the whole afternoon. We talked pleasantly about this and that as we scrambled along the creek, then agreed it was easier to stroll along the level grass at the top than to battle through the rocks and weeds with the others.

'Anyway,' remarked Johnny, 'I'm too fat for all this exercise.'

'And I'm too lazy,' I said.

'So am I. Or...no, I'm not exactly *lazy*. I just can't be bothered.'

One day we walked up to Nicholson Street to the monumental mason. I'd told them how dangerous the workshop was if they weren't extra careful: great blocks of marble swinging overhead or propped casually against each other, an immense thundering and sawing in the air, dust everywhere. Like all dangerous places, it was terrifically attractive. We got permission to go in, and the workers were explaining to the kids what they were doing, when the dusty air was rent by a frightful scream. Someone had bumped against a block of marble and knocked it on to the foot of Angelo, a chubby Greek boy. He shrieked with pain and fear. Two men lifted the marble and got his shoes off. His foot inflated instantly like a pink balloon. I got the others outside. Their faces were white. Angelo had stopped screaming, and was sobbing quietly. I put him and two of his friends into a taxi, and the rest of us walked back to school, gloomy and frightened. What worried them most was what would happen to me. 'It wasn't your fault, miss, it wasn't your fault!' they kept saying.

Back at school we found that Angelo and his friends had

taken nearly as long as we had to get back, because the taxi driver had driven round and round the Edinburgh Gardens, pretending he couldn't understand their directions. 'Miss we could even *see* the school, but he kept going round and round!' They were all nearly crying. We took Angelo to the office and called his mother who worked in a factory in South Melbourne. By the time she got there, Angelo was starting to enjoy himself, resplendently swollen outside the principal's office. His mother and I took him to the doctor to get an X-ray. We spent three hours in the waiting room, and she spent twelve dollars on the bill. Nothing was broken.

Next day the kids wrote the story of Angelo's terrible accident. Their hearts were hard and they turned it into comedy.

'"It 'erts! It 'erts!" shouted Angelo, tearing out his hair,' began Ronnie's unsympathetic version. 'In fact, he made such a song and dance about it that we had to go back to school.' When Angelo came back a few days later wearing a carpet slipper, he read the stories and knew he was a hero.

Every week I asked them to write what we called the weekly report. It was to be about anything they liked—something they'd done, thought, heard or read, or seen on TV. I promised that this report would be confidential. After a while, a lot of the kids were writing me what amounted to letters. Many of them even started, 'Dear miss.' They wrote about new cars, school rumours, love affairs, market prices, lost keys, relatives arriving from Europe, tears shed at airports, family fights. ('From 1860 comes this head you got,' one kid reported having said to his mother.) At first some of things they wrote scared me a bit, because I had to make up my mind finally which side of the fence I *was* on. I got to know who was wagging, whose parents didn't know, who was stealing and what and from who, who'd been sprung and who was in trouble with the police, who bashed who in the yard, who was in love and who was scared. I kept quiet about this.

One kid was sprung breaking into a house up in Carlton. The school had abandoned all hope of controlling him, and he'd been given an exemption from school to get a job before he was fifteen. He went to work in a shoe factory. He wrote goodbye in his last weekly report.

Girls who disappeared from school tended to do so with less administrative fuss, but more tears. Some were sent to all-girl Catholic schools because they'd become 'uncontrollable'. One girl simply vanished. Girls who were sprung shoplifting or wagging took their punishment with lowered heads, except for one girl I remember, Vera, a strapping Yugoslavian who was wrongly accused, by a furious man teacher, of having thrown something out of our room at his classroom window. She burst into screams of rage, right there in front of the class, spouted tears, sobbed aloud, and protested her innocence with such vehemence that she forced him to leave her alone.

Except for people like Vera and several girls from Clifton Hill, it was the boys who dominated the classroom and the yard with flamboyant outbursts of noise, violence and laughter. The girls, by twelve and thirteen already sharply aware of the roles they were expected to fulfil, were easier and less spectacular company. I seem to have fewer anecdotes about them because they were calmer, more constant, less concerned to impress and amuse me, and physically more at ease with me. When we went walking I had a girl on each arm. They'd hug me without embarrassment, sit crammed up beside me in the desks, ask me what was wrong if I looked worried. Once when I was sick at home with flu, at lunchtime three of the form-one girls burst into my bedroom carrying a wad of cotton wool and a bottle of metho. Ignoring my protests, they soaked the cotton wool in the metho and clapped it onto my throat with a scarf. 'There, miss,' they said severely. 'Now don't you take that off till you're better.'

There was a small group of French kids at the school. They stuck together in the yard, very smoothly dressed and a bit supercilious, standing like an island among the swirling mass of dark-headed Italians and Greeks. One French girl in my class wrote with what can only be described as ennui, 'God, how can I stand this place?'

It is a Greek suburb. When Theodorakis came to Melbourne, he and his band gave a free show at the Collingwood Town Hall for the schoolkids of the Collingwood-Fitzroy area. The Greek kids were silent with pride, the others with bewilderment at this intensely emotional music. By the end the Greeks were out of their seats dancing. They could hardly speak; their faces were shining. At the school's Greek night, girls danced in long skirts and blouses with coins hanging over their foreheads. Boys were not shy to wear costumes involving skirts, and shoes with pointed toes and pompoms. 'Oh, those boys will be teased tomorrow!' exclaimed an Italian mother standing beside me. But they weren't. Even the heavy-leather kids who watched from the doorway weren't laughing.

The popular pastime of the school was not speed or alcohol, but gambling. The younger boys gambled on scrabble, cards, and coins thrown against a wall. The sixth-form kids played endless games of poker. Boys who were big enough (though under-age) to get into what they called the spro bars gambled on the machines. George in my second form was fourteen and looked twenty. He won sixty dollars on the machines, and brought it to school and flashed it round the class. Someone else saw him with the wad of notes and dobbed him to the principal. He couldn't say where he'd got it because he knew if he told the truth the owner of the spro bar might get into trouble with the police—and certainly wouldn't open his door to George again. Everyone thought he had stolen the money. They couldn't break him down so they called in his parents.

After that everyone stopped talking about it, and George

left school and got a job. I saw him a few days ago, walking down Johnston Street, after work, carrying an airways bag. We didn't recognise each other until we'd almost passed, because he had a sharpie haircut, and I saw only that and kept walking. But he stopped me and said, 'Hey, miss! How are you going?' and gave me the old gentle smile.

You know you're losing touch when you see the haircut before the face.

1972

Why Does the Women Get All the Pain?

ONE AFTERNOON IN the spring of 1972, I settled my form-one class of thirteen-year-olds and we launched ourselves dutifully on an assignment about Ancient Greece. Using the only class set that wasn't too blatantly out of date, I'd managed to work up a little number on sex roles in ancient times compared with those of today. (I've explained this to account for having actually handed round eighteen copies of a book as pitiful as *Looking at Ancient History*.)

OK, everyone have a look at page 51. Rustle rustle. A moment of silence as we all stare, transfixed, at the defacements which other classes have perpetrated on a picture of a Greek athlete: in all but a few of the copies a monstrous cock has been added in heavy biro, with a colossal stream of sperm hitting the bullseye, the cunt of a woman on the facing page who is modestly demonstrating the folds of the Ionian chiton. Twenty-nine pairs of eyes meet mine.

'Miss!' ventures Tania. 'Look what's on my book!' She holds it up and a hiss of excitement flashes round the class. I turn my copy round to reveal similar adornments: their eyes are riveted on my face, waiting for the signal. I can't help it, in fact I don't even try. I start laughing and suddenly there's a riot, everyone's leaping out of their seats, Angelo is making violent rabbit-like fucking motions with his hips, Georgia's blushing and smiling at me sideways. Paul has his head on his arms with only his hysterical eyes peeping up to me. Cathy bellows enviously, 'No-one's drawn anything on *my* book!'

Calm down, everyone, let's see if we can get some work done. We read page 51 and turn over; God help me if there aren't two men fucking (under the pretext of being Greek wrestlers) and *stark naked*, not a stitch on. More ecstatic laughter, thumping on the floor, rolling of eyes, cries, cries of 'Miss! Miss!'

Then and there I'm obliged to face the fact. There's obviously no point in trying to get them to look at anything else on the page but these astounding illustrations. I realise that this is the moment I can't let pass. All the dreary arguments at staff conferences about the idea of sex education courses suddenly seem beside the point. So I say, look, the reason why people do these drawings, and why we laugh at them, is that sex is more interesting than just about anything else, and because most kids at school don't know nearly as much about it as they need to. Do you want to talk about it?

An incredulous silence. Georgia whispers, 'Can we ask you questions? *Any questions*? Will you tell us *anything we ask*?'

Yes, I will. Ask away. Silence. *Silence*? I've been with these kids every day since the beginning of the year, and the one thing they don't want is to be silent. What's the matter?

'Miss,' says Angelo, blushing puce, 'can we write the questions on paper?'

Of course you can. In an instant the desk lids fly up, Grace has opened the cupboard, biros and paper are shoved from hand to hand, there are four or five huddles of kids hissing furiously with their skinny bums in the air. Bursts of laughter and more whispering, furious scribbling, cries of 'Don't you know *that*?' 'Go on—ask her!' 'How do you spell…' 'Come on, hurry up!'

In five minutes there's a mound of paper scraps on my table and everyone is sitting still except Drago, who is writing steadily, his flushed face bent over his pen, his lovely silly smile darting round every few seconds at the impatient kids. 'Carn, Drago, *carn*! She's waiting, oh come on!' they groan. Paul dashes out with another question: 'Can we kill Drago?' At last he lumbers out to the front and pushes six questions across the table to me. His broad Yugoslavian face is shiny and sweaty with the effort of speedy writing, and red with his determination to ask it *all* in spite of the impatient abuse of the others. They're waiting for me now, and I pick up the first question.

WHY DOES THE WOMEN GET ALL THE PAIN?

Oh Georgia, oh Rita! I look at their open, eager faces and think of how their fathers beat them for talking to boys in the street, and how they are not allowed to go to church when they have their period. I spread out the papers and flick my eyes over their clumsy writing.

HOW ARE SPURM PRODUCED?

WHY DO MEN LOVE TO BIT LADY'S TITS?

WHY DO MEN LOOK AT GIRLS AND WANT TO FEEL THEM, WHAT DOES IT ALL MEAN?

WHY CAN'T A LADY HAVE A BABY WHEN SHE'S OLD?

DOES IT HURT TO HAVE SEXUAL INTERCOURSE?

Sexual intercourse? I'd better start here.

Before we can start, I want to make you understand that the words some people think of as dirty words are the best words, the right words to use when you are talking about sex. So I'm not going to say 'sexual intercourse', I'm going to say 'fuck' and I'm going to say 'cock' and 'cunt' too, so we'd better get that straight. Is that OK?

Without a word, Darryl reaches up from his desk by the door and clicks the lock shut.

And away we go. No, fucking doesn't hurt, it feels marvellous! and I'm drawing awkward uteruses on the board and pointing at my own body to where I think my uterus is, and explaining what a clitoris is and what it's for, and telling them that no, you don't always have to *ask* for a fuck, that often it just happens.

'Just happens, miss? Didn't your husband *ask* you?'

'Miss, is it true that there's a hole you shit from, and a hole you piss from and then another hole where you can do it with boys?'

CAN YOU ONLY FUCK WHEN YOU'VE GOT YOUR PERIOD?

WHAT'S A FRANGER?

CAN YOU FUCK EVERY DAY?

Every few minutes someone runs out with another question. Pretty soon they are saying 'fuck' with no blushes or sniggers. The more I answer, the easier it gets to be absolutely truthful. I'm not afraid of them. They are so hungry for facts that they're exhausting me. The bell goes and they all groan aloud—the end of the lesson. They trudge out reluctantly, thinking it's all over. 'See you, miss. Thanks, miss.'

I sit there at the table. My head is singing with the astonishing fact that this is the only totally honest lesson I have ever given, that not a second of it was wasted, that their attention didn't waver for a second, and that their curiosity made authoritarian behaviour on my part completely unnecessary. They asked, and I gave.

Next morning David and Chris, who'd been wagging the day before, ran up to me in the yard, grief-stricken. 'Oh miss, we missed it! Can't we continue this afternoon?' Yes, if you want to. When I walk in, the customary riot is not in progress. They're sitting like statues, and on my table is a stack of papers six inches high. I tell them that I'll get the sack if it gets round that I've been saying 'fuck' and 'cunt' in the classroom. They nod solemnly. I pick up the papers and we're away again. This time, most of them having absorbed the basic anatomical stuff yesterday, we're into refinements of one sort or another. Fears, too, begin to show.

WHAT'S A PERVA?

WHAT IF A MAN'S DICK IS TOO SMALL AND HE'S DYING TO HAVE ONE?

CAN A MAN'S DICK GET STUCK IN A LADY'S CUNT?

WHAT IF A MAN MISSES AND PUTS HIS COCK INTO A LADY'S DICK?

HOW DO YOU MAKE THE SPERM COME OUT?

It's the hardest work I've ever done. I'm drawing, I'm acting, I'm showing shapes and actions with my hands and body. Angelo wants to know how you actually get the cock *in*. As I explain, he nods and nods, miming a sympathetic motion of taking his cock and gently pushing it forward and up. No one laughs.

Lou in the front row fixes his beautiful serious eyes on me and says, 'Miss, what does a cunt look like?' I tell them, like a flower, and girls should get a mirror and look at themselves. Everyone laughs at this, but it's for pleasure and joy. The boys turn to glance at the girls, and their faces look both curious and tender. We are laughing a lot; we are making jokes that are sexy without being harsh. I try to draw a cunt and they call out to me to put the hairs on. Unfamiliar words roll of their tongues: 'pleasurable'. I can hear Georgia trying out the word herself.

It's easy to give facts, though I wished we had a man there for when my knowledge started to show gaps—for example, when David wanted to know what happened to his balls when he pulled himself. The most difficult questions were the ones that were really asking 'What is it *like* to fuck?' Drago wants to know, 'How long do you have to leave your cock in the cunt before the sprog comes out? An hour? Two hours?' I suppose he thinks it just lies there. I take a breath and try to tell them, but my description gets clumsier and clumsier and, looking at their patient faces, I simply die away. You'll have to wait till one day you do it yourself. I don't know how to describe it. Perhaps the only thing you're doing by answering kids' questions as honestly as you can is removing fear.

The girls are more reticent than the boys about their experience, no doubt because they've been fiercely protected since childhood by their fathers and brothers. Georgia has kissed a boy and she's regarded as an oracle in such matters. In subsequent conversations with the girls, several of them have told me about frightening encounters with men lodgers, and they are extremely sensitive about being stared and whistled at in the street.

What the girls ask me, again and again, is: CAN A GIRL ASK A MAN FOR A FUCK?

They eagerly search my face as I answer, of course, of course! and when I remark that men might be happy to share the job of initiating, the boys agree enthusiastically.

The conversation has been going on for a couple of hours when one of the girls writes: MISS, CAN A GIRL GET A DISEASE FROM SUCKING A MAN'S COCK?

As carefully as I can, I separate the two issues of sucking and venereal disease; I hope I manage to explain VD without scaring them off for good, while at the same time giving them a healthy respect for its nastiness. Then I talk about the pleasure of sucking anything—your mother's breast, a bottle, your thumb—then chewy, a pencil, lollies—and then various parts of a lover's body. They contemplate this earnestly. They want to know *why* anyone would do such a thing. Well, I say, when you love someone, or love fucking with them, there is nothing you can think of doing, short of hurting them against their will, that you wouldn't do.

'But, miss!' whispers someone. 'What if he comes in your mouth?' Everyone smiles but they're too involved to laugh and break the spell. I tell them that I used to be anxious about that too, but that you learn freedom, that it's another pleasure you can give or take.

There is a little flurry in one corner of the room. 'You ask her.' 'No, I can't. *You.*' Drago turns to me, blushing and smiling. 'Miss—have *you* ever had a suck?'

For a single beat I see the situation from a distance: *a kid has just asked his teacher if she sucks cocks.* I should be thunderstruck, outraged—but twenty-nine kids are gazing at me, waiting, their faces open and alight. Why lie? They trust me. They want to know the truth. Without a pause the answer simply rolls off my tongue, as undramatic as the next tick of the clock. Yes, I have. There's a second of amazed silence. To break it I say calmly, Well, I guess it *is* a bit hard for you to picture me with a cock in my mouth. And then, in room 8 upstairs on a Wednesday afternoon in spring, in the high school whose name I can't mention lest I get the sack—*would* they sack me? doesn't truth makes you strong?—the whole thirty of us burst into wild, joyful laughter.

The bell goes for the end of the day, and the kids pack up their things cheerfully and troop out, calling goodbye exactly as if it had been an ordinary day. One boy dawdles behind, the one who always chats with me while the others play. He wanders up to the table where I'm sitting. 'Hey, miss,' he says, pointing at the scattered pile of answered questions. 'Want me to help you destroy these?' Our eyes meet and we start laughing again. Without speaking, we tear the papers into tiny pieces and drop them into the bin.

1972

Postscript

'*Would* they sack me?' Of course they sacked me. This article appeared in the *Digger* in October 1972—anonymously, but I was pathetically easy to trace. On the second last day of that school year, I was summoned to the Education Department in Treasury Place, and carpeted by the Deputy Director of Secondary Education. He asked me if I had 'used four-letter words in the classroom'. Transparent to the end, I replied that I had. He dismissed me on the spot. I took the train back to school; I remember it was a high, hot, dry, perfect Melbourne summer day. By the time I got to our classroom, my replacement was already at the blackboard. The kids sat white and sobbing at their desks. We hardly had a chance to say goodbye.

Some of my colleagues passed the hat for me, some of the kids' parents wrote me kind letters, and early the following year the union called a one-day strike—but the heart soon went out of it, and life, as it must, rolled on.

It was hard for me to read this story again, let alone to decide to republish it here. People have forgotten how cramped and fearful and hypocritical Australian attitudes to sex were, in the early seventies. 'Sexual liberation', in the age of AIDS, has an almost comically dated ring, but back then it was an idea that really meant something. Now, in my fifties, I am jolted by the crude naivety of what I said and did. I know that to some people it will seem obscene. What I remember most about the conversations, though—and I wasn't a good enough writer, then, to render it—is the tenderness of the way we talked. The bluntness of the language, mine and theirs, obscures the delicacy and the urgency of their inquiry, the warmth and sweetness and gentle curiosity of the glances that passed between girls and boys, across a divide where coarse jocularity and abuse had always been the common currency.

And it seems important to add that between the conversations and the day I was sacked passed two months of absolutely ordinary school days, in that classroom. We didn't speak again about sex, or refer to the conversations; harmoniously we did our work, we studied and played and learned, as people do in schools. The conversations were an interlude, a strange, electric, privileged moment, in the working lives of twenty-nine children and their teacher.

My Child in the World

MY DAUGHTER ALICE, grade bubs Alfred Crescent Primary, is decked out in a bizarre array of garments, ill-fitting and brightly coloured. The gingham uniforms she thought she wanted, before she became a schoolgirl, she has stuffed away in her bottom drawer. Her hair is short and her legs, in black tights, are wiry and knobby-kneed. I hook her little case on to the handlebars of my bike, and with one arm swing her skinny body on to the cushion behind my seat. She sits there, effortlessly balancing, dreaming towards the pigeon cages on the shed roof, and grabs the back of my shirt in one hand as the bike bounces over the wide gutter and I push out into the traffic. Easy we roll, in the autumn sunshine.

Her dreamy litany begins. 'Con lives near here, and Angelos. I know where Angelos lives. Angelos is in grade three. She waits for me. I go to her house…'

I have never seen Angelos. I don't even know if Angelos exists. We rattle across the stones and sweep grandly into the crescent. Her ragged skirt flutters in the corner of my eye. The street is full of mothers and children.

'Can I come in with you today?'

'Oh yes!' she says. 'Will you stay till the bell?'

We chain the bike to the fence. A girl we know runs to the gate as we go in. Our mouths open to greet her, but she tears straight past us, yelling, 'Good morning, Mr Hitchcock! Good morning, Mr Hitchcock!'

'Where do you go now?' I ask.

'I put my case inside! Don't you know *anything* about schools?'

Kindly she takes my hand. The concrete floors are clean and we step over pools of water. She leads me to an old wooden locker, heaves her case to shoulder-height, and slides it, in. She turns her bare, pure-skinned face up to me and smiles. 'Now we go outside.'

I follow her black legs out on to the sunny gravel. Has she got a friend? Does she know I think it matters? She runs to the climbing frame and pushes through a crowd of small boys. One has a sugar cigarette in his mouth; she spots it and flashes me a grimace, from behind his back. I feel big and noticeable with my overalls and chopped hair. Some children stare at me, others are engrossed in their private thoughts, standing about waiting for the bell. No one has greeted Alice. My heart starts to thump. I make quick comparisons between her clothes and theirs. She looks wacky.

'Watch me!' she calls, throwing herself on to the climbing frame. 'I'll show you! Watch me! Watch! Watch!' She is fearless on the frame. Her limber body, taught by the grown-ups she has for friends at home, executes turns and flips. Again and again her shining forehead turns up towards me.

'Good, it's good,' I say.

She lands at my feet with a confident thump, and drags me to the fence. 'A big girl showed me how to do this.' She spans the gap between the ground and the first rail with a tremendous straining of one black leg.

Someone shouts her name. It's Raani, her pretend brother from the household where we live. But he's in grade one, he belongs over there in the big kids' yard. Alice gazes at him yearningly, through the mesh of the cyclone fence.

The bell, and they're scattering like rabbits. 'See you!' yells Raani.

He's only a blond blob among the running heads. Alice

leads me to a door outside which her grade is gathering. 'Watch me line up?'

I sit on a wooden bench among the Greek mothers in black.

Out of the chaos emerges a ritual: each child must have a partner; they march into school in pairs. I watch Alice approach the front boy in line and reach for his hand. He brushes her away without a glance. She whirls round with a skip and a terrible smile, and puts out her hand to a girl in white stockings. The girl frowns and shakes her off. Alice smiles again, flicks her hand and shakes her head and smiles and twirls to the back of the line. She comes to rest on her own, turned away from the line of perfect couples, her left thumb in her mouth, staring and searching out across the yard.

Is it a partner she is staring for? God, make a partner come spinning across the gravel for her, but the line is moving to the scratchy marching music and feet scrabble and the children march and the sun shines on the clean brown head of my lonely child with her thumb in her mouth, cracking hardy, looking over her shoulder at the yard full of purposeful pairs.

She drags along behind the others, still staring behind her, and as she disappears round the red-brick corner of the building I can't bear it, I jump up and run after her and catch her going up the concrete steps, last in line and very small between the drinking taps and the lockers.

I grab her hand. 'Alice!'

She spins round and sees me. 'Where *were* you?'

It's *me* she was looking for, in the yard. 'I was sitting on the bench! Couldn't you see me?' She is holding my hand tightly. She has been at this school every day for six weeks. Is it like this for her every day?

'Come into the classroom? Stay? Will you stay?'

'I'll come in for a little while.'

'No—for a long. Stay till we go out to play.'

The teacher nods and smiles to welcome me. I sit on a tiny chair at the very back of the room, and watch them twinkle fast and slow with their fingers, and sing, and draw a spiral, each on a little blackboard.

A boy is pushing Alice with his shoulder. I see her scowl at him, I lip-read her insult. He pushes, pushes, grinning at her, twice her size. I crouch foolishly on my little chair, watching her get up and move to a different place on the mat, watching him half-crawl, half-walk after her and push, push, push. I would ram my fist into his grinning face, I would strangle him on the spot, but for all the hope I've got of controlling anything that happens in this room, I may as well be back in the third row of Miss Lonie's grade in 1947 at Manifold Heights, Geelong, where I pissed my pants and soaked the shorts of the boy next to me because I was afraid to ask to go to the lavatory during lesson time.

But Alice's back is very straight. Her face is bright and open. She is drawing, as she is told, a curvy line on her blackboard with a piece of chalk. 'Blackboards under chins!' cries the teacher. Alice turns her board around and flashes a sharp look at the girl beside her. She turns and waves at me over her shoulder. She is smiling.

1975

Sad Grove by the Ocean

OCEAN GROVE IS a small town, or township, about fourteen miles from Geelong. It has no real *raison d'être*, or not of the sort we were taught about in geography classes. It is not on a river mouth, like Barwon Heads, nor is it, like Queenscliff or Point Lonsdale, near the Rip, the gap through which Port Phillip Bay opens into the sea. Ocean Grove sits about halfway between the Rip and the mouth of the Barwon River, on a long curved beach. It is just *there*.

Our family lived at Ocean Grove between 1948 and 1952, that is, between my sixth and tenth years, and from then on we spent all our holidays there. I don't know why we left Geelong for those years and then returned to it. Events of childhood have a hard shell of inevitability over them. They resist historical explanation. Why ask? They happened. Knowing why would not change my memories of the town, would it?

I told one of my sisters that I was going back there to write this. We had a mild argument about something called 'the Sheepwash'—about whether it was a particular spot on the Barwon Heads side of the river, or whether the name referred to that whole stretch of the river, taking in both banks. Neither of us felt any desire to consult an outside authority on this point: our father, a map. Happily and peacefully, we squabbled.

Ocean Grove was an ordinary place, an ordinary town full of ordinary people like ourselves. Our parents loved us: they must have, for they kept on having more. We went to school, we read books, we listened to the wireless, we were forced to help our mother with the housework, we went to the beach, we had roller-skates and glasses of cordial and plenty to eat and outings and friends to stay. Although I am the eldest of the six, and though the last two weren't born till after we left Ocean Grove, I can't remember a time when I didn't belong to A Big Family. A woman my mother did not know once laughed and said to her, watching us pour out of the car on to the beach, 'Cheaper by the dozen!' I think my mother probably laughed too, but her account of that event might well be different.

There is no pub at Ocean Grove, and when we lived there there was no licensed grocer either. To get a drink you had to go to Barwon Heads, two miles away.

'That's because the place was originally owned by an American Methodist church,' says my father. 'There was a strip of land a foot wide round the subdivision, past which you weren't supposed to carry any intoxicating liquor—not even a grapevine. Each title had a covenant on it.

'Bathing-box-type humpies people had, holiday shacks over at Barwon Heads. In the 1930s the South Barwon Council said they had to get rid of them, so people just picked 'em up and carted 'em over the river to Ocean Grove, where the Bellarine Shire was in charge—a poor outfit. That's why there's so many awful houses.

'When the migrants came, after the war, they put 'em into a place with holiday shacks and little cubbyholes. There wasn't enough room for 'em up at Bonegilla. They were putting them anywhere they could find. They can't have known what hit 'em —they got out of here as fast as they could.'

I remember the migrants coming. They must have arrived in a rush: in my memory it seems that they all arrived on one day. At Ocean Grove School No. 3100 we sat in double desks; when the migrants came we were suddenly three to a double. We called them Balts. We had no idea where they came from.

They were all blond. They had names like 'Wossle', 'Olger', 'Rocksanner', 'Beela', that even our teachers couldn't say. Years later, in books and films, when I came across those mysterious names properly spelt and pronounced, I felt sobered and ashamed, as at a lesson taught too late. We had never heard of garlic, let alone smelt it. We watched them unwrap their lunches: slices of bread an inch thick encasing slabs of high-smelling sausage. The girls wore their white-blonde hair divided into sections with the top bit rolled and pinned into a hollow tube that ran back from brow to crown, while we had ours, which was plain brown, cut short behind and held in a 'bunch' in front by a rubber band and a ribbon.

'Rocksanner' sat next to me. Under her skirt she wore what I thought were her pyjama pants. I felt sorry for her: so cold and so poor that she had to wear her pyjamas under her clothes. Nobody I have spoken to remembers this. Was it a folk costume? someone suggests, now, too late. Didn't anyone explain anything to us? Maybe our parents and teachers were like the soldiers in Ben Lewin's *The Dunera Boys*: essentially good-natured but profoundly ignorant. Wasn't it in the papers? As with the Sheepwash, I have a stubborn, sore reluctance to find out. I don't think it's laziness. If I poked even one rational hole in the thick skin of that closed-off world, who knows what would come squirting out.

The sea is still there, under everything else I saw and remembered. This goes without saying. There are no ugly bits of ocean. But I can't understand why it hurts so much to look at Ocean Grove. Other people in the streets don't seem bothered by its power lines, its desolate bareness of ground, its hideous shopfronts. They are going about their business unperturbed. Perhaps it's not really anything special, this ugliness. Perhaps it's no uglier than any other modernised town on that featureless coastline. Perhaps I've brought the ugliness with me. A clear hot day might have dispelled this cloud of sadness; or is there an Ocean Grove-shaped desolation that lives inside my head? Either way, when I get to Ocean Grove, I am not surprised to find the sky thickly covered and a fresh wind blowing, in early December.

We used to walk everywhere. So I leave the car at the motel (still no pub) and start to put one foot in front of the other. When I stick to the sealed road the colours seem all wrong: the ground should be yellow, but it's grey. I cut into the scrub and find a dirt road, badly eroded, leading up the hill in what I think must be the direction of the school.

I get to the school just before 9 a.m. Cars driven by women half my age are unloading small children. They are *driving their kids to school*. What's the matter with them? Is it too far to walk? Are they weak, or crippled? Has some danger unknown to me invaded the streets?

The old timber building is still there, but extensions have been built and stagger away down the sloping site. The dunnies, where we wiped our bums with pages torn from old copies of the *National Geographic* donated to the school library by parents, are nowhere to be seen.

Once I forgot something and my father had to ask the teacher to open the school building for us during the weekend. Several of my sisters came too. I was let in, and ran to get my cardie or my project or whatever it was while the others waited outside. I could hear the two men talking and the little girls shouting further down the yard. I became overwhelmed with a dreamy curiosity in the empty schoolroom by myself, and stayed much longer than I needed to. When I woke up and went to the outside door, it was locked. I ran to the side window and saw them all walking down the road. How did I get out? I forget that too.

I walk from the school to our old house. Looking Both Ways to cross Presidents Avenue, I wonder where we used to cross in 1948. Cross? We didn't have to. We used the road.

There were so few cars that we walked right down the middle of it, and it wasn't a road anyway, it was a *track*.

I pass through the shopping centre. Back then it was called The Shops: Kong's Bakery, Skinner's General Store, Miss Dorrie Wilson at the Post Office. Now there is a kind of mall and the street has been made one-way, for no reason that I can see. There are foreign restaurants: Chinese, Mexican. Back then it was exotic to drive over to Barwon Heads for fish and chips.

There used to be a milk bar called The Doo Duck Inn. The word 'duck' in its title was not written but represented by a head of Donald Duck enclosed in a golden and blue circle. I loved this and thought it clever. Later, bodgies and widgies used to loaf round outside the shop. One was called Wogger Whitfield. He looked like Elvis Presley and we thought of him as grown-up.

The street is now a string of real estate agents and take-away food shops. I go into the one I think must be the old Doo Duck, and order a steak sandwich from a Greek woman. A Greek! When I lived there the only Greeks I knew about were Theseus, Procrustes, Medusa. The woman, who looks exhausted, greets me with a beautiful, ironic smile. I sit at the formica table and eat the steak sandwich. I can hardly swallow for the lump in my throat.

Eight minutes from the school (not counting the steak sandwich) I am approaching the corner of The Terrace and Eggleston Street, where our old house used to stand and probably still does. An SEC truck blocks my view: some men are fixing the power lines. I slip between the truck and the thick tea-tree scrub, and there's the gate. The gate is still there. It is the same gate. It is so real, so much the same, I'm afraid that if I touch it I will get an electric shock. It is a wide metal farm gate that digs a little curved trench in the dirt with its corner and has to be hooked shut with a chain and a loop. We used to swing on this gate, four of us in a line, waiting for my father to come home.

The SEC men are watching me. I feel embarrassed by the state I am in, standing like a robber with one hand on the gate post.

Something funny has happened to the house. It has become confused, and uglier. It is divided now into two parts: the left side has had a second storey built on, and the other, though still fully part of the same building, has its yard divided off from the other's garden by a horrible brush fence, and has been allowed to Go to Rack and Ruin. Its weatherboard walls have been painted aqua and it looks hovel-like, with mean louvred windows and a low door, which I do not remember, halfway along the side wall.

The cement paths we used to rollerskate on are crumbled and overgrown. My mother's garage is a heap of tin under a cypress tree, and somebody seems to be living in the shed: a TV antenna droops feebly on its roof.

The SEC truck drives away. There is nobody about, though the door of the house's lower side stands open. People are going to ask me, 'And did you go in?' Why would I go in? It's just an ugly old house. If I went in my father would shout, 'Shut the flaming door!' and my mother would say, 'Go outside.'

So you'll just have to believe me when I tell you that, standing at the gate, I remembered part of a poem called 'Answers to Letters', by the Swede Thomas Tranströmer:

> Time is not a straight line, it's more of a labyrinth,
> and if you press close to the wall at the right
> place you can hear the hurrying steps and voices, you
> can hear yourself walking past there on the other side...

Except that I can hear not footsteps but the grinding of roller-skates with metal wheels, a gritty rolling; the feel of travelling on metal containing ball bearings; skating, skating for months on end, four knobby-legged girls, totally absorbed in our traffic lanes, our rules, our clumsy arabesques, our struggles with physics, with gravity; and the particular kind of jarring caused by a fall on concrete.

1985

At Nine Darling Street

In 1960 I believed that all Jews and homosexuals lived in New York. I was eighteen years old, dux of a provincial church girls' school. To my eternal shame I was dumb enough to let them railroad me into being head prefect: I was a miserable, lonely boss's stooge. I hit a tennis ball against a brick wall and despite my elevated status was always picked last in sporting sides.

I did not read the paper. I did not know what the word 'politics' meant, and none of my teachers saw fit to enlighten me. I was foxed by the faultless aplomb of our sixth-form English teacher who declared, as we pored mystified over Byron, that '*sensuous* means *of the senses:* but *sensual* is a bad, bad word.' I didn't know anything.

Our headmistress, who frightened me, spoke at assemblies (after the doors to the recessed altar had been trundled shut) about the goodness of the Lord. 'Think of it!' she cried. 'He made grass and trees green for the resting of our eyes. Imagine our discomfort, had He made them red.' This Valkyrie also informed us from the dais that people with backhand writing were untrustworthy. My mother wrote backhand and was of a transparent truthfulness.

In the gloomy dining room smelling of floor wax and neanderthal sausages we fifth and sixth formers gave one dance a year. I was a frump, a breastless creature barely past puberty with hair that wouldn't curl up at the bottom, who blushed in agony when addressed by man or beast, who was clad stiffly in cotton while others floated divinely in chiffon with the coveted shoestring straps.

Before the event the headmistress summoned us into the assembly room with its gold-littered honour boards (I always scanned them for Norah Linton, Saint Norah of Billabong, but stopped each time, incredulous, at someone called Daintry Gillett) and inspected us for *commonness*.

She dragged me out to the front in my square-necked, high-necked, frump-necked, flat-necked horrible cotton dress with wattle flowers printed on it, my ugly white shoes whose sandshoe polish was already showing cracks. 'Now why can't everyone be like Helen? Modest and plain.'

The boarders, strapping Western District girls with bosoms, sneered. I burned. I had a mole on my lip and my mouth was too small. I think that woman is dead now. Did she make us wear those long white gloves, or did we bring it upon ourselves? We were all in anguish, one way or another. Did I have a friend? I can't even remember. Under that sort of stress, friendships could be little more than temporary alliances.

So those innocent, patrolled affairs on school premises prepared us poorly for what happened at the end of the year in the great metropolis Melbourne forty-five miles away, in that supposedly magic time between exams and Christmas when anything seemed possible but nothing in particular was.

What use to us now were the counsels of our elders, distilled in whispers down the ranks of girls? 'Don't wear patent leather shoes: boys see your underwear reflected. Don't wear red: it excites them. Don't wear white: it reminds them of sheets. Don't smoke: it's common. Don't drink: there is no more disgusting sight than that of a woman drunk.'

We were going to the City of the Plain, where Merton Hall girls talked to boys in their drawling voices (we knew in our provincial hearts that they were more desirable than we were) and wore slinky dresses and had long voluptuous black hair and black eye make-up without being common and had probably been to jazz clubs, and one of them had even had an abortion, her cousin told us, because once you start doing it it's like a drug and you can't ever stop, you have to do it again and again.

Everybody knew that in the public toilets of Melbourne, girls from the country were injected with something and taken off to the White Slave Trade. Whatever that was.

'Get a guernsey, did you?' said my father, cruelly deflating me as I ran in the back door with my expensive embossed envelope. Who paid for those End of Year dances? For the printing of the invitations, the suppers, the bands of old men in dinner suits who could play 'The Golden Wedding'? The hiring of the Dorchester, of Nine Darling Street? There were strings of these dances, each school gave one, and it was rumoured that some girls had a different dress for each one. For mere children schooled as we were, kept in dumb ignorance, it was the massacre of the innocents, those hot December nights.

My mother had told me that Pimms No. 1 cup was 'what they call a leg-opener'. I only dimly visualised what this could mean. I was too scared and prim to drink, anyway, even if anyone had offered me any, which they didn't.

At Nine Darling Street, the steps were carpeted in red, as I recall them now, but perhaps I'm confusing this with the entrance of the stars to the palace at the Cannes festival. The tinselled significance was the same. My feet and hands in white were too big and the rest of me was too small. Who were those parents in the doorway? Where were the toilets?

My partner was a lumpy boy whose mother knew my auntie. We sat side by side, not touching, and discussed the exams and blushed during the long silences. He said there was an ice sculpture in the other room, with oysters in its crevices. We edged through the crowd to look at it. Everyone else seemed to be laughing. What would I do with an oyster, in these white gloves? I pretended not to be hungry and we returned to our seat.

He asked me to dance. I placed my pristine white glove upon his dandruffy shoulder, he seized a pawful of the back of my dress at the waist and away we clomped, enveloped in a malodorous cloud of Clearasil which even the piercing perfume of the gardenia (stalk wrapped in silver paper) pinned to the place where my bosom ought to have been could not disperse. Up to the end, turn 180 degrees, head back the other way, like a man mowing a lawn.

My shoes were blackened, my stockings torn and twisted, my knees ringing from collisions with his. Where he gripped me I was damp. I drew a vicious satisfaction from the fact that many of the successful girls dancing with future graziers and flashing their teeth in their big mouths had got badly sunburned that afternoon in the All Schools' Tennis Tournament at Kooyong: their backs under the shoestring straps blazed in ugly patterns of white and red. Poor things: perhaps their smiles were as fake as mine.

The music stopped, I turned around, and it happened.

A boy I knew (his cousin later married my sister) stood up suddenly and was sick all down the back of a stranger's dress. She sprang up appalled. Minutes later I went to the toilet and found her there, her back to the big mirror, weeping while her friends clucked about her mopping and scrubbing with roller towel yanked out of the dispenser. 'He's revolting, revolting,' she sobbed, 'and I don't even know him.' I pushed open the first toilet cubicle.

Two girls were lying face down on the floor, insensible, gardenia corsages bruised beneath their shoulders. They lay as if dead. They would not be roused. I stepped back and opened the second cubicle. A third girl lay there on her back, vomiting even as I stared. Who could I tell? There were no teachers present. It was all out of control. I poked the wretched girl with the toe of my ruined shoe. I rolled her on to her stomach, leaned down and shook her limp shoulder. 'Leemealone,' she groaned. 'Leemealone.' She had stopped vomiting and her eyes were closed, her greenish cheek pressed out of shape against the tiles.

So this was Melbourne.

Later a kind girl called Jenny Kerr brought me a glass of fruit-cup (had someone slipped something into it? I left it untouched) and a bowl of trifle. While we were eating and talking about the exams, a photographer appeared and took our picture. When I got my copy, I looked plain but not modest: I was grinning stupidly, mouth open, leaning back like an oaf in my seat with my knees apart under the skirt of my pink cotton dress. Jenny Kerr, on the other hand, had posed on an angle and looked soignée, relaxed, at ease.

I went home the next day to unfashionable Geelong. I looked at the photo many times, in many different lights. Then I burnt it: an act I have never regretted.

1979

A Scrapbook, an Album

Children with the same family, the same
blood, with the same first associations and
habits, have some means of enjoyment in
their power, which no subsequent
connections can supply.

Jane Austen, *Mansfield Park*

I WENT TO visit my four sisters, carrying a tape recorder and
my imagined map of the family. It was unsettling to learn that
each sister has her own quite individual map of that territory:
the mountains and rivers are in different places, the borders
are differently constituted and guarded, the history and politics
and justice system of the country are different, according to
who's talking. Now I'm in possession of the tapes and I don't
know what to do with them. I thought of adding them to some
as yet non-existent family archive—our father has burnt the
slide collection—but they are too…blunt. I don't mean bitchy,
though at certain points on each tape there are moments of
intense silence followed by sharp laughter. I encouraged bluntness. But I was surprised. The ones I expected to hold back did
not, while the usually talkative ones were discreet.

And because I, the eldest, was the one with the tape
machine and the pen, this account lacks a blunt view of *me*.
I got off lightly, this time. I tried hard to be irresponsible,
to vanish, to be swallowed up by the texture of the writing.
Because the one who records will never be forgiven. Endured,
yes; tolerated, put up with, borne, and still loved; but not
forgiven.

Already, a few weeks after we taped the interviews, regretful postcards, letters and phone calls are flying. 'What with my big mouth,' writes one, 'and your big ears...'

In the bunfight of a big family, each member develops a role. Everyone gets behind a persona and tries to stay there. Selective amnesia is required in order to maintain that persona. So the conversations on which this essay are based have stirred things up. And now I can't find a shape for the material I've got. The best I can do is a sort of scrapbook, or album. I certainly can't *analyse* my sisters. They keep taking over, bursting out of the feeble categories I devise to order the material: they keep heightening themselves, performing themselves with gusto. All I've done, really, is to tone them down. I feel panicky. We are five sisters and it doesn't even seem right to name us. The others wouldn't like it. 'The others', four women for whom I have feelings so dark and strong that the word *love* is hopelessly inadequate. I've used a chronological numbering system. We have one brother, by the way. He comes between sisters Four and Five. He's a chef. He makes the best lemon tarts in Australia. He has two sons. We love him, and we're proud of him. But he belongs to the male strand of the family: to a different species.

Work

I note that I have immediately defined our brother by mentioning his job. It would never occur to me to do this about my sisters. Work is what interests us least about each other. Work is our separateness, what we do when we're apart.

We know that good manners dictate an interest in other people's jobs, so we ask each other perfunctory questions; but often the questioner has tuned out before the answer is complete. (Four is the exception to this.) In childhood she seized the role of family clown, and every tale she tells is cleverly fashioned for maximum grip: 'He was wearing a rather bad porkpie hat. Get the picture? A real "bohemian". So I say to him, "Can I *get* you something? Like the *bill*?" '

Otherwise, each sister's working life is a mystery to the others. Two of us were nurses, but I have never seen either of them in uniform. Four is in a band, which is more public, so she is often cranky because her sisters rarely come to hear her play. The three of us who write and publish live in a cloud of unknowing: has anyone in the family ever *read* our stuff? We are brilliant withholders. We behave as if we subscribed to Ernest Hemingway's dictum from Paris in the 1920s: 'Praise to the face is open disgrace.' Praise from each other and from our parents is what we really crave; but we will *not* gratify each other. Our pride in one another is secret and oblique. One winter Four's funk band collapsed and she had to take a job selling donuts from a van outside the Exhibition Buildings. Far from complaining, she kept me entranced with stories about her workmates and their customers. Once, on her night off, we were driving downtown to the movies and passed the van. She detoured in to say hullo, and came running back with a steaming bag of free donuts. Behind her back I brag about her: 'Four can turn her hand to anything! She can pick fruit or pull cappuccinos. She's got no vanity about work. The people she works with love her because she makes them laugh.' But would I say these things to her face? That's not the way we do things, in this family.

'Three was complaining to me,' says Four, 'that whenever she visits Mum and Dad they never ask about *her* work, but are always reporting about the others, and praising them. Doesn't she realise that this is what happens to all of us? When *I* go out there, full of news, I have to sit in silence and be told in detail about One's latest book, or Five's new baby. I hate it, but I've got used to it.'

We are furious with our parents for their withholding, but *we* all do it too.

A Squad

Because I am the eldest, my sisters have always been behind me. My face has always been turned away from them, towards the world. I don't know what they looked like—that is, without photos I'd have no *memory* of what they looked like, though when I recently saw one of John Brack's etchings from the 1940s, of a tiny, sulking schoolgirl, I recognised her at once as me or one of my sisters: the chunky stance, the shoulders high with dudgeon, the scowling brow, the tartan skirt and the hair brushed back and held to one side with a ribbon. And yet I also have no memory of a time when they weren't all there— the first three, anyway. I have always been part of a squad. There are photos of me as a tiny baby, mad-eyed, box-headed, being held correctly positioned on the bent arm of my young, nervous mother, or bundled with my back against the chest of my grinning father, my blanket awry, my beady eyes popping with the force of his hug (see *The Favourite*, below); but now, when I look at these pictures, I am completely unable to believe that outside the frame my sisters aren't hanging around, squinting in the sun, picking at their knee-scabs or twiddling their ribboned 'bunches', waiting for me to climb down and turn back into a kid and come outside to play.

Laughter

Whenever I try to live in another town, my phone bill rockets; and when I look carefully at the breakdown of the call times, I see that I make the largest number to my sisters between four and five o'clock—that is, after-school time. I am fifty but I still have this habit, this longing to hear their stories of the day. I want them to make me laugh.

Two women are sitting in a fashionable cafe when their sister walks past, carrying a briefcase and looking cool and purposeful. She does not look in, but passes wearing the kind of expression one adopts when passing the grooviest cafe in town without looking in. The two sisters inside don't speak, but lower their heads to the table in silent fits. But we don't laugh *at* each other. We laugh *about* each other.

They knew that Virginia Woolf was about to crack up again when she wrote in her diary that she and her sister 'laughed so much that the spiders ran into the corners and strangled themselves in their webs'. Perhaps her case was extreme but I cannot say that such laughter is unknown to me and my sisters. There is something ecstatic, brakeless, about the way we laugh together. We laugh in spasms and paroxysms. Almost anything—a glance, a word, a mimicked grimace—can act as a trigger. When any (or all) of us are together we are quivering in readiness for the thing that will push us off the edge of rational discourse into freefall over a bottomless canyon of mirth; laughing together is a way of merging again into an inchoate feminine mass. (Again? When was this previously the case?)

Perhaps 'hysterical' *is* the right word: I've heard this wild laughter among nurses, waitresses, nuns. If you are not included in it, it can be alarming—not because you are the butt of it; it's not 'bitchy' laughter—but because there is something total about it, shameless; it's a relaxation into boundarylessness. Of course, as a spectacle, it is probably boring. It is ill-mannered of us to indulge in it in company. Sometimes two or three of us will withdraw from the table, at a big gathering, and be found in another room shortly afterwards, doubled up in weak, silent laughter. 'What, what is it?' the discovering sister will beg. 'What? Oh, tell me!'

The Favourite

'I was the favourite for eighteen months,' says One. 'I think I'm the only one who can categorically state that. A short blessed period which ended when Two was born and usurped my position. I've spent the rest of my life, in a warped way, trying to regain it through *merit*. Fat chance. This is the theory of the driven, perfectionist eldest child, and I subscribe to it.'

'I remember distinctly,' says Two, 'feeling that I was the favourite child. One and Three were in the poo for some reason, and I remember thinking, "Mum and Dad aren't cross with me—therefore they must like me best." It was a transitory feeling. Two years ago, when Mum and Dad were coming back from overseas, some of us went to the airport to meet them. Three had gone to the toilet, and Mum and Dad came out of the customs hall before she got back. We had the regulation pecks on the cheek, then Dad looked around and said "Where's Three?" He saw her coming from a long way away, and he put out his arms to her while she walked towards him. He gave her a huge hug.'

'Two turned to me as we all trooped towards the car park,' says Three, 'and she said to me, "You always were his favourite." What Two doesn't know is that for five years I'd been chipping away at Dad, after watching Grandma die lonely in that nursing home, looking for affection from anybody who'd give it, because she'd wasted her chances in life—I was with her when she was dying, and I couldn't *bear* it. I thought, "I'm not going to wait till Dad gets that old. I'll teach him if it kills me." So for five years I'd been *insisting* on giving him a hug and a kiss every time we met or parted. I even knocked on the car window and made him wind it down, when he'd got into the car to avoid doing it. I'd been pushing through that barrier. I was on some kind of mission, thinking, "I *will find* something on the other side of this." I didn't even need to earn acceptance or approval any more. I just wanted to break through that lonely barrier around him. I *never* felt the favourite.'

'Oh, Two was the favourite,' says Four. 'It was obvious. She was always the golden-haired girl. She was given a twenty-first at the Southern Cross. The *Beatles* had just been staying there. In 1965 it was the grooviest place in town. Later I remember Five being Dad's favourite. Ohh—indubitably. When she was little.'

'Everyone loved me endlessly,' says Five. 'I was born so many years after Four that I didn't have to fight anybody for anything. But sometimes now I feel a rather pathetic figure in the family—like the dregs of the barrel. As if what I've got to offer is somehow less. Everything's been done before, and better. If I'm patronised or ignored, I bow out. With my friends I feel more entertaining and clever than I do with my sisters—more relaxed and free.'

'Once,' says One, 'I was in the kitchen at Two's with Five and our brother. And in whispers we agreed that we were probably the three favourites: the eldest, the youngest, and the only boy.'

'Still, I had the best roller-skates, I thought,' says Three. 'Mine were German, and yours were only English.'

Are we in competition? And if so, what for? What's the prize?

Likeness
Once, during a visit, Three and One were standing behind Three's children who were watching TV. One grabbed the scarf Three had on, and Three put on One's denim jacket. Three called out, 'Hey, you kids!' The kids gave a perfunctory glance, looked back at the television, then swung round in a slack-jawed double-take. Yes, just for a split second they couldn't tell the difference. Why did Three and One find this satisfying?

What if each sister should keep an album of unflattering photos of the others? 'Ooh, she'll hate this. She looks like something by Francis Bacon.' No, we're really not that kind of family. But we all examine photos with meticulous care, glancing up with narrowed eyes at the subject, and down again.

We look like each other. Strangers stare at us in the street and say, 'You wouldn't be So-and-So's sister, by any chance?' For some, obviously, this is more flattering than for others. One, as eldest, embodies a version of the others' fates: a heavy burden. Covertly we check each other for signs of ageing, signs of *giving in*. When One started to wear what in our family are known as 'old duck sandals', a tremor of apprehension ran down the ranks. But our ex-sister-in-law saved the situation. She looked at the sandals for a long time, then said, 'Yes, they're daggy all right. But they're so daggy that they're almost *clever*.' A week later Four turned out to a party wearing an identical pair.

On tape our voices sound eerily similar.

Each sister manifests for the others a version of our common looks. Each performs her version of the inherited character. Each is a cautionary tale for the others, in different ways and at different times.

One day, when one of my sisters came and complained to me bitterly and at length, laying out in front of me what our mother used to dismiss as 'some great tale', I watched her in growing dismay. I saw the expressions that passed over her face and felt the sympathetic movements of my own facial muscles. I saw *myself*, my rigidity and pride, my pleasure in being aggrieved, my drive to power. And then, as we were saying goodbye on my verandah, under a climbing rose in bloom, each of us turned as if choreographed, picked a flower, and thrust it through the other's buttonhole. Perhaps after all we are not so horrible.

And it did happen that the 'rejected' one, when her life seemed to have collapsed, went to church one Sunday morning, wanting to be absolved, comforted, blessed, she didn't care any more who by. She went up to the communion rail and got down on her knees. She looked up, as the chalice approached her, and saw that the robed person offering her the wine was her sister.

'I saw you recognise me,' says One. 'It rocked you—I saw it go through you like a lightning bolt. I thought you were going to keel over.'

'I didn't even know you were in the church,' says Three. 'And when you put out your hands and turned up your face, for a second I thought it was myself.'

House
A certain humility is appropriate in a sister's kitchen. Respect is owed to the one wearing the apron. We enter each other's kitchens, however, as if we were coming home to our mother: straight to the biscuit tin, the nut jar, cram in a handful and stand there chewing, leaning on the cupboard and talking.

Our kitchen and household customs, while not identical, resemble each other strongly: the use and abuse of the dishcloth, the order in which things are done, the theory of storage.

But when Three has been minding Five's new baby, Five remarks, upon changing a nappy after the baby-sitter has gone home, 'Three always does the pins backwards.'

We are drawn to stand in each other's bedrooms. Perhaps it's simply for the scent of the place where a sister's body has slept. Even a husband's smell can't mask the deep familiarity of the first person you shared a room with. I love to put my head on my sisters' pillows, and breathe in. I like the smell of clean skin, something sweet and cottony. Maybe that smell is not just sisterly, but motherly.

'When I got my first period,' says Two, 'I told One. She laughed. But then she was nice, and took me out to the toilet and showed me how to put the pad on. I didn't tell Mum. Do you remember the toilet, at that house at Ocean Grove? It was like a brown coffin.'

'Do you mean the room, or the toilet itself?'

'The room,' says Two patiently. 'It was painted brown, and sort of curved.'

'I don't remember that,' says One. 'I thought it was white.'

Two visits One and they discuss the problem of curtains for the big back windows of One's kitchen. 'It faces south,' says One, 'so it doesn't get direct sun.'

'South *west*,' says Two, firmly. 'That's south *west*, so it *must* get direct sun, late on a summer afternoon.'

'Oh…yes, I suppose it does,' says One, 'in summer.'

Two is very happy about this. She sits down at the kitchen table and says, with a big smiling sigh, 'I'm *much* more of a sun and moon person than you, aren't I!'

Sisters have no truck with one another's finer feelings. Once I visited a friend and helped her in the kitchen where she was preparing a meal. I remarked, as I laid out the cutlery, 'This table is too low. Whenever I sit at it I knock my knees. You ought to get a higher one.'

She turned round from the bench and stared at me; her face was blank with shock.

'What's the matter?'

'That table,' she said, 'has been in my family for generations. I *love* that table.'

'Oh—sorry!'

We went on with our work. A week or so later she brought it up again.

'I think I was so shocked,' she said, 'because I've got no sisters. I'm not used to that bluntness. *Thwack*—you just *hit* me with it. But I realised later that you hadn't meant to offend me.'

There are no beloved historic objects in our family. There is no family home. Every time our mother gets settled somewhere, our father gets itchy feet and they sell up and move on. They have moved so often that some of their children have not even visited every house they've lived in.

Going in to Bat

'I remember,' says Four, 'when some hoon friends of Five's flatmate terrorised her one time, when she was home alone. After they'd gone she rang me up. Her voice was so faint that I thought she'd been raped. So One and Five and I found out the name of the main hoon, and we put on our best black jackets and drove out to his parents' house where he lived, to sort him out. Remember? It was a horrible cream brick veneer house, with a shaven lawn and no trees, and we presented ourselves at the front door, after dinner one evening, and asked for him. And when his mother said he wasn't home, One said, in a polite and icy voice, 'Perhaps we could have a word with *you*, Mrs So-and-so.' She sat us down in her lounge room on some fancy chairs, and we dobbed her son, in detail. She was struggling to look as if she didn't believe us; but I bet he *was* home. I bet he was hiding in his bedroom, letting his mother take the rap.'

'I was so nervous,' says Five, 'that I kept letting off huge odourless farts into the upholstery.'

'It didn't do much good, I guess,' says Four, 'but we shrieked and yelled all the way home down the freeway. And probably went out dancing for the rest of the evening.'

'I went in to bat for you, Two,' says One, 'at Ocean Grove State School in the 1940s, when someone had swindled you out of your best swopcard. I marched over and forced her to swop it back.'

'I don't remember that,' says Two.

'Three took me on a secret trip to Sydney,' says Four, 'so I could meet my boyfriend when he'd gone interstate to university. We went on the train. We walked around Kings Cross.'

'One took me to Bright and Hitchcock in Geelong to help me buy my first bra,' says Three. 'She protected me from those thin ladies in black with the tape measures round their necks. Because I didn't really have much to put *in* a bra. I needed one for other reasons.'

'When I came back from Sydney to live,' says One, 'Two arrived at my front door with a huge picnic basket full of wonderful food.'

'I was responsible for Five,' says Two, 'when Mum and Dad put her into boarding school so they could go overseas. Mum said to me, "You were wonderful to Five." I was, too. I liked doing it—but sometimes I get this narky feeling that I'd like to send in an account.'

'Three had dared to come to my first wedding,' says One, 'when Dad forbade everyone to go. And she took it right up to Dad when he called my husband a conman.'

'Wait till your father dies,' says somebody's husband. 'You'll be like the Baltic states at the collapse of the Soviet Union. You've been formed and bound together in opposition to him. When he goes there'll be hell to pay.'

'Let's try to keep it on sisters,' says One. 'Don't let's talk too much about our parents.'

'But aren't they sort of the point?' says Five.

'Yes, but it's obsessive. We all swerve and swerve back to our parents. I want us to talk about being sisters, not daughters.'

Other People's Sisters

I mention to a friend that I am trying to write this. She remarks, 'The best way for sisters to get on is to talk about their parents.'

Some sisters are sisters with a tremendous, conscious, public conviction. I remember a woman I knew, years ago, who would get up from the lunch table and retire to her room for the afternoon, saying, 'I'm going to write a letter to my sister.' We felt respectful, and tiptoed round so as not to disturb her. She would emerge, hours later, looking purged, satisfied, and slightly smug.

Another friend, one of whose sisters recently died in a freak accident, says to me, 'I've lost our shared childhood. I depended on her memory. I loved going out with her. When we walked down the street together with our youngest sister, the three of us, I used to be so proud and happy. I used to feel we were invincible—that nothing could touch us.'

This is the kind of story I think of as sisterly: once a woman was driving along a street in West Melbourne when she was attacked by severe abdominal pains. She tried to ignore them and drove on, but they became so violent that she was obliged to park her car outside a friend's house and stagger in, doubled over, to lie on a bed. Gradually the pains abated. When she was able to go home, she phoned her mother for a chat and learnt that, the same day, her sister had given birth to her third child in Geelong, and had had to agree to a hysterectomy because of unstoppable bleeding.

A striking example of telepathic contact, yes; and it happened, in our family. But the story is rarely told, sixteen years later, because this gut empathy had no practical application. The flaw is that when Three needed help, after that hysterectomy, none of the rest of us thought of offering any; she did not feel able to ask for it, and thus got none. The spirit of our family is 'Pick up your lip before you trip over it.' Is that sisterly?

The Different One
I asked my sisters, separately, to characterise themselves. Each of them, in slightly varying phrases, saw herself as the different one.

'I felt for years the rejected one,' says One. 'I couldn't go near the place without getting into a fight with Dad. But when I sent Mum a birthday telegram signed *The Black Sheep*, she got upset.'

'I remember feeling I was very different from the rest of you,' says Two. 'I was the first to marry and I lived in the suburbs, whereas you all (except Three) saw each other a lot and lived that sloppy rock&roll life, which was anathema to me, with a husband and two kids. I'm the only one who doesn't vote Labor. At family gatherings I still feel out of it, a bit. I dress differently.'

'I was always the odd one out,' says Three. 'I was a nuisance to One and Two, when I was little. Later I was the only one interested in having a spiritual life. Two came into the bedroom once and found me on my knees. I don't know which of us was more embarrassed. Then I struck out on my own and went to Papua New Guinea straight from school, and worked on the mission. It was a great shock, after growing up in a middle-class family. I was always looking for a way of doing life more simply. But then I burrowed into a conventional marriage.'

'I got the short end of the stick,' says Four, 'because I was the fourth girl. They must've looked at me and thought, "Bloody hell—not another one!" I've always thought that was the basis of my problem with Dad. Remember how when he was trying to tell childhood stories about everyone, at his birthday party? He couldn't remember anything about me to tell. I've constantly felt the odd one out—constantly. And I feel it now, specially since Five had a baby, because I'm the only one without children, and the only one who never wanted any.'

'I,' says Five, 'am the odd one out only in the sense that. I'm the youngest by ten years. Otherwise I don't feel that way at all. Oh—if you all get together and I haven't attended, I feel miffed or excluded. But I must have received a lot of attention when I was young. Mum and Dad had more time to spend with me. They took me travelling round the world with them. My relationship with them is different from the others.'

What Did You Pay For Those?
We are not so different that we can't wear each other's clothes. When one sister arrives at another's house, the first thing they do together is dash to the bedroom and starting trying on shoes.

At Christmas, One and Two arrive at Five's house for the big family dinner. They walk down the hall and become instantly aware of a certain quality of silence issuing like smoke from one of the bedrooms. They rush in. There stand Four and Five, bent over a table, heads together, backs to the door, working hard at something. They glance up as One and Two barge in, but their eyes are blank with concentration and without speaking they return at once to their task. One and Two push in beside them and see what is on the table: Five's six-month-old daughter, flat on her back, looking patient but slightly puzzled. Four and Five are trying to squeeze the baby's fat feet into a tiny pair of red leather boots. The boots are much too small, but Four and Five will not accept this. Quivering with suppressed giggles, they lace and tug, applying force to the leather and the flesh as if the baby's life depended on it. It is a bizarre initiation rite into the family passion for shoes. Shoes bought in haste, that don't fit.

One day in winter, One leaves her muddy Doc Martens on the front verandah. Next morning they are gone. She searches everywhere, then curses thieves and gives them up for lost. Several days later, in the afternoon, the doorbell rings. One opens the door and sees Four on the mat, beaming at her with a wicked look. Instinctively One's eyes drop to Four's feet. On them are the missing Docs.

'That'll teach you,' says Four suavely, 'to take better care of your possessions.'

In David Jones' 'perthume' department, Two says to One, 'Here—let me squirt this on you, in case I hate it.'

Four possesses an absolutely reliable brutality when it comes to clothes. 'Should I buy these trousers, Four? Look, they're only thirty dollars.' Four runs a cold eye over them, and turns away. 'Buy them if you want to look like a *stump*. Like a *mallee* root.'

One and Three enter a shop. Three scans, then heads unerringly for a rack of dark, sober, important-looking garments. One grabs her by the back of her jacket and steers her firmly towards a row of pretty, soft, pale, flowery dresses. The expression of suspicion, self-dislike and severity on Three's face, while she tries on a dress and examines herself in the mirror, reminds One so much of herself that it squeezes her heart. Three buys a dress. Next time One approaches Three's house, she sees a slender, long-haired girl standing out on the pavement, with the wind swaying her loose skirt. 'Oh, how pretty,' thinks One. She gets closer and sees that it's Three, aged forty-five, wearing the dress they chose together.

A Deeply Wounded Postcard

If there are five of you, you form a complex network of shifting alliances.

'For six months,' says Five, 'I'll mostly hang out with Four. Then she'll say or do something that shits me, but instead of slugging it out with her on the spot, I'll show her the door in a restrained manner and then get straight on the phone to One: "Can you *believe* what Four just said to me? Fuckin' bitch!" And then I'll move over to a different camp, for a while.'

'I was outraged,' says Three to One, 'by what you said about that African movie as we came out into the foyer. I'd been so moved by it—and you ruined it, in one smart crack. I had to get away from you, before you completely destroyed it for me. I came home and wrote you a letter about it. Which I didn't send.'

'I wrote Three a terrible letter,' says One, 'and I posted it. I quaked for a week, then she sent me a deeply wounded postcard. I apologised, and it was never mentioned again. But ooh, I'd love to have a fight with her.'

'Sometimes,' says Five, 'I despise myself after I leave one sister's house, thinking about how I've curbed my behaviour in her company. To please her. It's so easy to slip into a style of dialogue that suits the one I'm visiting.'

'Yes,' says Four, 'and when you get home you write the letter.'

'Five had the nerve,' says One, 'to write me an extremely snippish letter. I had to go for a walk to calm down. And then I wrote her a scorcher which said all the things I'd been bottling up for years and hadn't had the nerve to say before. I said, You listen to me. I said, How dare you. I said, I should come over and kick your arse right round the block. That sort of thing.

I censored the worst bits, and then I posted it.'

'When I got the letter from you,' says Five. 'I was paralysed. I also noticed you'd cut off the bottom of one page, so I realised there'd been even worse things. I sat on the end of my bed. I could hardly move for half an hour.'

'The bits I cut off,' says One, 'I pasted into my diary. That's how I remember what I originally said.'

'Why *don't* we yell at each other?' says Four.

'Because,' says One, 'we're so in love with the idea of our family continuing that to speak truly and honestly would jeopardise it.'

'Isn't that a bit pathetic, though? I think we should yell at each other.'

'You start.'

'All right. "Get out of my sight, you moll." How's that?'

'This is *serious*, Four—do you mind?'

'OK. Sorry. But you did yell at me once—don't you remember? I came over to borrow some money and you lost your temper.'

'I remember now I yelled at you that you were so selfish you never asked me how I was, or anything about *my* life—all you did was whinge about *your* problems. You bawled and howled, it was dreadful, and I said, "I'm sorry if this hurts you," and you said, howling away, "It's all right, because I need to know why nobody likes me." And that of course was so tragic that *I* started bawling, and then you looked at me with your red eyes and said in a weird, polite, choked sort of voice, "And how's work going lately?" We both cracked up laughing—and then I lent you five hundred bucks and you went home.'

'I had a fight one night with Two,' says One, 'outside Trinity Chapel after evensong. We'd gone to hear the choir. I'd left a cake in the oven before I came out of the house and I was worried about getting home in time. I was strapping on my bike helmet, and Two started in on me about the Old Testament readings, which had been about the parting of the Red Sea. She said, "It's awful. It's *racist*." I said, "Oh, don't be ridiculous." She said, "I am *not* being ridiculous! Imagine if *you* were an Egyptian and had to sit there listening to that!" I lost my temper and yelled at her. She didn't turn a hair. You can say *anything* to Two—she never takes umbrage, she just keeps on arguing. I realised how grotesque I must be looking, scowling and red-faced with my hideous helmet on, and I broke off and said "I've got to go straight home." Two said, "Yes, go on—go home to your *cake*." I pedalled away, to cross the university grounds, and I suddenly thought, "Goodness—we've had a fight!" But I didn't feel bad. I felt great. I felt exhilarated. And I yelled back to her, "The music was fabulous!" I could see her rippling along behind the fence railings as she strode back to her car—she didn't answer, but just waved and kept walking. I zoomed home on my bike, thinking, "Hey! Fighting's not so bad!" The next day I wrote her a postcard saying something to that effect. And she sent one back, quite cheerful and dignified, saying, "That wasn't a fight. It was a *disagreement*." '

'Yes, you can really have a fight with Two,' says Five. 'There's something thrilling about her bluntness. She's got no shame. And she doesn't get so *personal*.'

'It must be because she's done assertiveness training,' says One. 'I think it must teach you to do your best to get your own way, but if you don't, you don't sulk. You just cop it. It's quite impressive, in a gruesome sort of way.'

'I fought with Four,' says Five. 'It was very beneficial. I realised I wouldn't be able to go *on* with Four unless we had a fight. I said dreadful things. She was crying and crying—but she was taking it all on board. I had to respect her for that. I kept trying to put her to bed. She said, "Fuck you—I don't *want* to go to bed!" But I kept on trying to force her to.'

'That would've been because of what I said about Whatsisname, I'm sure,' says Four. 'He was a *pret-ty* vile guy, which Five later came to realise…whereas I knew it all along, and said so.'

'Three and I were building up to a smash,' says One, 'but we sidestepped it. She played the martyr, basically, and I panicked and became feeble and began to appease her.'

'We're always very quick to apologise,' says Three.

    'That's our way,' says One, 'of keeping everything on a safe, superficial level. We say, I've hurt her. I'll call it rudeness and say I'm sorry." Whereas if we were really going to have some form of intimacy, we'd yell at each other—"damn it, get that look off your face!" '

'I hold back from fighting, usually,' says One, 'because if I say to my sister what I really think about her, I'm licensing her to tell me what she really thinks about *me*. And I don't know how to defend myself against that. I'm afraid of it. Because sisters don't subscribe to each other's mythology. To the myths of each other.'

'I'm scared of you,' says One.

    'I'm scared of you, too,' says Three.

    They laugh, and look away. Then they glance at each other again, curiously. Gently.

Theatre
There is a tendency in our family to brood on slights. Each

likes to tell a story in which she appears more sensitive and more hard done by than another. We would rather be wounded, and glory in our outraged sensitivity, than take it up to the offender and make a protest to her face. Thus we end up with a series of shrines. Each of us (with the exception perhaps of Two, who is more robust, frank and fearless) keeps a private shrine to herself, with a little lamp inside it eternally flickering, and the oil that feeds it is the offences dealt out by her sisters. The misplaced smirk, the thoughtless crack is stored away, and for a while the little ego-lamp burns more brightly—until there's the shift, when the incident is related to one of the other sisters as a story, constructed and pointed with the primary aim of provoking laughter and a momentary sense of alliance. It becomes another chapter in our fanatically detailed, multi-track story about ourselves, which is hilarious, entertaining, appalling, obsessive. It is related in a secret language composed of joke pronunciations, silly accents, coded phrases whose origins were forgotten long ago but which are heavy with meaning and will always raise a laugh. We are major characters in the stories of each other's lives; we are all acting in an enormous comedy that will go on till we die. It has no audience but its own performers: our children and husbands roll their eyes and walk out of rooms. Its time scale is an endless, immediate now.

Obsession and Intimacy

'Once I was raving on,' says One, 'about my family to a bloke I know who's got four brothers. After a while he started twisting in his seat, and then he burst out, "Anyone would think you were the only person in the world who had a family!" I felt foolish. But I sort of couldn't *help* it.'

'I have to hold myself back,' says Five, 'with anyone I meet, from talking about our family. My friends are probably driven bonkers by the way I *go on* about it. They never seem to need to talk about theirs. I prod them. I say, "I didn't know you had a brother. Tell me about him." But they say they can't be bothered. "Why?" "Because he's boring." How can a brother or sister be *boring?*

'I think it's something wrong with *us*,' says One. 'I've spent my life trying to have friendships outside the family which will provide as much intimacy as I get from my sisters. It's a doomed enterprise. So I keep crashing and smashing and falling out with my friends. They can't stand the demand for intimacy and attention. I bore them, I irritate them, I wear the friendship out.'

'I don't think intimacy is the problem,' says Two. 'It's because you're too bossy. We're all too bossy.'

'I never got this intimacy from our family,' says Three. 'A lot of people say they envy me having four sisters—but no one ever hugged or cuddled, to comfort. It wasn't done. I was at a friend's place recently when her older sister came round, looking wretched. Between our sisters, a rough joke would've been made—Come on, pick up your lip before you trip over it! But the younger one had a good look and said, "Ah—what's the *matter?*" The older one shed a few tears and said: "Life's too difficult. I'm trying to work, and there's the baby, and I have to do a course if I want to keep my job—it's too much for me." And the younger one said, "Oh, come here"—and sat her sister on her *lap.* Can you imagine any of us doing that? Then they ran a bath and got in it together. I heard them laughing and shrieking. I felt terribly envious. Maybe you others had that sort of closeness. I never did. When I had a hysterectomy, I was abandoned. See? You hardly even remember it. One came down and minded the boys for a couple of days, but the rest of the time I was on my own, with a new baby and two toddlers, too weak to get out of bed. It was…desolate. I learnt not to look for help from the family.'

'Yes, that's shameful,' says One, 'but do you realise how perfect your marriage seemed, from the outside? You looked as if you had everything sewn up. You didn't ask for help. There's an art in asking.'

'I know how,' says Three, 'but I wouldn't.'

'Why?'

'I was afraid of indifference.'

'*Would* there be indifference, if you showed weakness?'

'It's not weakness,' says Three. 'It's need. It's better not to show need, if you're not going to get your needs met. I've learnt that. I worked out where people were going to care enough, and I went there.'

'It *is* rather uneven,' says One. 'I tried to tell Four my troubles once—we were driving downtown in a car. I talked for five minutes, and she cut across me and said, "Oh, shut up—you sound exactly like Mum." But whenever anything goes wrong in her life, the first thing she does is pick up the phone and dial my number.'

Four is the witty one. But as a child she was a tremendous howler. At the slightest rebuff she would throw back her head and roar; tears would squirt out of her eyes and bounce down her fat cheeks. One, Two and Three used to hold up sixpence at breakfast time, saying 'You can have this tonight—but every time you cry, we're going to dock you a penny.' By teatime Four would be once more heavily in debt.

'If we cried when we were little,' says Two, 'Mum used to say, "Stop it, you great *cake*."'

'I don't remember that,' says Five.

'Of course you don't,' says Two. 'You weren't born yet.'

'Three,' says Two, 'was the painful little sister we used to run away from. Once she tried to bribe us. She said, "I'll give you threepence if you let me come with you." But we took no notice and kept running.'

'I remember that,' says Three. 'I can remember the feeling

of the wire of the gate under the soles of my feet, as I hung over it and watched you two disappearing up the road. At least, I think I remember it. Maybe it's only because the story's been told so many times.'

'Maybe,' says One, 'it never happened at all.'

Endearments
Because endearments were never used in our family (Plymouth Brethren two generations back on our mother's side; grim-jawed Mallee stoicism on our father's), it has taken us all our lives to learn to say *dear, darling, sweetheart*, without irony.

'At school,' says One, 'when I was a boarder, I was sick with envy of girls who got letters from their parents that started with the word Dearest.'

A few years ago, Four sent One a telegram: 'Dearest Darling, happy birthday, from your Darling.' The telegram was read, marked, learnt and inwardly digested, then thrown into the rubbish bin. That night a strong wind blew, and overturned the bin into the running gutter. Next morning an angry young man knocked on One's front door. He thrust the crushed and sodden telegram in her face: 'Is *this* how you treat a man's heartfelt declaration of love? Shame on you!' 'It's not a man!' cried One. 'It's my *sister*.' He stared at her strangely, and stamped out the gate.

If one of us uses an endearment on the phone to a child, a friend, a lover, while a sister is in the room, she glances nervously behind her to make sure she is not being mimicked. None of us would dream, however, of mocking someone for doing this. In fact, we would (I believe) like to pet and treasure each other, to pour out floods of sweet words. But we are all engaged in the same struggle against inherited embarrassment, against a terrible Australian dryness. We maul and stroke each other's children: it's the closest we can get. And our children submit to their aunts' possessive handling with patient smiles.

Class
From the middle of the middle class there are paths leading in both directions. A family can rise or fall in class over twenty years, so that its eldest child is brought up at one level, and its youngest at quite another.

'I used to escape from the bedlam,' says Two, 'by going to my friend's place over the back lane. Her father listened to opera, and her mother always did beautiful ikebana flower arrangements that I loved—she was so creative. They had posh accents. The parents didn't just have single beds, like our parents did—they had separate rooms. I liked their accoutrements: engraved silver, crystal, a back sitting room. They had two spaniels called Kismet and Ophelia. They were what I aspired to be: Geelong Grammar posh people. We were down market. I wished our parents said *dahnce* and *cahstle*. Three always disapproved of my lifestyle, later on. Once I said to her, "I'd like to have a marblised wood dining table. I suppose they must be really expensive"—and she came back at me: "Even *poor* people have dining tables, you know!"—almost as if she thought my whole life was devoted to...acquisition. It probably is! I wouldn't deny it! I don't care about that now, but I used to.'

'Once I went with Two to a department store,' says Three, 'to buy our kids some pyjamas. I headed straight for the bargain bin, and she made a beeline for the quality shelf. When we met at the cash register, her stuff cost six times as much as mine. After I came back from Papua New Guinea I couldn't *believe* the way people in Australia spent money. Two Papuans from the mission where I worked came and visited Mum and Dad.

Later they wrote to me, "What a lot you gave up, to come to us. Your family lives in a huge house, with many comfortable chairs and two cars." I wrote back, "Yes, but in that house I have not learnt what I need to know." '

'One's friends,' says Two, 'were band-y, interesting, creative people. That got her into trouble with Dad. Whereas I had boring, stable, middle-class friends, which was approved of.'

'I remember asking and asking,' says Four, 'what the working class was. I mean—where was it? As soon as I got the chance I headed down market. I was desperate not to be middle class. Even my friends at school were rough as bags. I was smart but I was always in trouble.'

'Two was deeply offended, I think,' says Five, 'when I didn't marry X. She wanted me to marry an American and go and live on Long Island or in Hawaii. That was her fantasy for me. Frangipanis over breakfast for the rest of my life.'

'When Five was having her baby,' says One, 'I suffered for a while from ferocious jealousy. It was mostly displaced on to material things—on to shopping. Mum took her out to Daimaru for a swanky lunch at Paul Bocuse and then bought her a whole lot of fabulous baby clothes. When I heard about it I practically had to stay home in a darkened room for a couple of days. And Five's not even *married*.'

Afterbirth

With four sisters, there's one for most moods. Two is brilliant at cooking and gardening. Four is the adventurous one, to go out shopping and dancing with: at a certain point, whenever she and One went out together they witnessed a car crash. Five loves to talk about books and writing, and to compare the nibs of pens. In Three's company, the slightest incident becomes redolent with psychological and spiritual meaning.

Once, Three and One spent a day at One's shack in the bush. The purpose of the outing was to 'sort out some things', to have 'a conversation that was several years overdue'. Reproaches flew both ways. They sat sadly at the wooden table, looking at their hands. Then Three said, 'Want me to wash your face *with a warm washer?*' One recognised the childhood phrase. She presented her face, chin up, eyes squeezed shut, and Three rubbed and wiped, firmly; One could hear her quietly laughing. A little while later, One put some Oil of Ulan on Three's face. These things seemed very *symbolic*, as did everything else they did up there that day: tearing out the old ivy roots, sawing dead limbs off the shrubbery, making soup for the meal. Then, as they drove away towards the road home, One saw a cow in a paddock with a long red strand hanging out of her mouth. One yelled out, Three stopped the car. The cow had just finished licking the membrane off a new-born calf, which was struggling to its feet. They saw its blunt little head, its coat so matt and clean. The cow set about eating the afterbirth: the thing was clearly a membranous sac; the cow kept licking and chewing at the sloppy mound of it on the grass, dutifully gulping it down. One and Three imagined it already cold, slimy, strandy—it seemed a nauseous duty, and an image of the maternal labours they had been bitterly talking about. Neither of them remarked on this connection, but they sat there in the car, holding the dog by the collar, and watched intently for a long time. Then Three said, 'Oh *look*. All the other cows are coming over to inspect. To celebrate.'

Music

'Once,' says Three, 'I was combing Dad's hair with the comb dipped in Listerine and telling him that I wanted to learn the piano. One said, on her way past, "Be a jazz pianist." And Dad said to her, "Don't tell her what to do."'

'So *you* were the one who made them get a piano,' says One. 'How'd you do it? When I said I wanted to learn the violin they just laughed and made squawking noises.'

'Oh, I pestered and pestered,' says Three. 'And then I set up a stall in the street out the front, to raise the money to buy one. I think I shamed them into it.'

Back in the seventies, when there was such a thing as the three-dollar gig, Four and One used to go out dancing, with all their friends, several nights a week. It would never have occurred to One to imagine herself on stage; but Four watched carefully, then borrowed a saxophone from a man she knew and taught herself a few riffs. Next thing One knew, her sister was up there in a sparkly jacket, playing 'Suffragette City' with a women's band called Flying Tackle.

When Two's daughter decides to leave her medical course and study singing, Two invites Three and One over, one evening, to be a practice audience for the daughter's conservatoriurn audition pieces. Three and One jump in the car and rush over there, wearing clean, ironed clothes. They set up the living room like a little stage, and plump themselves on to the sofa in a line, hands folded, chins up, eyes bright. The daughter steps out to sing, sees them eagerly sitting there, and bursts out laughing. She leaves the room, and returns more composed. In the pause before she sings the first note, Two hisses to her sisters, *'Need a tissue?'*

'One came home from university for a visit,' says Three, 'and brought me a Vivaldi record. It was so *exciting*—I'd never heard anything like it before.'

Four is the kind of person to whom it matters how a backing vocal changes, in the bridge of the song, from 'shoop shoo wop bop' to 'bop shoo wop bop'. When she got of the plane at JFK she took a cab straight to Danceteria.

Three can sight-read. Three always remembers the words. Three goes to the trouble of making tapes and passing them round the family. Three must have been the only nurse at the Royal Children's in the 1960s who knew Mahler's *Kindertotenlieder*.

'In New York,' says Five, 'I heard some black people singing and playing in the street. I wanted to bawl. I said to the person standing next to me, "Are they from a religion? Show me where to join—I want to sign up."'

At school we were taught to sing in parts. Thus there were years during which, we would spontaneously drop into harmony, while washing dishes or on tedious car trips, or very softly in our beds at night when sleep was reluctant to come.

Then we were grown-up and nobody sang. Hymns and carols became embarrassing. We wiped 'The Lass of Richmond Hill' and 'The Ash Grove' from our repertoires and went to Europe or got married.

Decades passed. Then Two instigated a Christmas concert. It was fun the first time but soon degenerated into our children miming bad pop records. Anyway when we sang together now we sounded horrible. Our voices had dropped into a lower register and lost their sweetness. None of us could hit the top notes without screeching. We soon gave it up.

But Two secretly persevered, singing along to records of famous chorales. Three played hymns on her piano at night, telling herself she was just practising sight-reading. One, at forty, finally found the nerve to take piano lessons. Four, the only one with a serious musical talent and the drive to use it, took singing lessons, practised irritatingly in the car on the freeway, and was soon able to front her own band as a singer instead of just playing saxophone.

'I,' announced Two, 'am going to join a choir.'

She does. And she drags the rest of us into it too, a huge Christmas charity choir with a proper conductor. You pay your thirty bucks and are issued with a score and a practice tape to learn your part from, between rehearsals.

We work hard at it, separately, at home. Our first practice is at Two's place on a Friday evening. We belt out the carols in our terrible harsh (but in tune) voices, then tackle the harder stuff. Just as we roar to the end of the 'Hallelujah Chorus' and close our scores with sighs of triumph, One looks out the window and sees a huge pale full moon rising out of the trees.

When we sing 'The Shepherds' Farewell' from Berlioz' 'The Childhood of Christ', we think privately of our own children leaving us: 'God go with you, God protect you, guide you safely through the wild.' We hope that if we can sing right to the end without crying, the music will act as a blessing.

Every Sunday we drive or pedal to the Catholic Hall at the top end of Brunswick Street and sing the afternoon away. All altos now, we are within our physical range. It's important to position ourselves in front of older women, cheerful ones of sixty-plus who come in from the outer-suburban church choirs, who know the works and can sight-sing. We rush each week to get near these guides, the ones with calm, strong, bosomy voices, who won't fade out or get flustered when the timing goes complex, but who lean forward in the tricky bits, to keep us on track.

In a large choir—five hundred or more—a beginner can afford to take risks. You can take wild stabs at the intervals, and your mistakes will be swallowed up in the rolling tide of sound. We've learnt that in daily life we barely breathe; singing requires an intake and expulsion of air so much more rhythmic and profound that at times we become light-headed and have to grip the seatback for balance.

We are women who have always been fighting our father. Maybe this is why we love the way the men's voices surge under ours, a broad band of deeper sound, something stable and generous that supports the women in their sharper, more fanciful melodiousness. We are astonished by the ability of five hundred voices to sing softly, to make a sound like a whisper. We are learning the humility, the modesty, the indispensability of the alto part; accepting the limits and the strengths of maturity.

It's dangerous to look at each other. Two's hanky is always in her hand. If we catch each other's eye, our voices tremble, choke and die. So we are learning to stand beside each other, upper arms touching, looking straight ahead: part of the larger music.

Now that we can sing together, surely none of us will ever die—*surely*?

1993

Wan, Tew, Three, Faw

OUR FAMILY WAS not musical. Ours is not the type of family with an auntie who can vamp out 'Bye Bye Blackbird' and sing along in a high, trembling voice full of swoops and scoops. Our house never echoed with the squawks of amateur violins, or the running up and down of piano scales. One of my grandmothers did have a small grand piano but I never heard her play it. There was no musical instrument in our house until after I'd left home.

A musical family was one in which each child played a different instrument. The Brockmans down in Villa-Manta Street were such a family. Their father played the organ in a church. They all looked intense and tousled, with burning eyes. Our family was plain, fair and muscly. Our parents played golf.

All this silence got too much for me in 1977. I bought a second-hand piano for my eight-year-old daughter. A rock-and-roll bass player who lived in the house taught her a few riffs and she romped away. I was scared of the instrument and never touched it.

By 1980 I had got up the nerve to find a piano teacher for myself. His name was Greg. He was half my age and looked like Dr Dolittle. He was crazy about Bartok and started me off on 'Mikrokosmos'. I liked this very much but longed to play Bach.

I had been wanting to play Bach ever since I saw Manning Clark take up the piano at fifty and sit stubbornly at the instrument with *The Children's Bach* open in front of him, picking away at it, his ankles crossed under the bench. I bought *The Children's Bach* and read E. Harold Davies' pompous little introduction. 'Bach is never simple,' he wrote, 'but that is one of the best reasons why we should try hard to master him. It is only in overcoming difficulties that any of us can rise to greatness, and that, surely, is what we all want to do.'

Greg began to teach me 'A Song of Contentment', but then we moved house and I had to find another teacher. An old lady called Mrs Beryl T. Arroll took over. Above her piano she had two portraits, one of Schubert, the other of Liszt. She pulled a face when I mentioned 'Mikrokosmos'. John Thompson's method for beginners was more her speed. I limped through pieces with names like 'Runaway River', 'The Scissors Grinder', 'The Mouse's Party', 'The Wigwam'.

My daughter, meanwhile, had begun to learn the cello. Her pieces had dignified titles like 'Sonata in C'. Once again she galloped past me and I ate her dust.

The family Christmas dinner at my sister Marie's place was her idea, but the concert was mine. My motives were not pure. I was afraid of boredom on Christmas Day. I calculated the number of hours to be filled with social obligations: greetings and drinks, forty-five minutes: present-opening and exclamations, twenty minutes: dinner, ninety minutes: digestion and general conversation, several hours, and so on. Even if no clashes occurred between me and my father, the strain of this would be immense.

I said to Marie, 'We should have a concert.' She made no response, being preoccupied with a maintenance problem of the swimming pool. This was October. I let it pass.

Halfway through November Marie rang up. 'What are you and Alice playing at the concert?'

'What concert?'

'It was your idea. The Christmas concert.'

'It was only a joke!'

'You can't say that now. It's all organised. I'm making a list. Owen's sister is a terrific pianist, and her kids play too. They're doing something by Haydn, I think she said. What'll I put down for you?'

'I can hardly play at all. I only learn bubsy stuff.'

'That doesn't matter. What'll you play? It'll be gorgeous.'

'Everyone will laugh at me. I'm hopeless.'

'Of course they won't. Just tell me a title.'

'It's all right for you. You aren't playing anything.'

'No, but I'm organising. I want it all arranged in advance, so the kids' music teachers can help them prepare their pieces. Does Alice want to play in a trio?'

You don't argue with Marie. I may be the eldest, but Marie is the real thing, long-legged and elegant, wears real jewellery, married a doctor, has lived in America, keeps her recipes on an Apple.

I blackmailed Alice into accompanying me on 'Runaway River'. 'Just play the bottom line,' I commanded.

She rolled her eyes but obeyed. We would set ourselves up in the kitchen every evening while dinner was being cooked, and thump and saw away. Alice had to put a rolled-up towel under the cello spike to stop it from slipping on the lino. The weather got hotter and the piano went out of tune and started to jangle and buzz. I timed the piece: approximately twenty seconds.

Meanwhile the other members of the trio were preparing, with their teachers, for the big day. I took Alice out there for a practice. The cousins' music teacher, who called weekly at the house, put the cello part in front of Alice and away she went, bluffing like a trouper, her skinny legs clamped round the half-size Japanese cello, her face set in the fierce concentration of the sight-reader: eyes staring, teeth bared.

Back in our kitchen I plodded on. The daughter of a friend

happened to pass through the room one day. She came and stood beside me, watched my struggles, then leaned over and whispered in my ear, 'My mum can play better than you.'

Christmas Day that year dawned a scorcher. Alice felt ill but we set out anyway; my husband with a guitar and an iron determination not to play it; two of my sisters, one with a saxophone; Alice with her cello and a plastic sick-bowl; and me with John Thompson and a thundering heart.

'*La famille Rikiki va au concert*,' remarked my husband in his native tongue.

As we drove along Johnston Street, Alice vomited into the bowl. My sisters cried out in disgust and rolled the windows down. My husband pulled in to a closed service station and I got out and emptied the bowl down a gully-trap.

At Marie's there were dozens of relatives, by blood and marriage, running about screaming. Screwed-up paper and ribbons were strewn everywhere. I marvelled once again at the miracle of family resemblance. My family has Cossack legs and yellowish skin; Marie's husband's family a nutcracker jaw and piercing blue eyes.

Marie's children had made splendiferous programs for the concert. The first item was ' "Runaway River" by Helen and Alice.'

Alice was getting a lot of mileage out of the spewing story, but seemed to be in top form. Children in sopping bathers, skin scorched and hair dripping down their backs, tuned up their instruments. Someone was setting up a tape recorder.

'Keep that flaming door shut, you kids,' roared my father, who was born in the Mallee.

When the moment could be delayed no longer, I sat at the piano and Alice set up her cello. I was unnerved by having my back to the audience. I was dripping with sweat. My fingers stuck together and would not move independently; my hands were like two lumps of wood. I stared at the music and saw only black shapes dancing on a grid of lines, meaning nothing. It was the worst moment of my life, worse than a French oral exam. I thought I was going to die of fear.

'And now,' cried Marie from behind me in a cracked, excited voice. 'Helen and Alice will play—"Runaway River"!'

I sat block-like in the hush of attention.

'Come on,' hissed Alice at my side. 'Count us in.'

Fifth finger left hand, third finger right hand. I found them and put them on the notes. 'One, two, three,' I whispered. It was the softest piano I had ever heard. It was like playing a piano made of sponge. But some mechanism between brain and fingers was still working all by itself. The cello sang along. I could see my daughter's brow, her sinewy bowing arm, and nothing was going wrong.

By the twelfth bar I was enjoying myself. By the fourteenth I was Glenn Gould, by the sixteenth I was Bach himself. I struck the last note in pride and regret.

There was a silence, then a roar of applause. I stood up and turned to bow, and saw a room full of clapping hands and smiling faces. Marie was standing against the wall wiping her eyes with a huge red serviette; her mascara had run right down her cheeks.

Grown-ups played with children, child with child; piano duets, piano and recorder, violin and flute, the famous trio. In secret lounge rooms, in the kitchens and garages of rock-and-roll houses, in school music lessons, these ten years, an ordinary unmusical family had been doggedly transforming itself into something else.

My husband played the guitar after all and sang one of those melancholy, melodic French songs in three-four time, by Georges Brassens, that can break a heart. My father said it was marvellous and offered to become his manager.

Then Steve sat at the piano, my sister got out her

saxophone, and up stood the little ratbag, Adam, Marie's son. His huge teeth were chipped. His hair, matted and greenish with chlorine, shone like flax. He was holding a trumpet.

'Gawd spare me days,' said our father out of the corner of his mouth.

'Ssshhh, Bruce,' whispered our mother.

Marie, her eyes bunged up with crying, rose to make the announcement. 'Steve, Sally and Adam will now present—"Tamouree".'

'Wan, tew, three, faw,' said Steve. The blond boy and his blonde auntie poured forth a flood of brass. Their cheeks were fat with air, their eyes downcast. They leaned back to give the sound room. Their feet beat the rhythm, the boy's bare, the woman's in elegant open-toed shoes. The welkin rang. 'Tamouree' brought the house down.

'Ho, ho, ho!' roared our father.

In the pandemonium, the young trumpeter stood on his head on a cushion with his legs up the wall and played 'Mary Had a Little Lamb'.

Steve and my husband withdrew to a doorway. 'This affair is a bit ridiculous,' said my husband. Steve nodded and smiled and kept his eyes on the ground and his arms folded.

'Dinner is served,' shouted Marie.

'Still on the dole, are you?' said our father to my sister in the stampede to the table. She stopped and turned red.

'I get paid for playing, dad,' she replied.

Our mother said, 'Cut it out, you two,' and put herself between them.

'Oh no,' shouted Marie's husband. 'The tape recorder wasn't working.'

'Just as well,' said our father. 'Once is enough, don't you reckon?' He put on a paper crown, adjusted his glasses, and applied his thumbs to a champagne cork.

1982

Three Acres, More or Less

for Barbara Barnes: generous friend

If I had the Buddha's eyes and could see
through everything, I could discern the
marks of worry and sorrow you leave in your
footprints after you pass.

Thich Nhat Hanh

SHOULD THE EAGLES cruising on lofty air train their stern eye-beams down this way, they would see a puppet jerking pointlessly, trotting here and there, always on the move. This is me on my land. The *three acres, more or less*, as the title puts it, which I own *to the depth of fifty feet*, must thus be crisscrossed like the dirt of a mustering yard with the marks of my anxiety. Walking is easy. The hard thing is sitting still.

To get here, you travel across a landscape of volcanic plains. As a teenager dragged out on Sunday drives, I saw it as an endless stretch of colourless nothing which perfectly manifested my dismal inner state. Now, thirty years later, I see the cleanness of its lines, its puritan bareness and simplicity, the tremendous sweep of its low horizons. It is a weary, purified landscape, unambitious, worn smooth, covered in short dry grass the same colour as the sheep that eat it.

But at certain points the impersonality of the open, sheep-coloured plains becomes secretly complicated, crinkles briefly into more intimate creases in which a parcel of land like mine, once an orchard till the Apple and Pear Board standardised things and the unprofitable trees were uprooted, can be clung to by some stubborn old coot and preserved as personal though everything around it becomes state forest.

My three acres are on the side of a gully let into this rolling smoothness like a placket into a skirt, a modest echo of the wider, deeper, more twisting valley nearby in the bottom of which the Moorabool River, narrow and stony, slaves unconvincingly towards the Barwon. My gully is the bed of a creek which once probably slaved, too, to reach the Moorabool; but this creek has been dammed to make a little ornamental lake that I call 'the bottom dam', though its water is for looking at and not for pumping, drinking, washing or sailing. Below the dam wall is a stretch of mown grass with a couple of old apple trees left standing. I can't help thinking of this as 'a meadow', although I know this is a European word, a European phenomenon. Not only that, I think of it as a Russian meadow, and I have never been to Russia.

> *If I sit still, and if the wind is blowing from the east, I can hear the Moorabool toiling hopelessly among its stones. I shouldn't say 'toil', I shouldn't say 'hopeless'. It's just a river flowing.*

The place for sitting still is a bench that someone has left under the olive tree. I'll go down there in a minute, to the spot halfway along the gully rim, from which I can see the old rowing boat lying in the grass, and I'll sit still; but first I have to tramp up into the bush to collect some firewood, and walk to the top dam to check its level and the condition of the pump, and back to the ladder to peer into the high tank, and down to the house to disconnect the empty gas cylinder and connect the full one; and I have to heave the dunny can out from under its little wooden trapdoor and wheel it on its trolley along the path to the trench and shovel in some dirt to cover the sewage, and pile up the dead branches I drag in from the forest and cut some of them on my sawhorse and make a proper wood pile outside the back door, and then

I have to pull the old newspapers out from behind the fuel stove to see if that's where the rat's nest is; and if it is I have to clean up the mess of piss and chewed paper they leave behind, and then nail something over their hole behind the kitchen cupboard.

Then I have to get down on my knees to weed the front garden, and dig a proper drainage channel beside the steep track that brings rainwater tearing down from the ridge and deposits it under the back door, and heave up the rotting seagrass matting and lug it outside, and then I have to drive to the tip before it closes, and try to get the pump going so I can fill the tank from what's left in the top dam; and then I have to light the fuel stove and put the lamb shanks on to make stock for the soup I want to have for lunch, and get my bow saw and deal with the huge matted creeper that got blown down off the roof and is still growing although it's spread all over the grass outside the back door, and then...

If I sit still, my gaze comes to rest on the shifting treetops on the other side of the valley.

No matter how I squint and tilt my head, it is plain that the top dam is losing water. The earth here is shaly, yellow and hard; fissures are natural to it, and are encouraged by the roots of trees planted on and below the dam wall. Rabbits have tunnelled into the wall, their pellets give them away and when my father, arriving without warning from Geelong at 8 a.m., spots their droppings and the cracks made by the tree roots his mouth twists in scorn and he turns away to inspect the runoffs.

'What *is* a runoff?' I ask humbly, standing behind him with clasped hands.

He points. 'How the hell did you think the water got into the dam?'

'Oh,' I say, with the foolish giggle I despise in others, 'I thought it got filled from the—from the raining sky.'

He plunges away to the house, where I make a cup of tea and he tells me that frankly the dam is probably beyond repair and furthermore the place is a firetrap, that no one would be fool enough to insure it, that kero lamps are lethal, that the gutters are almost certainly choked with leaves, that if I went for a walk after dinner leaving the door ajar a draught could cause a flare-up and next thing the hut would be a raging inferno. As he speaks the cabin fills with huge noisy blowflies attracted by the smell of the shanks cooking.

After our tea he declines to go for a walk, saying he can see the eagles quite nicely from here, and sits with upright spine on a chair on the verandah, staring out over the gully. I take the blunt hedge-clippers and hack away at a part of the garden out of his line of sight, though from where I'm crouching I can hear the busy fidget and swagger of rosellas along the guttering where they are no doubt proving him right about its unkempt state, eating the grass seeds that have congregated there: but I wonder whether the pleasure of being right again will prevent him from losing his breath at the sight of the rosellas, whose feathers compress colour into essence and bring it squirting up into the senses from the depths of the mind.

I return with a bunch of very early violets. He must have seen the feathers for he consents to hold the flowers in his large blunt hand and even to have his photo taken in that pose. Then, departing, he says in a low voice, 'I could live in place like this, you know; but Mum wouldn't have a bar of it.' Later, in town, I get the photos back and there he stands against the verandah rail, contemptuous as a farmer, head back, eyes slitted; but in his coarse paw the tiny bunch of violets.

If I sit still, the wind blows, then there is a quiet moment.

I forgot to show my father the two commemorative trees in the bottom of the gully: the cypress planted when Phar Lap won the Melbourne Cup, the pine for Carbine—or is it the other way round? I forgot to ask him to show me how to start the pump. I forgot to shut the top gate after his car. I forgot to check with him whether there is any point in getting the place properly fenced, though I do remember him saying that a kangaroo can clear a six-foot fence in a standing jump: that he has actually seen this happen.

> *If I sit still, the koala hunches its grey shoulders round its bowed head and clings to the swaying trunk a few feet away from my table.*

While I am making a hasty list of things to do, the phone rings in its hiding place under the bed. An old friend is calling from the township, through which he is passing on a long trip round Victoria with his seven-year-old daughter. Directions are too complicated to give, so I tell them to wait at the crossroads till I come, and we drive in convoy along the ten kilometres of dirt road back to my place. The closer we get to it the prouder of it I feel, the more satisfyingly I imagine how beautiful he will find the timber cabin with its windows on all four sides and the high verandah on which we will sit together to eat our soup and from which we will gaze out over the timbered ridges, up into the sky with eagles, and down to the black triangle of the bottom dam lying deep and close in the view like a heavy brooch dropped into a loosely spread handkerchief.

We park the cars inside the top gate and his daughter prances down the track to the house, but he approaches slowly, with wary, even suspicious steps, looking this way and that, registering the arrangements of useful objects whose one-syllabled names, he used to say, make us love the English language: spade, boots, rack, hose, bin, rake, broom, saw, box, axe. From back door to front verandah, across the one-room house, needs only four steps, and there he stands on the veran-dah, confronted with all that air.

He turns his head to show a strange, pursed smile. 'I

thought you told me on the phone that it was beautiful.'

'Well, isn't it?'

'No,' he says. 'No, not beautiful. I'd say it was only pretty.'

This is the nature of our friendship, I now recall: as if by agreement, I inflate, he produces the pin.

'Everything's *small*,' he says, backing into a chair on the verandah and raising his brogues to the rail. 'It's too neat. I feel like someone on a film set—a Hollywood western. See the angle of that ridge? It's too perfect. It's tidy. Like a painted backdrop. Our place down the coast is wilder. *That's* beautiful. You must come down one weekend. Our front window there looks straight out over the ocean. Hey, Mini. I know it's probably not a very good question—but would you say you liked this place better, or our place down the coast?'

The girl drops her eyes. 'I don't think it's a very good question, Dad. I've only been here five minutes.'

'Yes, but just say you had to make a choice. Which would you say you liked the best?'

'I think,' she replies soberly, 'that I like both of them exactly the same.'

A pause; then he soldiers on. 'You ought to have a weapon up here. Specially as a woman.'

'I've got a waddy,' I say, 'and I keep the axe beside the bed.'

'No—you need a gun. You open the door at night with a twenty-two in your hand and they'll get the hell out.'

'But guns get fired.'

'I know that's what Chekhov says, but he wasn't a woman sleeping alone in a house with windows all round and no curtains. What if you woke up and found—anyway, I think you ought to get yourself a rifle.'

Very quietly I serve the soup and he tells us of the beauties and the histories of parts of Australia he has visited. While he is speaking I notice that the koala in the tree behind him has woken; it sashays backwards down its sapling, scrambles over the fence and heads off on all fours towards the forest. His daughter sees it too: its unexpected speed on the ground, its heavy head straining up to glance in all directions as it travels. The girl returns her gaze to her plate and continues to work away with her spoon.

After lunch, I suggest a walk to the opposite ridge so I can show them the eagles' nest which has been in this particular tree for nearly ninety years. When I point out to my friend the commemorative pine and cypress he is very impressed and stands gazing up into the scraggly branches with an expression of severe respect. There is a fair amount of soil erosion on the forest ridge which I have not noticed before: it looks shameful to me; I feel it to be my fault though it is not and there is nothing I can do about it, and I am afraid he will remark on it, but he plods ahead of us through the tussocky grass, eager for nature where it intersects with dated human history. 'Ninety years!' he says. 'They must have built this nest during the Boer War!' A kangaroo bounces away behind a clump of blackboys and we all cry out and follow it with our eyes.

Once we reach the top of the ridge and head along it, it should be easy to pick out the eagles' nest, which is in the fork of a tall tree growing so far down in the Moorabool valley that our eyes and the conglomeration of twigs ought to be on a level: but I can't find it. I sweep my eyes left, right, left again, trying not to strain, trying to let the nest present itself simply to me as it does when I am alone. No use. I have mistaken the spot. There is nothing for us to look at except trees, more trees, our native trees, and the usual mess on the ground.

It is getting chilly and they have to drive on to the next big town where they will spend the night. On our way back up to the house we pass the clinker-built rowing boat lying tilted in the grass. Painted a dusty Reckitts blue, it belongs in a dream of some Greek island where all the buildings are brilliant white.

The name fading on the stern is mythological too, but when asked I am unable to recall the story attached to the stranded boat, or to explain how it got so badly holed.

'You should remember these things,' says my friend. 'Your interest in this place is rather shallow, isn't it? I'm disappointed in you.'

The little girl's sole slips on the smooth grass and her elbow bumps my hip. She quickly finds her feet and plugs on up the hill between us, with her wilting stalk of a plait poking out over the collar of her jumper.

Although it is only mid-afternoon, the sun is dropping behind the ridge into which the house backs, and the shadow of that ridge rises up the face of the opposite one as slowly and as steadily as a tide. If boats could float on shadow, this blue one would be bobbing, then shipping darkness, then slewing and foundering with the weight of it. 'Goodbye,' we say at the top gate; the girl stands with hands in cuffs and face turned away towards the forest as her father and I kiss each other. Our cheeks are cold and our eyes averted, and no one mentions the sadness of a visit that has been a failure. In our hearts we are angry, and envious of one another for reasons we can no longer find names for, if we ever could; we have obliged a child to act as a buffer; and they drive away.

If I sit still, the afternoon sun fills the cup of the next valley with light, pours light into the cup of the valley till it is brimming over.

Cup? Pours? Brimming over? This is nature sentimentalism, verging on the purple. Is it really what late winter sun in a valley looks like? Yes. It is. And lovelier, and more peaceful, more comforting; and the light on the tufted grass is more tender, and the wind drops, and the whole landscape is holding its breath.

I walk along the rim of the slope that overlooks my gully, at the very bottom of which, a hundred yards away, the bottom dam shines like a drop of black ink. An old olive tree grows here on the grassy rim, and in against its trunk, under tough foliage, leans the bench for sitting still. I didn't put it there: it was here when I arrived, waiting for me to learn how to use it, It is still winter but before I take my place I check for snakes, and then I sit. I put my hands on my thighs, I count my breaths and tune them to my heartbeat, loosening the tempo as my pulse slows down and settles to andante. Whatever I needed to be comforted for stops hurting me. I close my eyes, and the space freed from what I saw is now gently filled by what I hear: the frogs carry on their cricketing down in the black bottom dam, and their cricketing forms a pattern round the silence of the pool like a complex lace edging on a cloth; but at the same time they are laying down a faithful rhythm track for the kookaburras who test the air with chuckles then decorate it with the absurd spasms of their evening's sociability.

After a long time, I open my eyes. The light is fading so steadily that I might be steadily going blind.

I walk up to the back gate and cross the road into the forest, to drag home branches for the fuel stove. Visitors always ask me incredulously why I have not got myself a chainsaw. I reply that it is against the law to cut down trees in a state forest, and that in fact even taking fallen timber is said to be forbidden, though I don't see the harm in a little gathering and collecting; but the real reasons are that up there it is still almost possible to maintain a connection between luxuries, like light and warmth, and the physical labour that produces them; that I hate the indignant cries of a chainsaw, its sneering; and that dragging and sawing by hand places another buffer between myself and the necessary: sitting still.

Tonight, if I hadn't sat still for so long, I could have tramped down past the bottom dam again, and up the slope of the forest ridge beyond it, among the airy timber whose parsley tops jostle and hiss whenever a gust of wind flows in and out of the gully.

For some reason the fallen branches under those trees are pale, dry, clean, and very densely textured: they make firewood that pleases the senses in the gathering and burns slowly with good heat, while the wood I collect here, in the bush up behind the house, is dark, crumbly, ugly, rotten, as if a cloud had hung over these trees for their whole growing lives; not simply that the fallen boughs have decayed on the ground, but as if the trees themselves were rotten in their being. But to get the healthy wood, I would have to walk a good kilometre, which is already out of the question as darkness fills the gully from the bottom. Tomorrow I'll get the good stuff. Tonight this rubbish will do, though I need more of it than the good, and its texture is repellent to the hand. My boots are so heavy that they encase my feet in two concrete bunkers. When I walk in them I crush things: but I can kick and plunge, which is satisfying, and wasn't that a car?

There is someone coming along the thickening road. I squat down behind a trunk. It's a ute, with a man at the wheel and beside him at least one other head dipping and rising. Although their eyes like mine must be webbed by the frustrating hour between dog and wolf, I stay down in a crouch till they've passed; and just as I heave a couple of branches over my shoulder and set off for the back gate, I hear the clash and whine of the vanished ute being thrown into second: he's a stranger then; he got a fright when the polite orange road dropped away on the turn and went stony, and in a moment he'll hit the ford in the almost-dark and then there will be cursing and gnashing of teeth.

The leafy plumes of the dead branches bounce lightly behind me on the uneven ground, out of sync with the rhythm of my walking, and the whispering they utter, full of agitation and pauses, steadies me with a sense of responsibility, as if I were a teacher in charge of a crocodile of small, serious girls. Though the fence on either side of it has long since collapsed into the soft grass, I close the gate carefully and force the rusty metal loop over its hook, meaning this for a sign.

From the sawhorse close to the gate, arranging the first branch across its double V, I glance down the slope and try to surprise myself with the familiar. How visible is the house? Would I notice it if I didn't know it was there? Would I respect the token gate, or would I take it into my head either to wrestle with its clumsy catch or to step round it? Would I have the nerve, the energy, the curiosity to walk all the way down the sloping track, seeing the small car there, and would I assume it was a woman's car, if I were a man? How do men think, at night, now, for example, when the light has been lifted clear of the gully and the house hunches itself in the deepening dark with its back to the track that leads down from the gate? (But I know that outside this gully there must be a beam of sun still in the sky, for the kookaburras have not quite finished their paroxysms, which tail off weakly as if they were exhausted by their own hilarity: Oh, stop! Don't say another word! I'll die!)

How *do* men think? I unhook the bow saw from the shed wall and as I begin to cut, quickly working up a sweat and having to strip off my jumper and tie it round my waist, I remember the body that was found last month in the bush along this road. It was a man's body, a long time dead, rotting and half-devoured in a plastic bag; the body of someone that no one missed; never identified, claimed or explained away. At the time I said to my father, 'Wouldn't you think a murderer would bury a body? Wouldn't you think they'd hide it properly?'

'They'd be in a hurry,' said my father. 'I imagine they'd just chuck the body into the scrub and go for their lives—but I don't know how to think like a murderer.'

I don't know how to think like a man. The poor wood crumbles and drops into ragged hunks beside the sawhorse, and I carry an armload of it, barely enough for the night, down the cleared slope to the house. I am still sweating from the work, and the dark air slides past my cheeks and my bare arms with the suaveness of a blade. The clammy breath of the bottom dam rushes up the gully side and surrounds me: the air consists (like water when you wade deeper) of waves of chill, bone chill, then stone chill: chill and chill again. This is the true arrival of night.

Both doors of the house are wide open and when I enter it the small room feels abandoned, hollow, only a tunnel through which night floods to join itself on the other side. I put my jumper back on, roll the sleeves down over my knuckles, and loop a woollen scarf twice around my neck. I have read that water is always the last thing to get dark, and notice with gratitude that the bottom dam holds on its black surface the reflection of a tiny, high streak of light, perhaps the one that has overstrained the kookaburras which now are silent, though frogs and crickets persevere.

The box of the fuel stove is small but fire grows in it quickly and I heat the remains of the soup and eat it standing up, straight from the saucepan, as people eat who have not yet arranged the habits of their solitude to suit an abstract ideal. I fill the lamps with kero and light them, and by the time I have got the enamel kero heater going at the other end of the room I have four combustion sites to keep guard over, so my eyes flick constantly from one to the next. The cold begins to crack in the roof iron of the house, making its mettle felt through the uncovered windows and unlined walls. It is barely seven o'clock.

> *If I sit still, the fuel stove burns with occasional crackles and soft, ashen collapses, and the kero heater sings a long breathing note.*

What will I do now?

I will turn on my radio.

On ABC-FM they are playing a sonata by Ravel for violin

and cello, and although I listen with pleasure, I am uncertain as to how I should dispose my limbs while listening: there is no immediate furniture between straight-backed chair, on which I feel foolishly formal, and bed, which can lead only to sleep and thus, so early, to an interminable night of dreams, or worse still, of no dreams at all. After each movement of the sonata the humble, persistent frog-music from the bottom dam reasserts itself, rising powerfully on cold washes of air. It makes me understand, as I hesitate on my feet between chair and bed, that not only shall the meek inherit the earth: they are in charge of it already.

I put out my hand to the kettle, and a hoarse gargling erupts outside the back door. My neck sprouts hackles, and my heart lurches into my skull and swells there to block my ears: yet when the radio on the table bursts into shrieks and whines, then fades to a dull buzz, I hear everything through these same ears, and I know it is the men in the ute, that they've joined forces with others in four-wheel drives with guns and spotlights and a CB radio which they're using to scramble the feeble intellectual signal of my transistor, that they're blazing down the hill to smash open my cardboard house, my pathetic little shelter. Though my hands are trembling and my head is deaf with panic I seize the radio and squeeze the button. It dies. Outside, the gargling sinks to a rattling growl, and ceases.

The frogs, unperturbed, cricket on.

Listen. Walk to the back door. Open it on to the blackness. The night consists of this blackness, and of a heavy, cold smell of eucalypts, grass and smoke. Something shifts in a tree. Pick up the axe. The tree gives a shudder: something in its central form groans and gargles. The lamplight works past my shoulder, diluting the night's absolute, and the lump in the tree fork throws back its blunt head and lets out an appalling cry of love or challenge: it is the bear, shaken in its sapling by a terrible passion, and the answering roar from the ridge is so urgent that, ignoring me and my weapon and barely using its braking claws, the animal skids down the tree and takes off at a clumsy trot up the track and into the dark.

When I lay the axe on the table and examine the radio, I realise that its batteries, by cosmic coincidence, had chosen that moment to give up the last of their power. The kero lamp nearest the open door suddenly flares, emitting a column of fine, sooty smoke which pours straight up out of the glass chimney and folds itself, on air, into smooth crinkles like pushed cloth. I rush to turn down the wick, then to shut the door, the click of whose latch sounds only half a beat before the crack of the first shot.

Its echo bounds away—*wah waah waaah*—across the cold ridges.

The woman who grabs the axe is me. Its handle has already lost the shallow warmth of my earlier grip and become cold wood, yellow, shaped and weighted for a hand much bigger than mine.

I am ashamed of what it means that I have grabbed an axe at the sound of a rifle shot in the dark.

Why is it so shameful to be afraid?

I wind the wicks right down, kick the stove door shut on a fresh hunk of wood, and step out my back door with the axe in one hand and the torch in the other.

Now the night odours are overpowering, and the frogs are very loud; but since they are able to increase the volume of their lacework without any alteration to its stubborn and yet endlessly submissive tone, nothing out here is different except the cold, which finds the joins between garments and touches me there with the unpleasant intimacy of a stethoscope. I move a few steps away from the building. A night-seeing bird would spot the anxiety I am leaving like phosphorescence in every footprint. A solo frog strikes a sudden ringing note in the bottom dam, then returns modestly to the chorus. No moon, no stars, and my torch makes so little impression that it's as if the air had drastically thickened. The totality of the dark disrupts my senses: my ears feel padded, and my skin has lost its elastic ability to report to me the whereabouts and nature of physical objects. I place the torch on the short grass: its beam clots like custard in the forest of blades. The air is thick, cold and utterly motionless. It strikes me with force that this thickness is the result of some kind of presence; that something is waiting all round me, round the house; that far from wishing me well or including me in its design and purpose, the universe is without meaning: stupid, askew, morally inert. Again my hackles tickle and stretch the skin of my neck.

The second shot comes as a relief. Its distortion, leisurely and attenuated, restores the perspective of the night: the gun must be at least a mile away, and so must the man holding it. The shot is not, after all, personal to me; and yet it was set in motion by another human creature for whose physical being, warm, muscular and engaged in purposeful activity, I experience a pang of comradely feeling, almost of gratitude. The balloon of awareness around me slowly inflates until I perceive that the sky has covered itself with clouds, that this explains the thick stillness of the air.

What was I afraid of? Was I afraid of the dark?

The house I stumble back into has no window coverings of any kind. I relight the lamps calmly, almost laughing, though my heart seems larger than it should be, and palpable in its beating.

On the high shelves the books I have chosen at a distance from the moment and mood of wanting to read look sober, selected according to criteria more severe than those of every day, as if I imagined taking myself very seriously here, freeing my mind for the bouts of extended concentration required to follow famous arguments. Instead, however, when I settle myself to read by the soft light of the lamps, though I force myself to continue for a good hour, I can barely concentrate at all. The dark outside turns every window into a black mirror, and me into a bad actor. I am *Reading Goethe*; I am a *Reading Woman*; I am self-conscious, exaggeratedly casual, and every movement of head, hand or torso, every clearing of the throat or rubbing of the forehead, every raising of the eyes from the page or pursing of the lips in thought rings false, a charade of nonchalance performed against the hostility of countless imaginary witnesses, all of them, naturally, men: for what woman would go out at night, with or without firearms, to trespass, to broach private property despite locked gates, to loiter outside lit windows, to confound the thoughts of those observed by entangling them in aggressive, scornful eyebeams? She's reading *Goethe!* She thinks she *understands* it! She believes it *means* something! *Here!* Each time I catch my own reflection my face is an inhuman white dish, without marks of experience or age, expressionless, a drowned girl's, surfacing in one or another of the treacherous panes.

In this public cube of light and warmth even breathing takes on a flamboyant quality. There is no point in prolonging the agony. I close the book and push it away, then I turn down the wicks, blow into the glass chimneys, and sit still.

I acknowledge the dark.

In one stroke the windows lose their power. The house lays down its weapons and surrenders. Its box of defiance collapses, gently and with relief, and darkness passes through it again and perfects itself on the other side. No longer held at bay by the lamps' hiss, and having known forever the pointlessness of argument, the folly of persuasion, the frogs flood the night with their patient, stupid cricketing, their endless embroidery round the borders of the black pool.

> *If I sit still, I feel the irregularity of my heartbeat, very close inside my ribs. I wonder what it is that powers the heart, what force drives it, and what for.*

In this darkness it is possible to undress without modesty, to drag off my clothes and throw them on to a dark chair and fumble under the pillow for my thick nightie, to crawl into the blankets and lie there shivering with stiffening eyelids and feet solidifying in the cold. The frogs work: they labour without looking for any reward; the shooting continues, sporadic cracks and splinterings that echo till they disintegrate between the ridges; and just as a rat begins to delve among the dirty dishes outside the back door, sleep comes suddenly to me in the form of an inversion of logic: rain flies upwards into maternal clouds, flowers shrink into soil and are swallowed up by their own roots.

When I wake, with a full bladder, it is still deep night and the frogs are stitching tirelessly. The guns are silent. A wild scampering outside the back door when I open it sends me back for my boots, in which I tramp with feet apart to avoid the dragging laces. On the first gulp of cold breath I know that something has changed. The lid has been lifted off everything while I slept: the clouds have slid away and now there arches over me and my house a tremendous emptiness which can only be called *firmament*, in which hang vast, tilting constellations. Squatting with my nightie up round my haunches, my mouth agape and my head craning backward, I feel the curve of the planet. I am aware of earth's roundness against this immense powdered screen of starlight whose patterns, nameless to me except 'Southern Cross' and 'saucepan', crackle with meaning: the starry sky is throbbing with form.

I squat here, unimaginably tiny, breathing out slow clouds, protected, forgiven, forgotten. I am no longer waiting for anything—or rather, waiting now for things so large and leisurely that they are beyond ordinary waiting: for my parents to die as they must, for my daughter to have children, for a god to come to me and bless me. The small heat off my stream of piss rises to touch the skin of my thigh, then disperses in cold.

The warmth hiding in the blanket folds is of my own making, even if I do not understand what for, and the dream I have is one that patiently unpicks all the knots in me and leaves without demanding to be remembered.

There may be no ocean here, nor even a river worthy of the name, and this morning the gully holds its mist veil over the surface of the bottom dam; but the sky turns a deep and secret pink, wrens spring about under the bare lilac bushes, and down in the hollow of the top dam, pushing my jumper sleeves back off my red knuckles, I yank and yank at the cord of the pump. It turns over, dies, turns, flares again, takes, and begins to chug.

Its note attracts me, there is a sweetness in it, and unexpected affection surges out of me to meet it: for the first time in my life I feel the charm of an engine. The dam surface trembles among its weeds, and the pipe gives a series of jerks as water begins to travel through it, heading for the tank on the high stand fifty yards away, near the back gate. I clump up the shaly yellow dam wall alongside the water-carrying pipe, panting and laughing, trying to sense the speed of the water and to keep pace with it. I start to shout, and as I top the rise and my boots strike grass, the sun sails out of a reef of grey and pink clouds, then scatters them in horizontal streaks a mile wide. I am striding towards the tank along the very edge of my land, parallel with the top road, singing and yelling out loud, dancing in my heavy boots to give the water time to catch up with me, when last night's ute comes flying by, scattering orange gravel. The driver, thickly rugged-up and laughing, bangs his flat hand against its door, and beside him two little boys in peaked caps scramble for a look and wave wildly till they are out of sight.

I scamper up the wooden ladder of the tank stand, forgetting the stiffness of my boots, and wait there, clinging to the tank rim and making my voice boom in its cavern, till through the view-slit in its lid I see the reflection of my own head start to shudder and break apart on the churning water surface: the stream from the dam bursts in, invisible and powerful.

I could get down and eat my breakfast while it fills, or saw wood or wash dishes or hunt rats, but instead I cut across the dew-flattened grass to the olive tree, spread my jacket, and take my place on the bench for sitting still.

It takes real discipline to close my eyes, but the frogs are helpful, pedalling away down there, eternally patient, eternally replaceable; and now the magpies, their virtuosos' minds distracted by something higher, let loose their blissful warblings, their variations so casual, so endlessly fresh, their insouciant scrolls and flourishes; while in the house, where I am not, where no fire has been lit, no disorder tidied, no great book read, the little round mirror beside the open door is hung so high that it carries on its cheap and perfect lustre the image of nothing but sky.

1990

PART TWO

Sing for Your Supper

Patrick White:
The Artist as Holy Monster

LET ME SAY that David Marr's biography of Patrick White is a grand and gorgeous book.* I hated having to maintain a reviewer's posture to it, reminding myself to take notes when I longed for the freedom to accept without reserve the biographer's seductive invitation to plunge into the river of somebody else's life. I read the book on planes, in buses, at meal tables: I became deaf, I laughed, I cried. Marr displays none of the modern biographer's anxiety about theory. He is not self-consciously watching himself perform the act of biography. He takes the gloves off and wades right in. It's a marvellous piece of work: the large sweep of it, how it rolls along, the subtle shape of its narrative, its poised breaths, its stabs and sparks of detail, its graceful syntax and richness of imagery: could a better match of subject and biographer be imagined?

To my warless generation, White's story seems extraordinarily manifold, as if he had lived half a dozen lives: the privileged childhood, broken by what he perceived as his mother's betrayal in consigning him to an English boarding school; the oddly domesticated, timid student years at Cambridge; a poofy, pommy, polo-necked, prewar period around the theatres and artists' studios of London; then the wide, light-filled rush of travelling, sexually freed, in America. The war completed, perhaps, this process of shoehorning him

* David Marr, *Patrick White: A Life*, Random House, 1991.

out of his comfy privilege. In the Middle East he learnt to muck in with the world at random. He discovered Greece, always the country of his heart; he met Manoly Lascaris, who was to be his life-long companion, and returned in 1946 to Australia, a 'familiar and at the same time hostile land', where he was to work out his fate as a man and as an artist.

So powerful and unflinching is Marr's creation that three-quarters of the way through the book my heart began to ache, I became foul-tempered, I snapped at people and said sharp things. I looked with horror and fear at portraits of White: that 'mineral stare', the shrinking, fastidious mouth. Memories of my own slight contact with White hurt me again: I recalled his gentle kindness to me at our first meeting, when he took me aside, sat me down with him, and questioned me on my reading, matching my tastes (especially in Australian work) against his, and sweetly, as if to establish common ground; but all this was exploded by the dismay of our second meeting when, hunched at a dinner table with his wooden holding-cross swinging round his neck, he excoriated certain people dear to me, savaging their moral characters, and I sat there, silent and trembling with shock, too cowardly (because of his tremendous presence and, I confess, his fame) to stand up for my friends. I cried with shame all the way home, and never saw him again.

Yet I learnt from this. Whatever his intention (and probably he had none: they were random, bitchy swipes) he showed me that although I have been vain about my 'honesty', I am in fact a coward; that under pressure I will kowtow to someone with a name and will slink away leaving my friends betrayed. This is something worth knowing.

To bear with, to bear a man like Patrick White one needs a steady belief in the idea—so out of favour in the universities—of the artist as holy monster. As a small child, White overheard a lady wondering whether the Victor Whites' strange little boy was 'a changeling'. This remark stuck in his mind, as comfort,

all his life. 'He saw writing as a cruel business,' says Marr, 'but
the changeling/artist is free of those loyalties and obligations
of kindness that make difficult truths hard to tell...He is *sans
famille*.'

White's periodic cullings of even his closest friends, using
tiny slights or hesitations as pretexts for a ferocious slashing
away of their links with him, make dreadful reading. Marr does
not spare White in his accounts of these episodes, but clearly
he can only countenance them because he believes them justi-
fied, when the chips are down, by the quality of White's work,
and the urgency of his needs as an artist. One is astonished,
repeatedly, by the generosity that some discarded friends have
displayed in their reports of the breaks. Others, like the painter
Sidney Nolan, responded in kind and thus lifelong feuds came
about.

Couple White's desire to be 'free of loyalties and obligations' with his terrible fear of loneliness, his belief (based on his
own wretched adolescence and early manhood) that *anything* is
better than loneliness, and the stage is set for a partner, a wife,
someone with superhuman powers of endurance.

The personality of Manoly Lascaris, White's companion
or (as Thomas Bernhard would say) *life-person*, lies subtly at
the core of the biography. Lascaris is the marrow in its bones.
Quietly present, quietly stable behind the monstrous foreground
performances of White, he glows, and grows in stature, in
sweetness and dignity as the story unfolds. In his modesty he
is able to make reverberating statements which are innocent of
the posturing they might, from someone less highly evolved,
imply: 'it is the pleasure of the disciple,' he says to Jim Sharman,
'to serve Christ.'

He is not, of course, meaning to liken White to Christ—
how could he, on the evidence this book provides?—but is
making a statement about the dignity and the satisfaction
of service, about an acceptance he has made of the proposi-

tion that some people have the nature to serve, while others, particularly those with a driven sense of mission, demand and desperately need to be served.

It's a measure of Marr's seriousness, and of Lascaris's depth and beauty of personality, that one does not brush aside the proposition here with a feminist's or a leftist's curse, but stashes it for further consideration. Which would we, in the end, rather have? Good manners, or great art? Are the two mutually exclusive? Women and men who serve the creators, as Lascaris did, gamble their whole lives on their instincts about their partners' abilities: a tremendous, dizzying bet.

The matter of religion—or *faith* is a better word, since White, though he was a great fan of nuns and took Anglican communion for many years, never settled into an established niche, and remarked that 'churches destroy the mystery of God'—is a strong strand of the biography. Marr points out that the most reliable love White experienced, as a child of the landed and socially ambitious rich, was that offered by devoted servants, and this equation of love with service deeply marks Marr's story, as it does White's work.

But whom did White himself serve, we might justifiably ask? It could be said, despite current fashions of thought, that he served art, as did the famous actress in Cilea's opera who sings 'Io son' l'umil' ancella' (I am the humble serving maid)—if one believes in art as a duty laid down. White certainly found art a hard master, and experienced the duty as an anguished (and sometimes exhilarating) slog. He returned after the war, with mixed emotions, to a culture which was not ready for what he had to offer it: but he shouldered the job, and dragged it some way out of its provincial bog, lashing and reviling as he laboured, fuelled by contempt for its fearful small-mindedness. Marr notes astutely that Martin Boyd was the kind of writer White might have become, had he chosen a life of exile in Europe.

Any writer in Australia who feels hard done by should take note of White's struggle. 'He deserved a VC for it,' one well-known novelist here has claimed. *The Tree of Man* was rejected by twenty English publishers. 'What is it about?' asked his London agent. 'It is about life,' he helplessly replied. Attacks on White by Australian critics have entered legend, of course; but it's easy for us, a luckier generation, to forget how painful his disappointments were. When *The Aunt's Story*, his third novel, was coldly received—dismissed, in fact—in Australia, Marr says that 'a fissure of bitterness opened in him'. His impulse to write was dying.

But he learnt—or was it already in his nature? he relished a fight—to use hostile critics as spurs and Marr shows us, above all, how absolutely White was a natural writer: blessed (or cursed, as White often said) by characters and stories that were not willed but 'boiled up in him'. Marr reveals brilliantly, and with the lightest touch, how each novel, as White slaved over it, provided him with a clue to the next, as if his work were an immense chain composed of linked and constantly developing obsessions.

Illness (asthma and its eternal complications) was always intimately entwined with his work. In reveries of fever and medication his characters would haunt him, talking themselves into life, and White would return to himself from these hallucinatory episodes armed with fresh material to labour on. (I laughed out loud to read that Brett Whiteley refused to believe, on meeting White after reading his work with delight, that White had never done acid.) He loved and needed music and painting: he envied painters especially, for being able to work direct with colour 'instead of grinding out novels greyly'.

Unlike many Australian artists, White went on producing powerfully original work till late in his life. He was nearly seventy when he published that audacious and weirdly beautiful novel *The Twyborn Affair*. Perhaps its clarified style was possible because White could now vent his spleen in public statements, the fierce political preaching that made him famous to people who had not read any of his books and which drew off and redirected his itching savageries, allowing him, in his last great novel, to reach a more dignified resolution of conflicts: in particular, as Marr points out, to produce something 'unprecedented in (his) writing: the entire acceptance by a mother of her child'.

Marr is scrupulous in documenting the decencies of White's domineering mother Ruth: 'like Patrick,' according to Lascaris, 'but with pearls'. She was the one who sponsored Lascaris as a migrant to Australia. She gave money to Inky Stephensen's tottering firm so he could publish Patrick's first book (of poems, which White later abominated, as he did his first novel *Happy Valley*). White battled Ruth all her life. It was apparently a fruitful struggle. Not a week passed without his writing to her. If I have one bone to pick with the biography, though, it is to do with Ruth. For all Marr says about her, for me she remained a puzzling presence: I did not really understand her, and I was never sure of what this often-mentioned mutual love between them consisted. They laughed together, it seems, at people who picked up the wrong fork at dinner, and when she was dying he entertained her with long recallings of all the servants who had ever worked for their family: but I have a much sharper picture of White's ineffectual father, who hardly plays a part in the story at all, except as a provider of money and, on one electrifying occasion, an object of suppressed desire.

White was, as he said himself, a monster: unbearable at times, and of merciless cruelty. But there are countless tales, some documented in the biography, others with word-of-mouth currency, of his generosities grand and small. When he was old and terribly recognisable, he would go into a bookshop and ringingly buy a dozen copies of some young struggler's latest novel. He bought a typewriter for someone too shy to show anyone what he had written. He gave away immense sums of his money to charity. He staggered along to hospitals to visit people who were hardly iller than he was. He used his Nobel Prize money to set up an annual award for writers who he considered had not received the recognition they deserved.

Marr's detailed account of the Nobel Prize workings gave me cold shudders. The matter of public recognition is a vexed one, bad enough within a writer's own culture, but when it reaches international proportions it becomes a nightmare of committees, hints, rival factions, baits dangled tantalisingly and then snatched back. There is a pathos in the human compulsion to rank, something scrambling and undignified which makes a mockery of the labour and meaning of art. I kept thinking of Thomas Bernhard's slashing attack on state prizes in *Wittgenstein's Nephew*; but I also thought of the painful fact that all our lives, in vain, we go on laying tributes at our parents' feet.

The memoir *Flaws in the Glass*, with its ferocious settling of accounts and its intimate revelations, appalled many people, not least the modest Lascaris; but, like White himself when Marr brought him the manuscript of the finished biography, Lascaris bit the bullet. He made no complaint and demanded no changes; and nor did White of Marr, though the biography made him weep. It is impressive how little White cared to control other people's images of him.

At the end of the day, monster though he was, White had the runs on the board. This nobody can deny. And the highest achievement of Marr's biography, with its subtle and enriching examination of the genesis of work in life, is that it turns us back, again and again, with eagerness to the novels.

1991

Sing for Your Supper

THE FIRST WRITERS' festival I ever went to was Adelaide Writers' Week in 1978. My first novel, *Monkey Grip*, had been published the previous spring, but in my ordinary life I didn't hang out with other writers. I was thirty-five, bringing up a child in a big communal household in Fitzroy, and the people I spent my time with were musicians and performers and photographers. I didn't even know there were such things as writers' festivals, until I received the invitation to Adelaide. I was flattered and rather awe-struck.

I owned a car but no suitcase, and I carried my clothes to Adelaide in a cardboard box. In a tent under the plane trees I gave my first reading, and delivered a stiff little paper which I read out in what someone I knew described later as 'best reader grade six' voice, taking up obediently the exact ten minutes I'd been permitted by the organisers' letter. An English writer on the same panel was surprised to learn that 'one' was expected to give a paper. He had not prepared anything. In a relaxed manner he cracked a few jokes about Johnny Rotten and Sid Vicious, then sat back smiling, leaving his Australian panel-partners looking earnestly provincial and over-anxious. We said nothing, but we had lips of string.

I spent whole days in the tent, listening eagerly. Best of all was a man from I forget which Eastern European country who read a wonderful short story about a wife, a husband, a child, an apartment and a light bulb. I have forgotten his name but the story is still fresh in my mind. It wasn't even spoilt by the brief encounter I had with the writer in the hotel lobby. Seeing him standing outside the lift, I ran up and tugged at his sleeve. 'I wanted to tell you how much I liked your story,' I panted, red as a beetroot; 'it was *beautiful*.'

His eyes glazed over, he opened his mouth, and out poured a stream of stunning cliches. 'Ah yes—it was a story about the alienation of the working-class family in modern society, blah blah blah.'

I let go his sleeve and stepped back. But I'll never forget the story. It was probably the first time I was struck by the power of minimalism—and by the way something read out loud can enter the mind and flourish there.

At night, in my tiny room, like a *chambre de bonne*, on the top floor of the Grosvenor Hotel on North Terrace where the writers (those of my low echelon, anyway) were lodged, I had to stand on a chair to see out the window; but the lights on the horizon twinkled fiercely in the dry summer air, I felt the thrilling proximity of desert, and I thought, 'How lucky I am! What a marvellous way to hear writers from other countries, and meet other writers from here, and have a little break from home!'

In 1992 I was in Adelaide again. Because of a contretemps with the organising committee I wasn't a guest of Writers' Week. My publisher paid for my plane ticket and my hotel room and I slaved away all day doing publicity for my novel *Cosmo Cosmolino* which had just come out. I had a minder from the publisher's PR division who put sandwiches in my hand and pushed me in and out of taxis.

Heavy rain fell without a break, day and night. I had so little free time that I heard only two sessions in the tent, and carried away one serious memory (Miroslav Holub saying, 'It is so hard to exterrrrminate somesing') and one flippant (Orhan Pamuk talking about 'the engaged Turkish writer who bravely goes to jail—by comparison I seem to be a spoilt young bourgeois who has fun and writes a lot'). A tight-lipped audience contemplated the young Turk's playful cynicism, but I couldn't help laughing. Feebly, out of exhaustion. When I looked out my hotel window I saw grey streets shining with rain. I thought, 'How miserable this is! I wish I could go home.'

Somewhere between 1978 and 1992 the gilt had worn off the gingerbread. Festivals had lost their festiveness and turned into work. Their magic had fled. Publishing in the '80s became internationally monstrous, and the festivals reflected this. Publishers and agents became as important as writers—behind the scenes anyway. The pleasantly daggy mucking in together of big and small names is a thing of the past. Internationally known writers—the male English ones, at least—tend to travel in tight groups of friends from home. They do their gig, fill the boot of the hire car with Grange Hermitage, and shoot through to the outback.

Writers are no longer humbly grateful for being noticed. These days 'one' would flounce home in a pet if one were shown into a *chambre de bonne* on the top floor of an old hotel. Nowadays 'one' expects at the very least a vast, impersonal room at the Hilton. I have learnt, through watching Ken Kesey stack on a turn at a Toronto reception desk, that international hotels have a certain number of rooms with *openable windows*: that 'one' does not after all have to endure meekly the choking claustrophobia of North American central heating.

When you think about it, there's something peculiar about the very idea of a writers' festival. Writers, in my experience, are not extraverts. They tend to be what Joan Didion calls 'lonely, anxious rearrangers of things'. Their work is by its very nature solitary—and when they're not actually in the workroom with bum on seat and door closed, they're mooching around the streets staring at people, listening in on conversations, sucking incident and meaning out of what's going on around them. Writers don't tend to hang out together. In fact, they repel each other. How can writers sit in a room together? They understand instinctively each other's horrible detachment and, out of what few manners are left to them, they struggle not to turn that dry-ice stare on each other. Thus, when they are together, their conversations tend to the trivial, to shop-talk. They talk about contracts, money, agents, sales figures. It's awful. But what can you expect?

It's a fantasy that writers discuss their work with each other. I remember a funny Frank Moorhouse story about a woman who comes from some blighted part of the outback to live in Sydney, and searches keenly for the pubs where, she is sure, people *discuss*. The narrator, astonished, touched, and perhaps slightly ashamed, is obliged to disillusion her. No one *talks* to anyone, round here! Perhaps occasionally an acknowledgment, a swipe, a furtive compliment, once in a blue moon a sudden phone call of warm admiration…but to imagine that writers sit around talking about *how to do it*, or about themes (those things which exist only in the minds of high-school English teachers), or *what they meant* or *what they'll tackle next*, shows a mistaken idea of what writing itself is like.

(Exception: I once had a short and fascinating conversation with Murray Bail and David Malouf, at Malouf's kitchen table, about punctuation—an occasion so rare that it felt almost indecent—we were *blushing*; we couldn't look at one another.)

'Everything you have deciphered,' writes the Israeli novelist Amos Oz in *To Know a Woman*, 'you have only deciphered for an instant.' Writers don't know how they did it. They certainly don't know how they'll do it next time. And when they're put into a group with three random strangers and called a panel, then given a topic and asked to discuss it in front of an audience, what they produce is some kind of strange heatshield, or smokescreen. Not *lies*. But everything 'one' says, however hard one is trying to tell the truth or say something useful, comes out askew, a little bit blurred, ever so slightly exaggerated or glib or beside the point.

This explains, perhaps, why writers rarely go to hear one

another read or speak, at these events. At a festival in New Zealand not long ago another guest laughed incredulously when I said I was going to hear the session of a writer I'd just met and liked. 'Surely you don't think people expect you to *go*! I wouldn't dream of asking anyone to come to mine.' When the American poet August Kleinzahler (who's my friend) spotted me in the audience of his panel at the Melbourne Writers' Festival one year, his face went blank for a second, with shock; I felt embarrassed, as if I had breached protocol. Part of this is the same neurosis that makes teenagers hate ringing up a stranger while someone they know well is in the room with them—someone who will register the exact amount of falsity in their special phone voice, their public persona.

Once at a publisher's dinner in Sydney where I was grumbling quietly to a fellow-writer about having to get up in a minute and make a speech, he laughed and said, 'Stop whingeing. Stand up and *sing for your supper*.'

Is that what writers' festivals are all about?

Everyone knows that these days writers can't just write books: they have to get out and flog them. There's a variety of ways to do this. A writer like Tim Winton will cheerfully appear on *60 Minutes* or *The Steve Vizard Show*, because he wants the audiences of those shows—people who wouldn't go to a writers' festival in a fit—to know that his book (a) exists and (b) was written by someone they don't need to suspect of being what Paul Keating calls 'a hairy-arse who's just dropped out of university'. He wants a forum where he can show himself as an ordinary bloke who's written a non-threatening book without any arty-farty pretensions. This, of course, is as false as any other persona. Tim Winton is in fact highly articulate and very widely read in theology and fiction; his books are rich and challenging. But he's also a family man and a terrific fisherman. With spectacular success he presents himself at the popular end of the publicity spectrum. Writers' festivals hover at the opposite end. Writers' festivals are for writers who are squeamish about deep publicity, or who don't want to get their hands dirty; or for writers escaping from a bout of doing those things in their own countries; or for writers who are tired and jaded, and need a little break from home.

What sort of *readers* are they for? What is this powerful urge people feel, that makes them not only buy books but pay even more money in order to clap eyes on the writers themselves, to hear them speak and read? Festivals 'make you part of something', one journalist bluntly stated after the Melbourne Festival. 'To observe and partake in...a discussion between two eminent writers, as though they were somehow in your own living room, is what writers' festivals are all about.' I found this oddly touching and tried to recall ever having experienced such a sense of inclusion, myself, while in an audience. I couldn't.

But it strikes me that there is a connection between the ever-increasing roll-up to writers' festivals and the question so often asked of writers by readers and journalists: 'Is this book autobiographical?'

Why *do* people always ask this question? I once saw Doris Lessing cop it, from a woman who stood up and shouted it from the back of a huge audience at the National Gallery of Victoria. Lessing glared. She snapped. She bit the poor woman's innocent head off, and the woman sat down in confusion. It was a distressing sight; but I had sympathy for both biter and bitten. I think that readers, specially today in a world so crammed with books that choice makes us dizzy, are longing for some guarantee of integrity. They want to know who they can trust. But does seeing a writer at a festival lead readers in the right direction?

The trouble is that the attractiveness or apparent honesty of the writer is no guarantee of the quality of the work. Plenty of good writers are jerks in person, while others who are charming and generous in the flesh are boring, phoney or feeble on the page. And the risk with festivals is that writers who hop up on stage to be 'spotlighted', to speak at length about their work and related matters, may be judged on their perceived performance, their gift of the gab, their persona, rather than on what they've written.

If all I knew of John Ashbery was the casual, stone-walling, rather hungover way he answered his interlocutor's reverential questions at the Melbourne Festival, I would never pick up a book of his, let alone buy it. I've been reading Marina Warner for years in the *Times Literary Supplement*, always with enormous pleasure and respect; I had her book *Alone of All Her Sex* on order at a bookshop before I went to her session at Melbourne, and now I'll have to grit my teeth and force myself to buy it because in spite of her manifest, sharp and ready intelligence in performance, I found her presence chilly and not very likeable. So what? Why *should* a writer in front of an audience be warm, open, likeable? Yet something about the modern writers' festival makes us likely to demand this, or to be disappointed if we don't get it. It's not fair. It's a bit ridiculous. It's got us barking up the wrong tree.

Writers, for their part, aren't supposed to get instant gratification. If they wanted that, they'd be in a different line of work—singing, or acting, or stand-up comedy. The danger of writers' festivals, for the writers, is that 'one' can get an inflated idea of one's importance. 'One' can go home with a fat head—or wake up next morning like someone after a huge party: wondering whether one has been a fool, revealed the nastier sides of one's nature, failed to recognise someone and thus created an enemy.

Worst of all, 'one' has forgotten how to be lonely, which is the *sine qua non* of the writer's life. It sounds as if I'm saying that writers and readers should be kept apart. That's not what I set out to say, but maybe it's not such a bad idea.

1992

Cypresses and Spires: Writing for Film

You can write a whole novel with your left arm curved round the page. You can get to the end of the last draft without having shown it to a single person or made one compromise. Even if you have to battle with an editor, the book reaches the reader pretty much as you intended it. All its mistakes and failures are yours, totally and forever, and so are its little glories. When the chips are down, you are the book, and the book is you.

Why would a novelist turn her back on this marvellous freedom, this privacy and independence, and sneak into the bunfight of screen-writing?

I did it for the money. That was my first reason, anyway. At a friend's wedding I met a producer I liked who asked me to contact her if I ever felt like writing a movie. Being broke at the time, I rushed home and rummaged in my folder of unexamined ideas. Out of it stepped Kelly and Louise, the young girls who became *Two Friends*.

But within a week I realised that though money is a spur, it's also only a mirage, once you've sat down at the desk. I found that filmwriting is powered by the same drives as fiction. You do it out of curiosity, and technical fascination, and the same old need to shape life's mess into a seizable story.

I've seen a lot of movies, but I hadn't a clue how to write a screenplay. The formal stages of its development—outline, treatment, drafts—were utterly foreign to me. When I write a novel or a story, I never plan. I circle round the dark area of life (mine, or someone else's) to which my curiosity is attracted, and I search for a way in. My method of work is a kind of blind scrub-bashing.

But now I found I was required to sit up brightly in a watch-tower and tap out a preliminary map of the territory. I had to turn my old, organic, secretive, privileged, hyper-sensitive work process inside out.

This was the hardest part of the change, for me. I'm used to working alone. It suits my nature. I can't stand it if anyone (no matter how dear) comes into the room behind me while I'm working. I have to cover the pathetic, scrambled mess on the page. I like to get the thing as perfect as I can make it, before I hand it over.

With movies, this won't wash. I had to learn to walk into someone else's room, whack down my idea like a lump of raw meat, and watch it quiver while it was rolled and prodded on the table.

This might easily have been as gruesome as it sounds; but in fact my brief experience of filmwriting has been an intense pleasure, because of the calibre of the people who introduced me to it: the directors Jane Campion (*Two Friends*) and Gillian Armstrong (*The Last Days of Chez Nous*), and Jan Chapman, who produced both these films. Long script sessions with these three classy, generous and challenging professionals taught me to drop my defensiveness and become more flexible at an earlier stage, before my thoughts could set themselves in concrete. They showed me the priceless art of the apparently dumb question, and the calm brazenness that is required in order to ask it. From Gillian Armstrong I learnt that before you can cut something out of the story you have to understand fully what it is, instead of dropping it because you're too lazy to think it right through. I learnt (from Jane Campion in particular) to follow and trust intuition, no matter how alarmingly it swerves. And, most valuably of all, because it applies to everything written in any genre, all three of them forced me to learn and relearn the stern law of structure.

What I had seen in a late draft of *Chez Nous*, for example, as a perfectly smooth narrative curve would turn out, under their skilful probing, to be more like a little Himalaya of mini-climaxes. Special effects a novelist might pull off on the page by bluff or flashy language simply will not transpose to film. Everything has to be re-invented through the eyes. It was very squashing to have to leave my precious prose at the door and be pushed back again and again to the bare bones of structure and dialogue. There is nothing else, it seemed at times. So hard, to be so stripped!

But, by the same token, how shockingly easy just to write 'Night, a desert motel', or 'She takes her father's arm', and to leave the rest, the complex labour of providing the detail that will fill the bare places and acts with meaning, to the director's incredibly numerous and expensive army of actors and techni-cians! The ease of it—it seemed criminal; I felt almost guilty.

Does anyone understand the alchemy of many imagina-tions that distils a film? An actor's wonky emphasis can throw a whole carefully crafted piece of psychology out of whack. The wrong brand of teacup on a table can skew a family's fantasy of itself. But by the same token, the tiny upward movement of one facial muscle, spontaneous, unconscious, impossible to write, can transform the emotional mood of an entire sequence. A director can take hold of your stick of an idea and make it blossom into a poetry your plodding typewriter could never have dreamt of.

I've read the horror stories and I know how lucky I've been with these two films. At the start I was hampered by pathetic gratitude that my work was even considered filmable. I didn't (and still don't) understand the writer's position in the hierarchy of the production army. I was often too proud to ask the ignorant question that would have taught me what I needed to know. I discovered in myself a passivity I never knew was there. I stayed away while the films were being shot, and when you're not present, when you're in another town, everything you think is always too late. I accepted without a struggle, over the phone, last-minute changes the necessity of which I was too inexperienced to judge. I still haven't learnt how—and *when*—to fight for what I see as crucial. I haven't yet learnt to foresee the flashpoints where imagination and budget might collide, and to take a stand long before the moment, on location, when the crucial is found to be impossible and the lesser road must be taken.

In *Chez Nous*, for example, there are the cypress trees.

From the main character's bedroom window I wanted a row of pencil cypress trees to be visible, growing in some distant and unidentifiable neighbourhood garden. These trees, to me, carry a heavy freight of meaning. They are Mediterranean, thus connected with the origins of our culture. They are calm, sturdy, graceful. They are a reminder of darkness, of stillness, of death—and thus of the question of God, and the soul. At certain charged moments in the plot of *Chez Nous*, people glance out the window and see the cypresses. Once, Beth speaks of them to her pregnant friend in a way that tells us a good deal about her.

But you will not see the cypresses in the film of *Chez Nous*.

When a terrace house in Glebe was chosen for the film it was perfect in every way except one: there were no cypress trees. The cypress trees, it seemed, would not be possible. I went to the house with Jan Chapman and Gillian Armstrong, and we walked from window to window, looking for something to replace them. Then, from an upstairs room we saw, beyond the thick summer foliage into which the house backed, the tip of a church spire, just floating there. The building to which it was attached was completely hidden by leafy branches. The spire was grey, rather pale, almost insubstantial. At that anxious moment it seemed a gift, and we persuaded ourselves that the spire would do.

And in a sense it did do—but a resonance departed. A spire, no matter how indistinct and beautiful, is literal. It represents a known religion, a particular theology, with all the sectarian and social meanings that this entails. The mystery of the image is lost.

So when I published the script of *Chez Nous* I removed the spire, and put the cypress trees back in.

The qualities of air and light in a certain place, I now realise, are more than purely aesthetic. They form the tone of people's lives, the way people move about and behave towards each other and feel about themselves. Both these films were imagined in Melbourne and shot in Sydney. I didn't think this would matter, but the experience has taught me that the two big cities of Australia are tonally as distinct from each other as Boston is from LA, or Lyon from Marseilles. The very image of *a house*, on which both films heavily depend, bears one sort of psychological emphasis in warm, open Sydney, and a completely different one in Melbourne, where dwellings are enclosing, curtained, cold-weather-resisting: more like burrows.

These are only a few of the lessons I have learnt. I don't know yet whether I will have another chance at applying them to a film. I think I will always prefer to write fiction. Collaboration, if you're used to the long spells of obsessive loneliness that fiction demands, is weirdly over-exciting. You go home each day suspecting that you have made a complete fool of yourself. It feels illicit. All that laughter! Can this really be work? People hang around whose job is to *bring you a cup of tea*! A sandwich on a plate! And to clear away the crockery afterwards while you go on writing! You are afraid of being swallowed up by the seductive machinery of it, the intricate balancing of forces that you barely understand.

And as for the money—the appalling sums it costs, to

make your ideas visible—I will never get used to this. Thinking about it nearly makes me keel over. Yes, at the beginning I really thought I was doing it for the money. But now I know that if I do it again, it will be for the slightly crazed pleasure of collaboration, and for the subtle little quiver of possibility that the enterprise gives off at the start—the distant flicker of a not yet perfected story that might end up satisfying and deep, if the chemistry is right. And, of course, for the moment when you sit down in the dark and see your characters walk and talk, with tones in their voices and expressions on their faces; when you see them spin away from you and out into the world of strangers.

1992

Dreams, the Bible and Cosmo Cosmolino

YEARS BEFORE I wrote *Cosmo Cosmolino*, its title came to me in a dream.

My friend, in this dream, was in the last stages of pregnancy and I ran about looking for a doctor as she began to labour. Slow-motion frustration: no doctor or nurse to be found. I would have to deliver the baby myself. My friend was quiet, she was not panicking, she was ready to give birth. 'Squat, squat,' I said, remembering stories of peasants. I spread out two old blue sleeping bags and a towel in the hallway of a terrace house. I took hold of her shoulders. She was perfectly calm and at ease. I held a mirror under her: her cunt opened like a shitting arsehole and the top of the baby's head appeared. It didn't move, or come further out, so I squeezed her cunt as one squeezes a pimple; with pressure from a small distance away, and pop! out it came, the strange bald head, as far as the nose, through which it immediately took a breath. The rest of the baby slithered out into my hands: suddenly there we had it, the child, already wrapped up and quickly old enough to crawl about and eat an apple. We called it Cosmo, Cosmolino—world, little world.

I had been keeping a record of my dreams for a long, long time. I had always been interested and attracted by dreams, decades before I realised that they spoke a kind of language, a poetry—and that they had something to do with *me*. Long before I realised there was a way of getting a handle on them, I loved their vividness and their weirdness. I used to keep a book beside the bed, and would sit up straight out of sleep and write them down, in that precious and brief state between sleep and full wakefulness.

Later, when I reread them, I'd often envy that me, the half-awake me who had grabbed the pen and written a whole page before the reasoning, embarrassable mind got back into the driver's seat and jammed on the brakes. I used to think, 'These dreams—the way they express themselves, their bluntness, their bare-faced frankness, their utter lack of irony, shame or guile—these dreams are better than anything else I've ever written.'

I felt both responsible for them—I mean pleased with them—and at the same time innocent of them—as if I shouldn't take credit for them because they weren't exactly *mine*. It was more as if I were theirs. I had a strong sense that they were passing through me. (I once read an interview with a saxophone player who said, 'When I play badly, it's my fault, but when I play well, it's got nothing to do with me.')

The daylight me, who sat at a desk, fed, watered, fully dressed and wearing shoes and socks, who laboured to produce articles and reviews and stories and novels—this working me longed to recover that state of being in which I was able to dash off these dreams. The dream writing was writing without effort, without strain, without ambition.

I don't mean, though, that it was automatic writing, or gibberish like someone talking in tongues. My half-waking mind was able to construct sentences of syntactic grace and correctness. Better still, the language it used was completely without embarrassment or social constraints. It could handle sexual ecstasy or excretion or shocking physical cruelties or tremendous natural phenomena (floods, earthquakes) without the slightest hesitation. It was equal to anything, of any scope, vast or tiny, complex or simple. Nothing was too squalid or too glorious for it to express. It found (or possessed—there seemed to be no struggle involved) a language appropriate to whatever spectacle it had witnessed or taken part in, while I slept.

And most enviably of all, it had a style which I longed to command. This style was urgent, direct, simple; stripped of ornament yet rich in imagery, correct in syntax and grammar, and graceful in its movement; muscular in its verbs; laconic without being desiccated; capable of fine distinctions without nit-picking or pedantry; able to move easily between high diction and blunt serviceable everyday speech.

In short, it was everything the daylight me wanted, as a style, and could not have.

So, when I started working on what was eventually published as *Cosmo Cosmolino*, one thing I wanted was to find a way of incorporating dream into the writing.

I say 'into the writing' rather than 'into the story' on purpose. It's easy enough to put a dream into a story—that is, to make a character have a dream. (One writer I know says he's suspicious of dreams in novels. 'As soon as someone in what I'm reading has a dream,' he says, 'I either skip it or put the book down.' He thinks that to make your character dream is a kind of cheating.)

What I tried to do, in *Cosmo Cosmolino*, was to enrich the texture of the story, to get beyond the fairly simple psychological realism I'd been writing previously and out into a more wondrous world that would still stubbornly be *this* world. I wanted to write something that had all the squalid panic, the wild swerves of narrative, the radiant emblematic objects and the passages of swooning bliss that I had found in dreams.

It was not easy.

But I found another source—the Bible. I began to read it, partly, I think, because one of my characters was a fundamentalist Christian, and I wanted to become familiar with his territory before I tackled him. But it was also because—

At this point I recognise a false tone in what I am saying. I mean the sort of not quite lies but not quite truth either that a writer can slide into when speaking about her own work. I am starting to talk *as if I knew what I was doing* when I wrote the book. In retrospect, one starts to take credit for things in the work which, at the time of writing, were desperate stabs, blind lurchings, or steps off cliffs into thin air. The truth is that I forget why I started to read the Bible. What makes us pick up one book and not another? I do remember buying for a dollar a battered old copy of a 1950s translation of the New Testament in the Cat Protection Society op shop on my way along Enmore Road to work. I remember taking it to my work room, reading a few pages, then deciding—*because my writing was going so badly*—to get hold of the King James Version and the Jerusalem Bible as well, to go back to Genesis, to sit there and read the whole damn thing. I remember realising it would take months, and deciding that since I had a two-year Literature Board grant it was the perfect time to do it.

I also remember being relieved at having set myself a serious task that would remove for several months my appalling attacks of guilt at not being able to write the novel I was trying to write—that I had been given *taxpayers' money* to write.

I remember being astonished at the intensity of the reading pleasure I got as a writer from the Bible—I mean technically. It would be too neat to say that I found in it something approximating to the style my half-waking self commanded but which was beyond the range of my daylight self. But there were passages of narrative in the Bible that made my hair stand on end—with horror, bliss, and *technical awe*. The Book of Tobit, for example. Chapter 5, verse 16: 'The boy left with the angel, and the dog followed behind.' This is a story in which an angel just stands about casually in a doorway; a man unwittingly *hires* an angel 'at a drachma a day'. I found, too, certain brilliant ways of *launching* a story, of grabbing the reader's sleeve and commanding his attention: 'A man had two daughters' or 'Consider a carpenter, who...' This blunt, urgent address reminded me of fairytales.

And I recognised, often, the emblematic objects of my dreams: things that seem to radiate a tremendous, mysterious meaning: the cloak that Elijah throws over the ploughboy's shoulder; the hem of Jesus' garment, through which the 'virtue' runs out of him when the sick woman touches it; the staff that puts forth shoots and leaves; a little pancake; the details of sewing and carpentry in the building of the temple.

(I took notes, and later, when I did find a way into writing *Cosmo Cosmolino*, I shamelessly borrowed and stole.)

Dreams and the Bible have certain things in common. One is violence. Some days I'd come out of my workroom white and shaking after reading one of those hideous tales of rape and butchery that the Old Testament is sprinkled with—just as we wake from certain dreams in a lather of horror. What could be a more practical gift, to a writer of my age who has been brought up in a civilised, peaceful country, a member of a generation that has not had to go to war?

When I compare *Cosmo Cosmolino* with the half-waking dream-writing I still do, I see the very wide gap that lies between my waking, working self and the unselfconscious scribbler sitting up in bed. *Cosmo Cosmolino* got away from me, somehow. It went into the purple. I had a huge amount of fun with it, slinging the clauses this way and that; but I didn't come within cooee of my longed-for dream-style, with its simple urgency and directness. Still—at least I figured out how to get dream into the texture of the story. And I got far enough past my pragmatic Australian inhibitions to find the nerve to write a world in which angels stand about casually in doorways, or steal money, or accept a massage, or fly away straight after breakfast.

A few mornings ago my husband said to me when we woke up, 'You talked in your sleep last night. I noted it down. Look—here's what you said: IS IT SPECIAL LOOKING?—DOES IT REALLY EXIST?' If I was talking about my wonderful dream-writing, I believe it is special-looking, and it does exist—but I haven't found it yet. I'm still searching.

1992

Elizabeth Jolley's War

'IN THE MIDDLE of the journey of our life', when we start to feel the weight of the crimes we are hauling behind us, we might turn to literature for wisdom. It is not readily available, but I have always found it in Elizabeth Jolley, even before I knew what I was looking for. The Old Testament, in one of its great hymns to wisdom, calls it (among other things) 'manifold, subtil, lively, clear, undefiled, plain…' and adds that its 'conversation hath no bitterness'. All these things apply.

I picked up My Father's Moon with eagerness.* I had noticed over the preceding year or so the appearance in magazines and anthologies of new stories by Jolley which entered territory her work had hinted at before but not yet fully broached: in particular, the world of nursing, and not the shonky little rip-off nursing home of Mr Scobie's Riddle, but a big British training institution, a military hospital in wartime.

Now here is the novel and it richly rewards the wait. All the elements of Jolley's previous work, its familiar (even obsessive) moods, motifs and subject matters, are swung into balance with each other. It becomes clear that it was this early experience of training as a nurse in wartime England which, though she held back so many years from tackling it directly, was all the while sending waves of subdued power through everything she wrote, imbuing it with a personal and particularly female authority of tone—the authority of

* My Father's Moon, Elizabeth Jolley, Viking, 1989.

someone who has bitten the bullet, learnt to bear things and to be useful—an authority sometimes missed, or misread as whimsical headmistressliness, by those unmoved by her simple statements of pain and stoicism, or untickled by her crooked, skidding humour.

It is sad when senses of humour fail to meet, for nothing can be done about this, and how tedious the straight-faced must find it to be told of the spasms of enfeebling hilarity her work can provoke—something like the wild laughter of nurses, or nuns. But when one reviewer disobligingly remarked that the book reminded him of Rachmaninov, I was astonished. If there's any composer Jolley brings to mind, it's not a grandiose tear-jerker of a Russian but someone more like Satie—always resolutely human in scale, modest, thoughtful, quirkily melodic, with flashes of oblique humour and a light touch.

The plot, if it were wrenched against its weave into a rough chronological form, would go like this: Vera, a plain, naive girl with a German-speaking mother (social and patriotic embarrassment) and an English father, is sent away to a Quaker boarding school then on to train as a nurse during World War II; at the hospital she does well at work and study but is socially a flop, resorting to dobbing, sucking-up and petty sabotage, until she is taken up by a reputedly promiscuous doctor and his gushy wife; she falls in love with him, gets pregnant, is abandoned (the doctor vanishes as the war ends: 'dead or believed missing') and, rejecting her parents' offer to take on the illegitimate child, stubbornly drags the little girl away into a dismal life of privation and precarious survival.

Vera's first-person narrating voice shifts back and forth in time among these events with a suppleness that keeps us hovering several inches above the ground. Its loftiest vantage-point, the brief *now* which encloses the story, is that of the middle-aged Vera who sees on a train a woman she believes to be a nursing companion from that wartime hospital: Ramsden, a slightly senior nurse, also slightly superior in social class, who, though Vera at the time was too proud and too ashamed to accept what the older girl offered her, has remained a symbolic focus of unconditional generosity and grace throughout Vera's memories of that world without comfort in which she struggled.

A sentence that stays with me from one of Elizabeth Jolley's earlier books is this: 'It is a privilege to prepare the place where someone else will sleep.' In *My Father's Moon*, too, certain remarks resound like quietly struck chords.

> The strong feeling of love which goes from the parent to the child does not seem a part of the child which can be given back to the parent.

> There is something hopeless in being hopeful that one person can actually match and replace another. It is not possible.

> However much a person resembles another person, and it is not that person, it is not of any use.

If, as Emerson says, prayer is 'the contemplation of the facts of life from the highest point of view', these remarks, still showing in their hesitant or repetitive syntax the effort that has gone into their formulation, function as prayers, and for me they have the same calming, if not comforting, power.

> She said…that love was infinite. That it was possible, if a person loved, to believe in the spiritual understanding of truths which were not fully understood intellectually. She said that the person you loved was not an end in itself, was not something you came to the end of, but was the beginning of discoveries which could be made because of loving someone.

Stendhal, in his charming if not very helpful book on love, declares that there are some things which even the most resourceful and experienced woman would not be able to face: for example, 'just how beastly a wound can be'. Later came nurses. Perhaps Jolley has been working her way back, all these years, gaining skill as she went, towards something she needed to write about a soldier, hardly more than a boy, whose legs have been amputated above the knee and who also has a terrific wound in his stomach. He begs the nurse to put the crucifix from around his neck into the wound: the prim Quaker girl, gold-medal nurse, refuses 'because it isn't sterile'.

> I brush something small and white out of his bed. It seems to roll up like a soft bread crumb. As I swab the wound it seems something is moving in it. It is a maggot. I pick it out quickly with the forceps trying not to show my shock. Suddenly I see there are maggots everywhere. It's as though he is being eaten alive. They are crawling from under his other bandages and in and out of his shirt and the sheets. I lean over him to try to stop him seeing and I ring the bell, three rings for emergency...I try to cover him but the maggots have spilled on to the floor and he has seen them. I see the horror of it in his eyes.
>
> The charge nurse comes around the screens straight away. 'Fetch a dustpan and brush nurse,' she says to me, 'and ring for the RSO.' As I go I hear her raised voice as she tries to restrain him and to say words of comfort—that the maggots have been put there on purpose, that they have cleaned his wounds and yes of course she'll put the gold cross wherever he wants it—yes, she'll put it there now...

What is the detail that screws this scene into its tightest focus? Isn't it the comically humble dustpan and brush?

The book's surreal quality undercuts me whenever I start a sentence that is even faintly psychological or sociological. Yes, Vera is isolated and cramped by class, the story is riddled with it, but how can I soberly examine this when the characters who outclass Vera are nurses with names like Diamond and Snorter who 'never wear uniform and…sing and laugh and come into theatre in whatever they happened to be wearing—backless dinner dresses, tennis shorts or their night-gowns'? The book itself will laugh if I become pompous about it: it ranges so liberally, it's so *flexible*.

There are striking passages about the actual process of learning. 'It's like poetry, I want to tell them, this anatomy, this usefulness of the pelvis… "Describe the acetabulum, and do it without looking at the book". "A deep, cup-shaped cavity, formed by the union of three bones…"' The acetabulum, when I look it up, is the socket of the thigh-bone, and in Latin means 'vinegar cup'.

Under a sequence about study, the pleasure of hearing the pennies dropping, bubbles the half-hysterical meanness of schoolgirls:

> As I write the essay, the staff and the patients and the wards of St Cuthberts seem to unfold about me and I begin to understand what I am trying to do in this hospital. I rewrite the essay collecting the complete working of a hospital ward into two sheets of paper. When it is read aloud to the other nurses, Ferguson stares at me and does not take her eyes off me all through the nursing lecture which follows.
>
> I learn every bone and muscle in the body and all the muscle attachments and all the systems of the body. I begin to understand the destruction of disease and the construction of cure. I find I can use phrases suddenly in speech or on paper which give a correct answer. Formulae for digestion or respiration or for the action of drugs. Words and phrases like gaseous interchange and internal combustion roll from my pen and the name at the top of the lists continues to be mine.
>
> 'Don't tell me you'll be top in invalid cookery too!' Ferguson says and she reminds me of the white sauce I made at school which was said to have blocked up the drains for two days.

> She goes on to remind me how my pastry board, put up at the window to dry, was the one which fell on the headmaster's wife while she was weeding in the garden below, breaking her glasses and altering the shape of her nose forever.

Schoolgirlish? Jolley upends every silly book I ever read as a child about merry boarding school pranks and (later) nurse-and-doctor romances. Her schoolgirls are tight-lipped savages with sliding eyes, measuring and preying on each other. 'We both shake with simulated mirth, making, at the same time, a pretence of trying to suppress it.' She knows the warped forms that ingenuity can take in lonely children or unpopular girls, and the self-disgust of those who, forced to adopt protective colouring, discover in themselves unexpected depths of cruelty and yet carry on practising the art of survival.

Vera, starved of affection and hopelessly lacking in 'Sex Appeal', becomes a weird gremlin loose in the hospital, wreaking havoc among prettier and more popular girls, plundering secret food stores for dainty treats with which to woo her oblivious superiors. These splendid, crazy chapters flash between bright and dark moods with a bizarre energy: they dive in and out of surreal horror, the panic of having to learn a job by doing it, the pleasure of order achieved, the longing for revenge and for intimacy.

> In a fog of the incomprehensible and the obscure I strive, more stupid than I have ever been in my life, to anticipate the needs of the theatre sister whose small, hard eyes glitter at me above her white cotton mask.

> Isolation…is approached by a long, narrow covered way sloping up through a war-troubled shrubbery where all the dust bins are kept… When I go out into the darkness I can smell rotting arms and legs, thrown out of the operating theatre and not put properly into the bins.

Night Sister Bean…is starch-scented, shrouded mysteriously in the daintily severe folds of spotted white gauze. She is a sorceress disguised in the heavenly blue of the Madonna; a shrivelled, rustling, aromatic, knowledgable, Madonna-coloured magician; she is a wardress and a keeper. She is an angel in charge of life and in charge of death. Her fine white cap, balancing, nodding, a grotesque blossom flowering for ever in the dark halls of the night, hovers beneath me. She is said to have powers, an enchantment, beyond the powers of an ordinary human. For one thing, she has been on night duty in this hospital for over thirty years.

Every day, after the operations, I go round the theatre with a pail of hot soapy water cleaning everything. There is an orderly peacefulness in the quiet white tranquillity which seems, every afternoon, to follow the strained, bloodstained mornings.

When the attention of the glamorous doctor is momentarily turned her way, she seizes it with the greed of the deprived, though she knows she is a lesser creature and that these 'very long and very sweet kisses' can't last. But their effect, what they lead to, is related obliquely in choruses of nurses' gynaecological gossip—ignorant, pitiless and (for the reader) hilarious—which whip the final section into a disorienting coda of distress. This thins out into one piercing line of dialogue. Lois, an erstwhile friend or perhaps even lover, spots the sixpenny wedding ring Vera has bought in an attempt to legitimise her still secret pregnancy. As the nurses are about to go on duty, 'Lois, in her cloud of smoke, extinguishes her cigarette. "Whoever," she says leaning low across the table, "whoever would ever have married you?"'

The book's final page, only twenty-five lines, returns in a calmer key to the silent woman on the train, who may or may not be Ramsden. It is *important* that she should be Ramsden, not for sentimental reasons but because Ramsden was the only person in that insane world of the wartime hospital whose behaviour endorsed Vera's knowledge that music can be a channel for grace, that words can be arranged to form poetry, that love can exist and have a meaning. If the woman is Ramsden, then something can be salvaged, the past can be made to yield up something that is pure. Thus the bleak, delicate question, the intake of breath on which the novel ends: '*Is it you, Ramsden, after all these years is it?*'

1990

Germaine Greer and the Menopause

WHAT A STRANGE secret the menopause is. I would need the fingers of both hands to count the women of my age (forty-nine) and slightly younger who, when I mentioned to them that I was reading *The Change*, dropped their eyes with a shudder and said, 'Ugh—I don't want to *know* about menopause. I don't even want to *think* about it.*

'No, no!' I'd cry. 'It's not what you think! It's wonderful! We'll be free!'

Some laughed and turned away. Some hastily changed the subject. Some looked at me with sidelong, sceptical smiles. And one said, 'Not now. Not yet. I'm in love. I'm getting on a plane next week to go and meet him'—as if she feared that menopause was like a fire-curtain in a theatre: boom, it drops, and overnight you are cut off forever from energy, light, risk-the place where things are burning.

But *The Change* is full of energy, light and risk. The whole work is that rare thing in modern public discourse, a passionate argument for spirit. Its trajectory describes a beautiful curve through indignation, anger and grief, and out the other side to a vantage-point with a high, calm view towards death. One English reviewer I read, a woman, remarked crabbily that she 'could have done with less talk about "soul" and "spirit".' In fact this is the central concern of the book, stated early and many times repeated: how a woman can learn 'to shift the focus of

* Germaine Greer, *The Chance: Women, Ageing and the Menopause*, Hamish Hamilton, 1991.

her attention away from her body ego towards her soul'. To wish for less of this is to miss the point entirely.

The word around the traps is that Germaine Greer is against hormone replacement therapy. For many, the core of the book has seemed to be her chapters about HRT and its purveyors, an assault vastly documented and couched in the language of fierce irony that we have come to expect from her; and yet somehow, despite its vigour, this attack I found confusing, almost perfunctory, as if, while she knows her obligation to deal with the chemical question, which the world sees as central, her heart and her real thoughts were focussed elsewhere.

Her critique of HRT has raised hackles, particularly among women who have read only reviews of the book: for as women of my age approach the end of ovulation with its aura of ill-defined dread, and as the first symptoms of the change 'from the reproductive animal to contemplative animal' begin to manifest, we are now routinely urged, by female and male GPs alike, to start taking replacement oestrogen, even if what we are experiencing is only mildly distracting, and physically not traumatic at all.

The peculiar fear of menopause, which this book has dispelled for me but which many otherwise well-informed women will admit to in private conversation, tends to bathe the proffered HRT in the alluring light of a rescue. A rescue from what? We barely know—and that is why Germaine Greer has written this book.

In her view, the prevailing attitudes towards menopause in our youth-obsessed culture fall into two broad strands: on one side, a brisk denial that women at this stage of their lives go through anything significant at all; on the other, an insistence that menopause is a deficiency disease, that the cessation of ovulation and menstruation hurls a woman into a chasm of mania, suicidal melancholy, foul temper, inappropriate lusts (or lack of any libido at all), malice, ugliness, uselessness and despair. It is hard to know, she says, which picture conceals the cruder misogyny: the no-nonsense materialist approach to the climacteric as nothing in particular ('the goal of life,' snaps Greer, 'is not to feel nothing'), or the catastrophe model, where femaleness itself is seen as pathological, and treated accordingly.

This is how menopause appears to men. In vain we ask the older women we know how it appeared to them: they go shy and vague, or claim to have forgotten. Women, Greer argues, know themselves so poorly, have adapted themselves so thoroughly to men's (and children's) requirements of them, and have allowed their own version of their intimate experience to be so muffled and distorted, that the whole phenomenon of menopause has been whisked away from them and defined for their own purposes by men, to women's infinite loss, and cost.

Our reliable knowledge of what menopause actually is and does remains disgracefully slight, Doctors are not yet able to distinguish symptoms of hormonal change from the effects of ageing. And one cannot fail to notice the punitive nature of medical treatments meted out to menopausal women, or the eagerness with which surgery is applied: 'A man,' says Greer, 'who demands that his penis and/or testicles be cut off will be immediately understood to be deranged; a woman who for no good reason wishes to extirpate her uterus will be given every assistance.' The only thing more shocking than Greer's catalogue of the carnage visited on the persons of menopausal women over the last two centuries is the conniv- ance of women in this charcuterie, their readiness to endure and request invasive, mutilating procedures for ailments which, according to Greer, might well have derived directly from the unbearableness of their female lot, or which could have been temporary manifestations of hormonal upheaval that in time, given patience and gentle treatment, would have eased gradually, as the natural change completed itself.

Greer unearths certain gruesome and pathetic case studies

and applies to them a broader reading, more patient, and more *womanly*—feminist, if you like. She carefully examines the woman's particular social and family situation, her history of loss and grief, details of which were present all along in the file but which the doctor, in his narrow focus on symptoms, had failed to take into account; thus, suddenly, these women in the grip of rages or depressions that looked like insanity become people struggling with bereavement—people whose motives are utterly understandable.

She calls oestrogen 'the biddability hormone', and suggests that at menopause, when the body ceases to secrete it, women may find themselves back in touch with a rage 'too vast and bottomless' to have been allowed expression during the thirty-five years of altruistic family life—that long process of 'censorship by oestrogen'. 'Many women only realise during the climacteric,' she says, 'the extent to which their lives have been a matter of capitulation and how little of what has happened to them has actually been in their interest.'

Yes, perhaps it is only at menopause—or towards the age of fifty when age shows in their faces and bodies—that women begin to grasp how deeply their lives have been defined and limited by men: by the physical fear of men's violence, which has circumscribed their freedom of movement (and a daily glance at the newspapers shows us that even extreme old age offers us no immunity from this); but still more thoroughly, if more subtly, by the gaze of men. How can it ever be measured, the shaping, the formative effect on women's lives and intellects and imaginations of being, for more than thirty-five years of their lives, under constant sexual scrutiny?

Around fifty, according to Greer and as many an older woman has observed, this gaze ebbs, and is withdrawn. One becomes, in the outer world of street and work, and often too within the family and the home, all but invisible. It is disconcerting, this gradual removal of a ubiquitous force against which, in order to survive as a social being, a woman has been obliged to learn to define herself. Invisibility is a very humbling thing, no matter how many times during the decades of eyeballing one cursed one's fate and wrestled with it, becoming 'strident', 'unfeminine', 'dikey', 'badly dressed', 'hostile', 'castrating', and so on, in the process. But invisibility, writes Greer, which feels for a while like formlessness, like a non-existence, is the first taste of the freedom that is to come.

She slashes away in a most gratifying and invigorating manner at women's fear of ageing, and more ferociously still at our spineless collaboration with *men's* fear of women's ageing, that pressure which slides many a woman towards an unthinking grab at the proffered hormone replacement therapy. Greer is not 'against HRT'. She states plainly that if certain symptoms have been identified as menopausal, and if they become intolerable, they should be treated with hormones, and welcome to it. But she urges women not to rush in. She challenges us to examine our motives for taking HRT with more self-respect and scrupulousness than she believes we do. And what she is against is the proposal now being seductively articulated: that menopause is somehow old-fashioned and unnecessary: that menopause should be eliminated.

She insists that it is not a disease, but an essential stage in a woman's journey towards death. Our children, at this time of our lives, grow up and leave; and we shall have no more. The end of motherhood, potential or actual, *is* a little death. The death of the womb brings with it a grief that is, in Iris Murdoch's impressive phrase, 'an august and terrible pain'. Menopause is *serious*. At the exact point where our external culture loses interest in her, menopause presents a woman with a challenge to respect and define herself in a new way. It may be a sombre way. 'Calm, grave, quiet women,' says Greer, drive youth-obsessed men 'to distraction'. When I read this I thought it an amusing exaggeration. A week later I was being interviewed by a male journalist who, learning with surprise that it was a long time since I had gone out dancing in a club, bristled with disapproval, then burst out, 'You don't *laugh* much any more, Helen, do you!' Yes, I do—but not at the same things; and I don't feel obliged to crack jokes and kick up my heels just to keep a stranger comfortable.

Twenty years ago, when I was ploughing my destructive way through a series of 'love' affairs, I was taken aside one evening by a woman in her late forties who taught a yoga class into which I sometimes blundered. She wanted to give me a piece of advice, though she must have seen I was too addicted to emotional upheaval to be able to hear it. She said, 'Helen—if you learn to know yourself, you may not even need a partner.' The advice itself, at the time, went in one ear and out the other, but I have never forgotten her way of delivering it: she *whispered* it, as if it were too subversive to be spoken out loud. Germaine Greer does not lower her voice, but the advice is the same; and it's the kind of thing that people do not want to hear, because in our impoverished culture nobody can imagine anything more terrible than being solitary.

While reading *The Change* I did a little browsing through our suburban library's sparse holdings on the topic of menopause. In one bracing text I came across the expression 'sex-lazy'. *Sex-lazy*, apparently, is what a lot of women (and some men) become as they grow older. It's not that they *dislike* sex. They sort of can't be bothered. Sex has slid to a low position on their list of activities, and this the writer of the tract severely deplored. The term brought to my mind something I spotted a while back in a *New Yorker* piece on comparative attitudes towards clothing in France and the United States: the French, said this woman fashion writer, look with horror on American women's loose, comfortable dress, and believe that such women are not facing up to their 'erotic responsibilities'. I would like my disappointed journalist to know that *this* made me laugh, till tears ran down. 'The very notion of [the older woman] "remaining attractive", writes Greer, 'is replete with the contradictions that break women's hearts…Is one never to be set free from the white-slavery of attraction-duty?' Be sexy, or be alone. Is this the choice that women are presented with, at fifty? If it is, suggests Greer, we should seriously consider the more challenging option.

'Menopause doctors,' Greer goes on, 'see as one of their chief functions the curing of ailing marriages.' An ageing wife loses interest in sex, while her similarly ageing husband is still keen. What is to be done? Why, drug treatment for the sex-lazy woman, of course, and a lot of *work on herself*, of a cosmetic, sartorial and surgical nature, so that the husband's failing interest in her might be revived, or his straying eye brought back within the fold: because, after all, people will 'persist in the irrational belief that regular psychosexual release is essential for the proper functioning of all individuals'. This is the attitude to which Greer most forcefully and satirically objects; and at this point many a reader thus far sympathetic might part company with her contentions. What about long, loving monogamous relationships? they ask. What is the husband to do with his sexuality?

Greer spins out an anthropological phantasmagoria of Asian and Middle Eastern and African extended families, matrilocality, polygamous set-ups and the like, in which ageing women, she claims, are not obliged to remain sexually active against their will in order to be accorded status and dignity. It makes fascinating reading; but much good may these speculations do us, here where we live. They serve merely to highlight what we in the developed world have given up in exchange for relative health and prosperity, and to point up our lack of proper rites of passage, as well as the bleakness of our landscape of isolated, helpless little nuclear arrangements where, if sex is 'the [only] cement of the family', its decline (should this occur with the wife's ageing) can cause the tight, inflexible structure of the couple to collapse.

To tell the truth, Greer is not very interested in long-lasting couples. Her experience of them is slight. Though she writes gripping accounts of splendid old women—Madame de Maintenon, Diane de Poitiers, 'neither of [whom] would have looked good in shorts'—who despite their physical decrepitude kept the love and respect of kings until they died, her whole imaginative drive is towards solitariness.

And why not? For even the strongest partnership, these days, is liable to end in widowhood. Women live longer than men. We are likely, at an advanced age, to find ourselves alone; and then everything Greer has told us will apply, whether we were happily married or not.

Many chapters of this book sizzle with vigorous polemic. For example, Greer takes it right up to the late Simone de Beauvoir, who 'aged ungracefully and ungratefully' and 'wasted time in bitter regret'. Greer sorts her out mercilessly for the 'futile repining' at growing old which fills and sours her memoirs. 'Simone de Beauvoir is, she tells us repeatedly, an intellectual; notwithstanding, she faces the future as unprovided as any empty-headed beauty queen…It is as if she has no interior landscape…[Her] vanity and poverty of spirit…undermine the importance of her thinking, which could not bring her serenity or self-command.'

But the finest writing (and thinking) comes in the book's two final chapters, 'The Old Witch' and 'Serenity and Power'. With her generous intelligence working at full spate, Greer draws together material from women's poetry, fiction, memoirs and letters into a beautifully complex and challenging statement, funny, calm and wise, which I know I will read again and again. Who could have predicted that Germaine Greer would reach this point? She looks poised to become not a witch, but a mystic.

1992

On Turning Fifty

EARLY IN 1992, the year I turned fifty, my fifth book, *Cosmo Cosmolino*, came out. The fact that there had been a gap of eight years since my previous novel, *The Children's Bach*, was much remarked upon by journalists, although in the intervening time I had published a collection of stories, written two screenplays and had them produced, and continued to earn a living by various forms of journalism. One critic said that to let such a gap occur 'in one's career' was 'dangerous'. This way of thinking about work—a *treadmill*, never relaxing, always looking back over your shoulder, hearing footsteps—seems to me at worst exhausting and corrupting, and at best simply beside the point.

The word 'career' is one I can never imagine applying to what I do. 'Career' is a word that can only be applied from without. It's a word with connotations of speed and certainty, of a smooth forcefulness, like the trajectory of a comet seen from a great distance. How can one speak without irony of one's own career?

It's unimaginable, to me, to use the word 'career' to refer to this daily slog; the absolute inability, while you're working, to judge whether or not what you're doing has any value at all—thus, the blind faith and grim stubbornness required in order to keep going; the episodes of elation, the occasional sense of hitting your stride, or of being in tune with the force that creates—the feeling that *now* you've got it, *now* you can't put a foot wrong—then the guilt you feel, when your work's going well, that you are *allowed* to spend your days having this much fun and ultimately being paid for it, while others have jobs in offices or schools, and bosses, and laid-down work hours they have to stick to—then the arrival next morning at your desk, the dropping away of the floor from under your feet as you see the thinness of what yesterday seemed so rich and right; the picking up of the pen, the dogged *keeping going*—the sickly envy of people with jobs, because they *have* got bosses to tell them what to do next, and work hours that finish at a certain regular time so they can go home, and *holidays*, and *secretaries*, and *superannuation*—and they're allowed to ask for *help*; the pathetic pleas for encouragement you make, invariably to the wrong person—a child, a husband, a parent—someone who can't possibly know the right thing to say, or who is in the grip of some barely conscious hostility towards you that they can't help expressing at the most destructive possible moment; the hatred of your own name, because of its connection with this slogging labour and with the expectations which you have caused the outside world to have of you, and that you're afraid you'll never live up to; the despair of feeling trapped inside your own style.

This last may be a particularly middle-aged despair; or perhaps it's one that strikes just before a new surge occurs in your work. The Caribbean writer Clarice Lispector said, 'Even one's own style is an obstacle that must be overcome'; and the Cubist painter Georges Braque, 'One's style is one's inability to do otherwise.' I once wrote to Manning Clark, grumbling that I was 'sick of my style'. He wrote back a postcard saying bluntly, 'Your style will not change until *you* do.'

I like to think that if there was a big gap in my so-called career, it was for the simple reason that I had nothing to say.

The idea of career also ignores something that my working life has taught me: you write a novel, and you think, good, right, now I know how to write a novel. WRONG. You found out how to write *that* novel; but what you nutted out for *that* one is not going to help you to write the next. Each new bout of work demands a new approach. You have to teach yourself everything afresh, every single time, and then when you've learnt that, you have to teach yourself a whole lot more.

This too may be specially true of middle age. Because at middle age, life gets serious. At middle age you have to learn the language with which to speak of death. This is the time when a kind of sombre colouring can enter your thinking and feeling, and thus your work. It can also be a difficult transition—and perhaps it's just as difficult for your audience.

Once an artist has become reasonably well known in her society, specially if it's a rather small one, like ours, there's a danger that she will be pinned down. People dislike change. If they've settled into your already established content and style, they like you to stick with it. They want the comfortable feeling of opening your new book and settling down to an afternoon of what they've come to expect of you.

There's a problem, too, specially in Australia, or if you belong to my generation and kind of education and social experience, anyway—a problem of embarrassment. People are embarrassed, for example, about religion, they're embarrassed about God, they're embarrassed by biblical imagery and angels and ideas of redemption and salvation. The people I'm thinking of want materialism and realism, and if that's not what you've written this time, they'll bloody well distort your book till that's what they get out of it—anything rather than read what you're actually trying to say.

I used to suffer a lot from what critics said. But after *Cosmo Cosmolino* I was able to see the reviews as a cavalcade of attitudes. I enjoyed them as a spectacle. They fascinated me and made me laugh. This is how I knew that suddenly I was a grown-up. I did not shed a single tear.

The grand thing about being fifty is how tough you can be.

You don't have to care what people think. You can let things rip, in your work, that good manners and being lady-like would once have inhibited. At fifty you can stop wanting to be *nice*.

And, anyway, who was ever silly enough to imagine that you could be an artist and a nice person? How can a *woman* be an artist and nice in the way women are supposed to be? Who can be the oil in the social machine when she's got the fiercely over-developed observing eye that the artist has to have? The two don't match. They can't. The nice thing is not to notice. But artists *must* notice. They have to stare coolly, and see, and remember, and collect. That's their job, their task in the universe.

I don't see how you can be an artist without causing pain. I don't mean hurting people on purpose, for revenge, or idly, or to settle accounts. But what you see, if you're really looking, is often what people wish you *wouldn't* see.

A good friend of mine recently reread, after twenty-five years, Flaubert's novel *Madame Bovary*. I asked her, 'How does it last?' She looked uncomfortable, then blurted out, 'I *hated* it. It's cold, it's horrible, it's cruel—I couldn't *bear* it.' We were both shocked. To two educated readers of our generation this was heresy. Soon after this, my friend went to visit a wonderful old woman we know who is a tremendous, voracious reader. In her eighties, she's the widow of two painters and has known many writers. This is a woman who, when I once admired her trenchant turn of phrase, laughed and said, 'The men in my life, when women spoke, had an attention span so short that if I wanted to be heard I was obliged to *haiku* everything.'

My friend phoned me after her visit to this woman. 'I told her,' she said, 'about hating *Madame Bovary*. I thought she'd be scornful of me—but she laughed and said, "Good. When a woman realises that she hates *Madame Bovary*, darling girl, that's when she knows she's come of age."'

Perhaps we 'come of age' rather late in Australia, or in my

generation—but I never expected to find, in my fifties, this marvellous freedom. Women may be late starters, as artists, but perhaps a strength that develops late lasts longer. Where once you rushed at things like a bull at a gate, now you know how to be patient. Things still hurt, but you are stronger. At fifty, you are developing a steady nerve. You can discriminate. You can stop worrying about exteriors, and start to look inward for meaning. At fifty, the age when you thought you would be on the scrapheap, you find you are just entering your prime.

1992

PART THREE

The Violet Jacket

At the Morgue

IN EVERYONE'S MENTAL image of a city there is a dark, chilled, secret place called the City Morgue. We know these exist because we've seen them at the movies. If you had asked me where Melbourne's mortuary was, I wouldn't have had a clue. I might have gestured vaguely towards the murkier end of Flinders Street—but like most Melburnians I had no idea that half a mile from the leafiest stretch of St Kilda Road, in there behind the National Gallery and the Ballet School and the Arts Centre with its silly spire and its theatres and orchestras and choirs, stands a wide, low, new, clean, bright, nautical-looking structure, with a cluster of slender steel chimneys and a crisp little landscaped garden: the Coronial Services Centre, which was opened in 1988 and houses the Victorian Institute of Forensic Pathology. This is where I found the mortuary.

If you die in an accident, or unexpectedly, or by violence, or in police or state custody, or by suicide, or in a fire, or if no doctor is prepared to sign a certificate stating that you have died of natural causes, your death is called a reportable death. Your body is taken to the mortuary, where you enter the juris-diction of the coroner. He, on behalf of the people of Victoria, wants to know exactly why you died. And until the cause of your death has been established to his satisfaction, in most cases by means of an autopsy, your body will remain in his care. You have become what is known as a coroner's case—a coroner's body.

The first one I saw, from a raised and glassed-in viewing

area, was lying naked on its back on a stainless-steel table in the infectious room of the mortuary. It was the body of a young man. Because he had been found with a syringe nearby, he'd already had a battery of tests. He was infected with hepatitis C, a virulent form of the disease for which there is no vaccination and which eighty percent of IV drug deaths are found to be carrying: thus, the lab technician was not only gowned up and gloved like a surgeon, but was wearing a hard clear perspex mask which covered his whole face and gave him the look of a welder. The other actor in this odourless mime-autopsy was also a man, a pathologist. He wore no mask but was otherwise dressed like the technician. Both of them moved around on the spotless tiles in big stiff white rubber boots.

Before I could get my bearings (and my notebook was already hanging by my side, forgotten) the technician stepped up to the corpse's head and sank a needle into its left eye. The first sample of fluid laid aside, he moved down to the dead man's hip, plunged another syringe into his abdomen just above his pubic hair and drew out a sample of his urine. Then he picked up a scalpel and walked around to the right side of the dead man's head.

I would be lying if I claimed to be able to give a blow-by-blow account of the first autopsy I witnessed. The shock of it made me forget the sequence. Time slid past me at breathless speed. The pathologist and the technician moved as swiftly and as lightly as dancers. My eyes were too slow: they kept getting left behind. If I concentrated on one thing, another procedure would suddenly be launched or completed elsewhere. So this is not official. It is not objective.

I saw that the scalp was slit and peeled forward over the face like a hairy cap, leaving the skull a shining, glossy white. The skull was opened by means of a little vibrating handsaw. The brain was lifted neatly out (so clean, perfect, intricately folded—so valuable-looking), but also, before I could contemplate it, the torso was slit from the base of the neck to the pubis in one firm, clean-running scalpel stroke, then someone seized a pair of long-handled, small-beaked shears and smoothly snipped away the arcs of ribs which protect the heart and lungs—and there it lay, open to view, the brilliantly, madly compressed landscape of the inner organs.

It can't be, but I thought that the two men paused here for a second, to give us time to admire.

Out come the organs now, neatly scalpelled away from their evolved positions. The technician, working blind in the hollow cave of the torso, lifts them out in glistening slippery handfuls. I recognise small and large intestines, liver, kidneys: but there is plenty more that I'm ignorant of, an undifferentiated collection of interior business. The technician lays it all out beautifully on the steel bench for the pathologist, who is separating, checking, feeling, slicing, sampling, peering, ascertaining. Each organ is put on the scales. Its weight is scribbled in blue marker onto a whiteboard on the wall. The contents of the dead man's thorax are heaved out: his lungs, his heart, his windpipe, even his tongue, the topmost muscle of this complex mass of equipment: to think he used once to talk—or sing! Now his neck looks hollow and flat.

His intestines, his organs, all his insides are examined and then placed between his legs on the steel table. I can't believe all this has happened so fast. But the technician is scouring out the hollow shell of the skull, using the same rounded, firm, deliberate movements of wrist and hand that my grandmother would use to scrub out a small saucepan. At this moment I think irresistibly of that action of hers, and her whole kitchen comes rushing back into my memory, detailed and entire. I have to shove it out of the way so I can concentrate.

The technician balls up several pages of the *Age* and stuffs the cleaned skull with them. He slots into its original position the section of the skull he removed earlier, and draws the peeled-down scalp up off the face and over the curve of bone where it used to grow; he pulls it firmly back into place. He takes a large needle and a length of surgical thread, and stitches the scalp together again. He stuffs the hollowed neck with paper, forming and shaping skilfully and with care.

He places the body's inner parts into a large plastic bag and inserts the bag into the emptied abdominal cavity; then he takes his needle again, threads it, and begins the process of sewing up the long slit in the body's soft front. The stitch he uses is one I have never seen in ordinary sewing: it is unusually complex and very firm. He tugs each stitch to make sure it is secure. The line of stitches he is creating is as neat and strong as a zip.

At some stage, without my noticing, the pathologist has left the room.

During the sewing, most of the watchers in the viewing suite drift out of the room. Only two of us are left behind the glass, standing in silence, keeping (I suppose) a kind of vigil: it would be disrespectful, having witnessed this much, to walk away while he is still half undone. The stitching takes up more time (or so I calculate, in my semi- stupor) than all the rest of the process put together. The meticulous precision of the job is almost moving: the technician is turning an opened, scientifically plundered coroner's body back into a simple dead one, presentable enough to be handed back to the funeral direc-tors and to his family, if he still has one—his family who are presumably, at this very moment, somewhere out there in the oblivious city, howling or dumbly cradling their grief.

It's almost over now. Outwardly, he is whole again. The technician turns on a tap and hoses the body down. With wet hair the young man looks more life-like and more vulnerable, like someone at the hairdresser. But the water flows over his half-open eyes which do not close. Yes, he is dead: I had almost forgotten.

His fingertips and nails are black. As the technician raises the body slightly to hose under it, its right arm flips out and protrudes off the edge of the table in a gesture that makes him look more human, less like a shop dummy, less obedient. The technician replaces it alongside the torso, and once more the young man is docilely dead. The technician dries the young man's face with a small green cloth. This closes his eyes again. His mouth moves under the force of the cloth just as a child's will, passively, while you wipe off the Vegemite or the mud; his lower lip flaps and then returns to a closed position.

The technician removes from under the young man's shoulders a curved block of wood which, yoga-style, has been broadening out his chest and keeping his chin out of the action throughout the autopsy. His head, released, drops back onto the steel surface. The table is tilted to let the water and a small quantity of blood and tissue run down the plug-hole near the corpse's feet. His genitals are long and flaccid. His hands are scrawny. He is very thin. As the technician pulls the trolley out of the dissection bay and swings it round towards the door, the sudden turning movement displaces the young man's hand so that it flips over his genitals, covering them as if in modesty or anxiety.

Now, because of the danger of hepatitis C infection, the technician must manoeuvre the body feet first into a thick, white plastic bag. It's hard for someone working on his own. It's like trying to work a drunk into a sleeping-bag. It takes a lot of effort and muscle. At last he has the body and the head encased in plastic. He draws up the neck of the bag, grabs a bit of it in each hand, and ties it in a neat knot. He slaps a sticker onto the outside of the bag. It's big and I can see it from here. It reads: BIOLOGICAL HAZARD.

The technician opens the door of the infectious room and wheels the trolley out. The room is empty. I look at my watch. I have been standing here, completely absorbed, for forty minutes.

On my way home I would have liked to jabber to stran-gers about what I had seen in the mortuary, but at the same time I felt I should keep my mouth shut, probably forever. I stopped off at the Royal Women's Hospital to visit some close friends whose baby daughter had been born early that same morning. The labour had been long and hard, and they were all exhausted, but calm. The baby was still bruised-looking and rather purple. Her struggles to be born had left her head slightly lop-sided, an effect which the doctors said would soon correct itself. Somebody said, 'Her head is shaped like a teardrop.' We all laughed.

I didn't tell my friends where I had spent the morning. I stood beside the baby's cot and gazed down at her. Her eyes were closed. Her hands were clasped near her cheeks. Her mouth moved constantly, and small waves of what looked like expression kept passing over her wrinkled face. The baby and the corpse did not seem to be connected to each other in my mind. They inhabited separate compartments, and my thoughts skipped and slithered from one to the other and back again.

The people who work at the mortuary are not used to being interviewed. They know that the picture the general public has of them is a macabre cliche. But they are not the skulk-ing ghouls of legend. Far from it: they are as ordinary as can be. And they are young. Except for the coroner himself, Hal Hallenstein, a sombre, chastening man in a dark suit, I am at all times the oldest living person in the room. The more time I spend with the manager, the scientists and the technicians, Rod, Jodie, Barry, Kevin and (although she is a Bachelor of Science) 'Little Alex', the more impressed I become.

Just as well. You need somebody trustworthy for a guide when you're taken into the big storage chamber called 'the fridge' and confronted with a long row of dead bodies, twelve or fifteen of them, laid out on steel trolleys.

I experience an atavistic urge to make a sign of reverence.

Only one of the bodies is covered: a very small baby, wrapped up, as firmly as if it were alive, in a pastel cotton blanket, and laid on a metal shelf at eye level.

A dead body, stripped of clothes, makes perfect sense of itself in no language but its own. It packs a tremendous wallop. In its utter stillness it seems preoccupied with some important matter that you are ignorant of. It has an authority, in its nakedness, which transcends whatever puny thoughts you, the stranger, may entertain about it. It has presence. And yet it is no longer a person.

But it takes me more than one visit to realise this. At first I keep pestering for each body's story. Oh, what happened to this poor man? Look at this lady—oh, poor thing—what have they done to her? To the technicians and the pathologists, these matters are of academic interest only. They are patient with me and, because I'm their guest, they oblige me by calling up the details of 'the circumstances', as they call them, on the computer. Fell off a truck, they say. Suspected heart failure. Looks like a suicide. MVA (motor vehicle accident).

But their tone is abstracted. They can't afford to dwell on the personal or the tragic. They get at least one suicide a day—'we've got bags and bags of ligatures out there', somebody tells me. They have to perform autopsies on dead babies and murder victims. Their detachment is very highly developed and they have to maintain it. It is precious to them. It is their only defence.

So after a while I control myself and try to copy them. Some of their composure begins to rub off on me. It's amazing how quickly you can get used to the company of the dead. Of course, I am in the privileged position of an observer. Later, Barry, a brilliant dissector who worked and studied his way up from being a porter at Charing Cross Hospital in London to his current position as senior technician, remarks to me, 'You never get completely detached. I've been in this work for eight and a half years. Every now and then I say to myself, "Well, now I've seen everything"—and then next day a case will come in that'll shock even me. You never get used to the homicides—what people will do to each other.'

'It's not such a different job as other people think it is,' says Jodie, who at twenty-five is senior scientist in the mortuary. 'Often I think our lab's just the same as any other, except that our specimens are bigger.' She is sitting in the manager's office in her blue surgical gown and her socks, having left her huge white boots behind at the mortuary door. Like all the technicians who spoke to me, she has a very direct gaze, and an air of unusual maturity and calm.

'I was the first woman here,' she says. 'The guys taught me everything. The first day I was here I went home all worked up, I'd had such an interesting and exciting day. Day two, it caught up with me. It was the smell, maybe, or the blood. They were doing eight post-mortems at once and everyone was busy; they were all gloved and gowned up, and someone looked at me and said, "Jodie, you're going pale." I walked into the change room and passed out.

'But the techs were fantastic. Someone said, "Come over here. I'll make you concentrate on one small area." I did, and then I was all right. But it took me a while till I could step over that red bench into the lab without thinking, "What am I doing here?"'

She laughs, sitting there quietly with her hands folded in her lap. She is not what you would call tough: she's got a rather sweet, open face, with intelligent eyes; but she has the firmness of someone who's had to work out a few important things earlier than your average Australian twenty-five-year-old. She commands respect without having to try.

'Staying detached,' she says, 'is hardest with the kids that come in. The cot-death babies, or kids that die in accidents or fires. It's terrible. With every grown-up case you can manage to convince yourself that there's a reason, but with kids—they're innocent. They haven't done anything. One day I was working with Barry, who's got young kids. We opened up the little coffin, and when we saw the baby in there, so young, wrapped up and holding a furry toy, we looked at each other and we both had tears in our eyes.' She shrugs, and drops her glance to her lap. 'We quickly started work. You can't afford to feel those things. You'd go crazy.'

'With the SIDS babies we take extra time. We wash and powder them. And during post-mortems we're really careful not to damage them. You feel they've been through enough. We rebuild and reconstruct them really carefully. Funny—when you're holding a dead baby in your arms, you know it's dead, but you still have the instinct to support the head, and not to let it drop back.'

'You've got death at the back of your mind all the time,' says Barry. 'Like when you're backing out of the drive, you're extra conscious. The child that gets crushed by a car in the drive is always after a toy that was under the car. It's always a toy.'

'You realise how easily death can happen,' says Jodie. 'And there's a certain case for each of us—something you see that you relate to in a way you don't…like. It might be a shoe on someone that's brought in, a shoe like ones you've got at home, or the sort that your brother wears. Only a small thing…but it can trigger something in you. You have to keep a split between your natural feelings and what you do.'

Everything the technicians say stresses their mutual respect and their sense of being a team. I ask why they appear to be doing all the cleaning of the mortuary, as well as their scientific work. 'There's a lot of weird people in the world,' says Jodie. 'People you wouldn't want to trust around dead bodies. And other people refuse to come in here. Sometimes we can't get tradesmen to do maintenance work. They won't come in unless we can guarantee they won't see anything upsetting. Still, our floors are shinier than the ones in the rest of the building—did you notice?—shinier than the ones the contract cleaners do.'

To spend hours in the eight-bay lab, standing at the elbow of Barry as he works in silent absorption, or beside David, a pathologist and assistant director of the institute, is to realise that it's a place of study, of teaching and learning, of the gathering and organising of information. David is a natural teacher. He chatters to me as he works on a body, wanting me to notice the creamy-yellow, waxen globules of subcutaneous fat, or the weak, exhausted-looking muscle of a damaged heart, or the perfect regularity and beauty of the striations of windpipe cartilage. 'Exactly like reinforced garden hose —look!'

The radio is on softly in the far corner of the room, spinning out a long, dated guitar solo. Someone in the corridor whistles along to it. Somebody else, going to the shop, calls out for lunch orders. It's not so different from the outside world after all.

'After I'd been working here for a while,' says Rod, 'I found I'd lost my fear of death. I don't know what the soul is—that spark—and no one knows what happens to it at death. But it's certainly gone before people reach here.'

'You have to realise,' says Jodie, 'that what we deal with here isn't really death. We see what's left behind after death has happened—after death has been and gone.'

For days after my visits to the mortuary my mind was full of dark images. At first I kept thinking I could smell blood, on and off, all day. Once I tore open a paper bag of pizza slices which had got squashed on the way home, and the dark red and black of their mashed surfaces reminded me of wounds. My bike helmet knocked lightly against the handlebar as I took it off, and the sound it made was the hollow *tock* of a skull being fitted back together after the brain has been removed. In the tram my eyes would settle on the wrinkled neck of an old woman: she'll soon be gone.

There is nothing so utterly dead as a dead body. The spirit that once made it a person has fled. But until I went to the mortuary I never had even the faintest inkling of what a living body is—what vitality hovers in its breath, what a precious, mysterious and awesome spark it carries, and how insecurely lodged that spirit is within the body's fragile structures.

1992

Sunday at the Gun Show

On a Sunday morning, hours after a man was arrested for the knife-murders of three young women near the bayside suburb of Frankston, I went with my husband to the twenty-sixth Melbourne Gun Show. *Australian Shooters Journal* promised '250 tables of antique and modern firearms, Edged Weapons and Militaria'; its editor depicts this extravaganza as 'often the favourite of many due to the intimate atmosphere of the venue'.

Entry cost nine dollars fifty each. Just inside the door, a Salvo lady, middle-aged, smiling hard, was rattling her tin. As I dropped in my coin I remarked, 'You're a bit out of your element here, aren't you?' She made no comment, but intensified her glassy smile and murmured, 'God bless you!'

The organisers in the vestibule had safety-pinned official Gun Show ribbons onto their chests, just over their hearts. As they walked briskly about or paused near the open door, the blue and white ribbons would flutter merrily. These spasms of bright movement made a striking contrast with the carefully controlled male faces above them. One might speak, another might briefly smile, but, on the whole, expression was at a premium.

My husband plunged through the main doors and I followed him into the big auditorium. Intimate atmosphere? Maybe, compared to a wind-swept parade ground, a waist-deep swamp at dawn. For intimate, read crammed, muffled, dimly lit. The palace of weapons was packed with men. Blokes of all ages were shuffling, hands in pockets, along rows and rows of trestle tables, on which flat glass cases held displays of medals, daggers, drill manuals, stained desert maps, ancient bullets, firing pins, mysterious screws and springs, and other treasures. Bizarre assortments of second-hand books were sprinkled about; unread hardbacks with titles like *Dentist on a Camel* lay alongside well- thumbed paperback copies, at three dollars, of reputable Australian novels such as *1915* and *My Brother Jack*.

In here, facial expression was outlawed. The social tone was blank and affectless. Moustaches were plentiful, in a narrow range of styles: barbered grey, Civil War, semi-reformed bikie. The universal response to 'Thanks' was 'No sweat'.

My husband, who is as interested in guns and warfare as the next fifty-two-year-old erstwhile air cadet, moved smoothly past the sentimental memorabilia and into the area where the handguns began and the vibe darkened further. He seemed to be able to read the weapons, to get a distinct meaning out of each piece—though, like all the other men in the room, he was keeping strict guard over his facial features.

'Look,' he said, pointing to a double-barrelled shotgun in a battered case. 'A Hollis. That's what Hemingway shot himself with. Or was it a Purdy?'

To me the displays were just a lot of lumps of metal. I concentrated hard. Yes, that one was pocket-size, and this one, by an effort of the imagination, I could call 'pearl-handled'. Caught in the slow-flowing river of men, I kept shuffling sideways. Two buffs behind a table were talking. One of them, who had a big gut and drooping whiskers, was saying, 'I don't have friends. I get emotional when friends let me down.' The other nodded, stone-faced.

I came to a display of knives, very slender, gleaming, about eight inches long. They looked as if they were designed to slide neatly between some poor bastard's ribs. I picked one up. It was terrifically sharp. The fat blond in the dark blue tracksuit who was selling them kept his eyes on me. To make conversation I said, 'I wonder what you'd use these for?' Holding my eye, he drew in a huge sigh, let it out slowly, took two beats, and said in a voice that was at once toneless and heavy with irony, 'Opening letters?' I put it down hastily and shuffled on.

In the next part of the hall a sort of bottleneck had developed. Men were lingering over a particular glass case as if spellbound. I squeezed through, but it was only another spread of handguns. Were they better, cheaper, made by someone more famous? It was as baffling to me as if these men had been contemplating relics of some god whose name I didn't even know. I accidentally caught the eye of the man in charge of these guns. Like the blond knife-seller, he maintained eye-contact in such a way as to lock me into his level, hard, challenging stare. He, too, let fall a significant pause, then said in a low voice, without the slightest intonation, 'G'day. How you going?'

'Good, thanks!' I piped. I actually blushed.

I caught up with my husband at a table where bundles of bumper stickers were on sale. He was reading them with grunts and clicks of incredulity. '*Annita has one—Paul is one.* Look at this, will you? *Take my gun? The contents come first!* It's paranoid. It's bloody moronic. It's pathetic.' The sticker-seller, a callow youth, glanced up. My husband stepped towards him, then changed his mind and walked away in disgust.

A girl knelt beside her boyfriend, who was sitting on a folding stool behind his display. She was watching him open a little present she had brought him. 'It's Chinese,' she said. He glanced at whatever it was, quickly rewrapped it, and sat unmoved while she threw her arms around his neck and passionately kissed him on the cheek. She let go, and knelt there, gazing up at him, exuding speechless adoration. He glanced nervously behind him. No one seemed to have noticed. He eked out a narrow smile.

We passed a video of a burly backwoodsman in a landscape

of snow. He was casually dismembering the corpse of a large furry beast. Paying close attention to the screen was a young Vietnamese man in full camouflage gear. His eyes in his blank face were unnaturally bright, almost blazing. Beside the video screen a thick strip of leather hung in a wooden frame. One was invited to slash it to shreds with a sample of the same knife the backwoodsman was using to skin his prey. We both had a go. Ooh yes, it was very sharp indeed, and cleverly shaped into a vicious, chunky little curve.

Round the next corner, in the Ultimate Arms stand, hovered two young women dressed in blacktie, and caked with make-up, blusher and vivid lipstick. Their sparkling smiles, as they referred inquiries about the importing of weapons to their less attractive male colleague (also in evening dress) came as a shock in this cavern of grimness. Closer in, we saw that under their swallowtail jackets the girls were wearing black leotards and towering heels. The counter was exactly low enough to reveal them from the crutch up. Around this stand ran a hectic little frisson—but only in the movements of eyes. Faces remained frigid.

Shuffle, shuffle.

A silver-haired old man ear-bashed his fellow gun-fancier about security: how not to look like a tourist, where to carry your money, how to react when mugged, how to park your car so you never have to walk to it alone at night. 'I tell my kids,' he said, 'and I think as they get older they're starting to listen. I say, "Listen to your old dad and you'll live longer."'

Is that what this is about—fear of death? 'They're all brooding on death and destruction,' said my husband. But there was another quality in the silent, tense concentration of the shuffling blokes. They were as scrupulously expressionless as men you see in adult bookshops, contemplating sex aids and pornography. The air was thick with suppressed anxiety, a sort of dull belligerence.

I went out to the vestibule and waited there for my husband. Near me, also waiting, stood a young woman with frizzed blonde hair holding a small girl by the hand. The three of us shifted from foot to foot, glancing occasionally back into the slow, milling stream of men. Several times the young mother caught my eye. Once she tilted up her chin and opened her mouth, as if she had something she wanted to say to me: but no words came, only nervous glances and smiles.

To get out of the hall we had to submit to a metal-detector, and a man inspected my bag without meeting my eye. We drove home in silence. As we rounded the corner near the Aberdeen Hotel, my husband gave a sigh and said gloomily, 'But there *was* some craft. Some people were better than that mob—like those two blokes who made the beautiful stocks, out of good timber.'

While the dinner was cooking, I sat at the kitchen table and flipped through *Australian Shooters Journal*. A chap from Queensland called Mr C had written in with an idea. 'Frisking passengers by means of an electronic gizmo at the departure lounge is not the way to go. On the contrary, no passenger should be permitted on board who is not armed or at least willing to defend himself. Picture our terrorist who has boarded at an intermediate stage and doesn't know the rules. In mid-flight, the maniac stands up and says he is taking over in the name of the Mongolian Mother Molesters' Movement. Next thing there is the sound of three hundred hammers being cocked, and the following day the Japanese tender for the mineral rights to the last hijacker!'

'This bloke' commented the *Journal*'s columnist, 'has a delightful turn of wit. Why this little yarn made me chuckle all afternoon is hard to say...Was it because, like you perhaps, I am well and truly fed up of [sic] being kicked around by scum?'

I called my husband to eat, but he had turned on the TV and got interested in a documentary about the World War II campaigns of the great Russian general Zhukov. I carried the meal into the living room and sat down beside him. He took his plate and thanked me. I said, 'No sweat,' but he didn't laugh. His eyes remained fixed on the screen, where the camera was roaming disconsolately through the gashed and gaping ruins of Berlin.

1993

The Violet Jacket

In Hobart, on my way to a more remote spot for some walking, I went to a bushgear shop to buy myself a waterproof jacket. A young man in his early twenties served me, friendly and knowledgeable. He showed me a jacket of a pretty violet colour. 'It's specially designed for women,' he said. 'The sleeves are not too long, but they come right down over your wrists, to keep you warm. And the whole thing isn't too...voluminous.'

I put it on.

'See how it's made?' he said. 'They've sewn it so that even when your rucksack strap comes across here, in front on your shoulder, you can still get things out of your top pockets.'

'How clever—isn't it clever!' I was zipping and unzipping and ripping the strips of velcro. I got it all done up and swanned about in it, in front of the long mirror. The young man laughed. Together we admired the ingenuity of the jacket, its simple practicality, the outcome of somebody's careful thought. The price tag made me wince, but I said, 'I'll take it.'

As I slipped it off, I noticed among the wall display of heavy hiking boots a strange shoe, which was dangling toe down, hooked to a peg by a little loop of leather stitched to its heel. Its upper was of stiff cloth firmly laced, and its sole was made of black rubber, moulded so closely to the curves of a human instep that it looked as light and tight as a ballet slipper, but tougher: springy, graceful and peculiar. 'What sort of shoe is that?'

'It's for rock-climbing.'

'You'd think it was made for a dancer,' I said. 'It's strong, but it's almost dainty.'

'Beautiful, isn't it,' he said, taking it down and passing it to me. 'You have to buy them tight. Your foot has to be right up against the end, so that when you get the top of the shoe over a hold, your toes are over it as well. You have to be able to get a *grip*.' He made clawing movements with his bent fingers, laughing, and glanced back over his shoulder as if into a yawning chasm. My hair stood on end. I put the shoe back on its hook and followed him to the counter.

'Are you going walking?' he said.

'Yes—do you think the weather will be good?'

He flashed me a joyful look. 'Last weekend I was down at Freycinet,' he said, 'and I could see snow on the Hazards! Maybe you'll be lucky!'

At the cash register a woman customer was telling the other shop assistant, also a woman, that she had just that morning got out of doing jury duty.

'Didn't you want to do it?' I asked.

'I would have—but I was challenged.'

'Why?'

She shrugged. The woman assistant and I ran our eyes up and down her. She was in her forties, with a lot of flustered wiry blonde hair and a big smiling mouth full of uneven teeth. She wore a rain jacket, a money belt, heavy boots.

'Maybe you looked a bit…alternative?' I suggested.

'Or were they getting rid of the women?' said the assistant. 'Was it a rape case, maybe?' She shuddered. 'I'd hate to have to do a rape case. I'd be so outraged—I don't think I'd be able to be objective. Or imagine if you were on the jury of that bloke who killed his wife and cut up her body into pieces.' She lowered her voice. 'He put bits of her down the drain. Some of her he put into a blender.'

We three women looked at each other without speaking,

our eyebrows raised and our lips stretched back off our clenched teeth, through which we sharply sucked in air.

'A friend of a friend of mine,' continued the woman shop assistant, who was wearing spectacles with unusual, sophisticated frames, 'knows someone who knew the social worker that the wife went to. Apparently the social worker warned her. The wife came to her and said, "I'm leaving him." And the social worker said, "Well, get help—because you could be in real danger." But the wife said, "Don't worry. I can handle it."'

'She *told* people he was violent,' cut in the rejected juror passionately. 'She *told* people, but no one would do anything about it.'

During this exchange, the young man was right in the middle of us, shoulder to shoulder with his colleague, working modestly and efficiently, keeping his eyes down and filling out the credit card docket, folding my new coat and sliding it neatly into a big paper bag with string handles. He waited till there was a pause, then handed me the pen, to sign.

Our eyes met. The sparkle had gone out of his open, cheerful face; it was closed and sombre now. He was carrying in silence the load of the horrible story. I signed quickly, thanked him, took my parcel, said goodbye, and hurried out on to the street.

There are two men in this story. Two. Out of all the many sorts of men that exist in the world. And so I'm determined that I will acknowledge and value and remember the young man who laughed with me and showed me the clever jacket and the beautiful shoe, for at least as long as I'll remember the other one, the murderer and dismemberer.

1993

Killing Daniel

WHAT SORT OF a man would beat a two-year-old boy to death? Paul Aiton, thirty-two, who stood trial in Melbourne in 1993 for the murder of Daniel Valerio, is a very big man, a tradesman who wears colourful shirts, thin ties and boots decorated with chains; but at first glance, in the dock, he looked oddly like a child himself. On his heavily muscled body, with its overhanging belly and meaty hands, sat the round, hot-cheeked face of a boy who'd been sprung, who was in serious trouble, but who glared back at the world with eyes that sometimes threatened to pop out of his head with indignation and defiance.

Often his head, with its moustache, its reading glasses, its hair cropped short in front and curling over the collar behind, would be invisible behind the dock, where he appeared to be doodling or taking notes. Outside the court, especially during the retrial, when a spirited performance by the defence QC led many to believe that the verdict might be the lesser one of manslaughter, Aiton would occasionally make mocking gestures, leering and waving, towards the dead boy's father, Michael Valerio, a huge, simmering but powerfully restrained man who attended court each day with his wife. Something about Aiton persistently called to mind the word *infantile*.

At least there was a certain intensity in his demeanour. When Cheryl Butcher, the dead boy's mother, was called to the witness stand, she displayed the dull eyes and defeated posture of a woman whose path through life is joyless and without drive. She had her first child at seventeen. Her relationships with men have been chaotic and soon broken. Now she has lost one child through violence and had two others (Candice and Benjamin, then seven and four) taken from her and given into the custody of her previous de facto, Michael Valerio.

Cheryl Butcher has not been charged with any crime. But she intrigued people who followed this case through two trials. How could she not have known what was being done to Daniel? What deal did she make with herself to allow her child to suffer the brutality of her boyfriend Aiton in exchange for his company, his pay-packet—for the simple fact of not being manless? And how could she, the night after her little boy died, agree to marry the man who had killed him?

Butcher was out of the house when Daniel met his end. At lunchtime on Saturday 8 September 1990, on the Mornington Peninsula, southeast of Melbourne, she drove to collect her other son from his grandparents, leaving Daniel in bed sleeping off the remains of a three-day wog. Aiton had been out in the yard all morning running a garage sale. When Butcher returned half an hour later, Daniel had been rushed to hospital by a family friend. By the time Butcher got there, the boy was dead. The doctor at casualty refused to sign a death certificate. He took a proper look at Daniel and called the police.

An autopsy that evening showed that Daniel had died of internal bleeding from abdominal injuries. A pint of blood was found in his abdominal cavity. Many of his organs were bruised, his duodenum was ruptured, and the mesentery (the membrane that anchors the intestines to the back wall of the abdomen) was torn in several places.

Aiton was taken in for questioning. He held out for quite some time. According to Butcher, when she visited him during these hours he was 'very clinging' towards her. He told her several times that he loved her. He asked her to marry him. She asked him whether he had hit Daniel. He said he had not. But on the Sunday morning early, after a second conversation with Butcher,

Aiton at last admitted to the police he had struck Daniel.

He claimed that he had not meant to harm the boy, and certainly not to kill him; that he had merely wanted to stop him crying. He had been having a bad morning: he was stressed out by the garage sale, by the fact that the toilet had blocked and by an angry phone call from a tradesman about a cheque that had bounced. Daniel had started to cry and scream just as Aiton was passing his bedroom door. Aiton had gone in, slapped him, then when he would not shut up, punched him several times in the stomach while Daniel lay there on his back.

Everybody knows that a child's crying has the power to derange, and that some people—especially those who, like Aiton, have been mistreated as children—lack the resources to control their own violent tendencies. It seemed at the time a simple case of a bloke's having 'lost it', as Aiton put it, gone berserk under pressure, lashed out. The charge at first was manslaughter.

But Daniel's end was not so short and simple. At the morgue they counted one hundred and four bruises on his tiny corpse, inside and out, distributed liberally over his head, face, neck, chest, abdomen, arms, legs and back. Both his collar-bones were broken, and had partly healed without ever having been diagnosed, or treated. Many of Daniel's injuries, said the pathologist, were more than twenty-four hours old. He spoke of 'bruises upon bruises'. Daniel also had an undiagnosed condition of the bowel that would have caused him, doctors said, bouts of excruciating pain, and which appeared to have been present for some time. Daniel's slide towards the day of his death, it now became clear, was a long, slow process.

Through the witness stand at the Supreme Court poured a stream of people who had seen on Daniel Valerio the marks of the violence that infected this already broken family, once Aiton met Cheryl Butcher through an introduction agency in February 1990 and soon afterwards moved into her house. People who noticed the boy's afflictions—monitored them, in some cases—included neighbours, tradesmen, social workers, teachers, family friends, doctors, nurses, police, a photographer. Over these months, Daniel was seen by twenty-one professionals.

These witnesses are not 'bad people'. They are ordinary citizens who go about their daily business as best they can, trying to sleep at night. They saw the marked child, they harboured suspicions. Their instinctive response was correct. What stopped so many of them from speaking or acting?

Was it fear, squeamishness about dobbing? Were some of them inured to suffering by the terrible things they encounter professionally every day? Or were they captives of the resilient myth of the nuclear family, the ability of the most pathetic and vicious collection of children and parents to throw up a stockade around themselves, a force-field that repels outsiders?

The doctors, for the most part, impressed in court by their lacklustre quality. Their manner appeared limp, their language feeble and non-committal. What they conspicuously seemed to lack, and what Aiton perversely seemed to possess, was *energy*.

From about June 1990 Daniel was exhibiting an ever-renewed array of black and blue marks. Three different doctors at the local clinic remarked on this. The tenant in the flat behind the Aiton–Butcher house used to hear screaming 'over the sound of the television'; it was so intolerable to her that she would go out driving in her car until it was over.

So frequently did Daniel display bruises to the temples, eyes, forehead and back of the head that a family friend and sometime babysitter, Wayne Williams, bought some strips of wetsuit material and constructed for the little boy a child's version of a boxer's headguard: a lime-green strip of rubber ran round his skull, a dark blue one passed over the top of his head, and the thing fastened under his chin with a black velcro strap. When this colourful contraption was shown to the jury, onlookers sobbed. It seemed a gesture of helpless kindness by a good, gentle man—but wasn't it misdirected? Wayne Williams used to change Daniel's nappy. Hadn't he seen the bruises in places where the normal bumps and trips of toddlerhood don't reach?

Williams' wife Sylvia was Cheryl Butcher's best friend. She had a special feeling for Daniel, who called her 'Mum'. Sylvia found a large scrotal swelling on Daniel. She said Cheryl told her 'she didn't know it was there'.

Cheryl repeated to the court—as she had over these months to anyone who asked her about the child's constant bruisings, black eyes and mysterious pains and stumblings—her explanations that Daniel was 'clumsy and accident-prone', that 'all small children bump into things', that his older brother 'headbutted him and played roughly with him', that Daniel 'often fell from his stroller', that he often 'walked into the furniture' (in particular, a dangerous table with edges at the exact height of his temples). The theory she was most at ease with was one that several doctors took seriously: that Daniel must be suffering from 'a blood disorder'. They put him into hospital and ran tests.

During his five days in hospital Daniel displayed, according to his paediatrician, the classic behaviour of the neglected, emotionally deprived child: not at all shy, he would go eagerly to total strangers, such was his need for cuddling and attention. No fresh spontaneous bruises appeared on Daniel in hospital; on the contrary, he put on weight and 'generally blossomed'. The only thing the tests picked up was a slower than normal blood-clotting time. Daniel was discharged on 29 July. Cheryl Butcher did not bring him to his follow-up appointment. Daniel's blossoming period was brief. Around this time, Wayne Williams, who was fond of Daniel, backed away from any further babysitting. He said in court that Daniel was too sick for him to want to take the responsibility.

Aiton, according to Williams, 'was a big man, and he

talked loud'. He worked and travelled manic hours as a foreman in a painting and decorating firm. Three of his workmates told the court that Aiton had boasted to them about his rough treatment of his girlfriend's kid. Two of them would apparently listen without comment to Aiton's laughing tales of hitting Daniel on the penis with a wooden spoon, pushing Daniel's face into his own shit, picking up the sleeping child by the hair and the seat of the pants and dropping him face-first on the floor. The third workman, however, when Aiton bragged about his custom of making Daniel 'do a stary'—stand with his legs and arms spread, upon which Aiton would kick him so hard between the legs that he flew across the room—finally jacked up. This workmate told the court that, distressed, he had 'spoken very sharply' to Aiton. In fact, he had sworn and said, 'People like you should be put away.' In this bleak story of moral paralysis and missed opportunities, even a few sharp words stand out like an act of goodness.

About a fortnight before Daniel died, the family moved from Rye to a house Aiton had bought not far away at Rosebud, in a street with the Proustian name of Swans Way. The police video of the house's interior gave onlookers a pang of sympathy. Everyone can imagine the strain of moving into an unfinished house with three small kids in tow at the end of a Melbourne winter: the thronging plastic bags, the stained and sheetless mattresses, the incongruous pale pink leather lounge suite, the unconnected electrical wiring poking through holes in the plaster.

The wiring might have saved Daniel, if Victoria's police and welfare bureaucracies had been better co-ordinated. On his way home from work one night, Aiton stopped at a local florist to buy Cheryl some flowers for their six-month anniversary. It chanced that the florist was also an A-grade electrician. Aiton asked him to do the wiring job at Swans Way, and over the following week he visited the house several times. What the electrician saw there—the way the children were controlled and disciplined and, on his last visit, the bruised, silently stumbling, 'man-handled' Daniel—upset him so much that when he got home, on 30 August, he phoned the Rosebud police and made a report. At last, someone had broken through the force-field.

When the community police came to the house to do a welfare check on Daniel, Cheryl Butcher was 'distraught' at the suggestion that he was being abused. The photos that a police doctor took the next day are almost as horrific as those taken at the morgue after Daniel's death; and yet the doctor's report was not delivered to the police until four days after he died. Three days before he died, Cheryl took Daniel along to the open day at the school of his half-sister, Candice. Candice's teacher sobbed in court as she described the 'picture which still haunts' her: Daniel's 'ghostly white' face, his bruised temple, his unfocused, listless stare, his utter lack of response.

The rest of the story reads, now, like a race between heavy-footed bureaucracy and a sleeker, livelier force. The boy was adrift. The people with the power to save him strolled, fumbled and tripped; and Aiton got there first.

Paul Aiton's first jury—eight women and four men—could not reach a verdict, and was dismissed, many of its members in tears of apparent frustration. The second one, an older, more sombre panel of seven women and five men, took less than four hours to convict him of murder. Late in the first trial, his new girlfriend had come into court holding on a stick a heart-shaped silver balloon with the defiant red words I LOVE YOU. In the second trial, the senior defence counsel's flamboyant style of presentation had made Aiton seem cocky, and towards the end even brought a tiny smile of hope to the faded face of his adoptive father who sat in court beside the girlfriend almost every day.

'This man,' cried the QC, flinging a hand towards the dock, 'brought flowers for Cheryl Butcher on their anniversary. I ask you, is this the behaviour of a sadist?' One of the older women on the jury, in unconscious rejection of this line of rhetoric, set her lips and slowly, firmly shook her head. It was clear at that moment that Aiton was a goner; that the defence's theatrical appeal to the complexity of human psychology, and to our lack of right to make moral judgements, was missing its mark. It was clear that the muffled, phlegmatic summing-up by the prosecution, with its central image of the man's huge fist pounding into the sick child's tiny, aching abdomen, had entered the souls of that jury, and lodged there.

Ferocity against children is not rare. Why did the murder of little Daniel Valerio pierce the public heart, pack the court, even bring some of the first jury back to the retrial to hear the outcome of this haunting story?

I think it's because Daniel's fate was not confined within the pathology of his fractured family. It escaped into the wider community. It unravelled slowly, offering multiple entry points to at least twenty official agents of what we like to think of as our collective decency. And yet Daniel was lost.

In a strange way, Aiton's conduct is easier to understand than Butcher's: we may loathe it, and believe it should be punished, but we can *see* what he did. Action is easier to grasp than inaction, somehow. Cheryl Butcher's behaviour remains enigmatic, the kind of thing that people lose sleep over, trying to puzzle out the meaning of such passivity, such apparent abdication of responsibility.

What happened to Daniel Valerio reflects on us all, on our private and public natures. It stirs up deep fears about ourselves, and makes us frightened and ashamed. I don't see how it is possible to contemplate Daniel's story without acknowledging the existence of evil; of something savage that persists in people despite all our enlightenment and our social engineering and our safety nets, something that only philosophy, religion or art can handle: the worm in the heart of the rose.

1993

The Fate of The First Stone

MANY YEARS AGO I came across a remark made by the poet A. D. Hope. He said, 'With hostile critics of my work, I am always scrupulously and cheerfully polite.' Professor Hope's subtle resolution came back to me in March 1995, when my book *The First Stone* finally appeared, and I had to stand up and defend ad nauseam my attempt to discover the truth behind a sexual assault case at one of Melbourne University's residential colleges. I hung on like mad to the poet's tactic, and I'm happy to report that it's possible, in the face of the most intense provocation, to keep your temper for months on end. I bit my lip and gnawed my fist and went on taking deep breaths and counting to ten—partly because I wonder if, when the chips are down, courtesy is all we have left; but also because I knew that, if I waited, a time would come when I could put forward calmly some thoughts about the furore provoked by this book, and about the things I've learnt from the strange experience of publishing *The First Stone*.

Our culture at large is obsessed, at the moment, with matters of sex and power in the relations between women and men. Given this, and given the attempts by the two women complainants from Ormond College to get access to the book in the courts before its publication, I shouldn't have been surprised by the *extent* of the response to the book. But what did astonish me, and still does, is the *nature* of the response—its primal quality. Primal things lie much deeper in people than reason does. People in the grip of a primal response to the very existence of a book like this will read it—and if they consent to read it at all—between the narrow blinkers of anger and fear. I realise now, having had it forced on me by this experience, that there are as many versions of *The First Stone* as there are readers of it. And yet there *are* certain words and sentences on its pages, put there on purpose in a certain order by the hand of a certain person—namely, me. So I'd like to take the liberty, here, of briefly and firmly listing a few of the things I did *not* say.

I did *not* say that the two young women who brought allegations of assault against the Master of their college *ought* to have agreed to be interviewed by me. I was terribly frustrated that they wouldn't, and in the book I often express this frustration, but right up to the end of the book I continue explicitly to respect their right not to speak to me.

I did *not* say that women should 'go back to wearing ankle-length sacks'.

I did *not* say that the correct way to deal with sexual assault or harassment is to knee a man in the balls.

I did *not* say that women are responsible for the way men behave towards them.

And I most emphatically did *not* say that women who get raped are asking for it.

I know it's the fate of all writers to feel themselves misread. I hoped I was writing in such a way as to invite people to lay down their guns for a moment and think again—and not only think, but *feel* again. I wanted people to read in an alert way—alert to things between the lines, things that the law prevents me from saying outright.

The book is sub-titled not 'an argument about sex and power', but 'some questions about sex and power'. There are more questions in it than there are answers. Because it declines—or is unable—to present itself as one big clonking armour-clad monolithic certainty, it's not the kind of book that's easy to review briskly. Because it's a series of shifting speculations, with an open structure, it's hard to pull out single quotes without distorting it. What the book invites from a reader is openness—an answering spark.

But I found that many people, specially those who locate their sense of worth in holding to an already worked-out political position, are not prepared to take the risk of reading like that. Perhaps they can't, any more. What is not made explicit, for readers like these, is simply not there. Being permanently primed for battle, they read like tanks. They roll right over the little conjunctions and juxtapositions that slither in the undergrowth of the text. It's a scorched-earth style of reading. It refuses to notice the side-paths, the little emotional and psychological by-roads that you can't get into unless you climb down from your juggernaut, and take off your helmet and your camouflage gear and your combat boots. It's a poor sort of reading that refuses the invitation to *stop* reading and lay down the page and turn the attention inwards. And it's always easier, or more comfortable, to misread something, to keep it at arm's length, than to respond to it openly.

Thus, several prominent feminists have used the word 'sentimental' to dismiss the scene in the book where the ex-Master's wife speaks, through inconsolable tears, of the devastation these events have brought to her and her family. Less doctrinaire critics have been able to recognise, in this scene, a terrible example of the human cost of political action which narrows its focus to the purely legal, and thus divorces thought from feeling.

Many feminists, even, incredibly, some who teach in universities, have declared it correct line not to buy *The First Stone* or to read it all. This position is apparently quite widespread, judging by countless reports that have reached me of bitter arguments round dinner tables, in women's reading groups, and at bookshop cash registers. This sort of feminist, while refusing to sully her party credentials by reading the book, also knows, however, or has absorbed from the ether by some osmotic process, exactly what the book 'says', so she is able to pontificate freely on how I have 'betrayed the feminist cause', and 'set feminism back twenty years'. One woman, representing the student body of an institution in the town where I was born, wrote to let me know that, the minute she heard I was going to go ahead with the book, she had purged her shelves of all my other books. She rebuked me for having 'profiteered' off other people's misfortunes, and suggested in a challenging tone that I should donate my ill-gotten gains to a worthwhile feminist organisation. Here I permitted myself the luxury of a coarse laugh.

The question of money in this context is fascinating. The accusation of 'profiteering' is the last refuge of one's enemy—a reproach, densely packed with psychic content. If *The First Stone* had been a jargon-clogged pamphlet bristling with footnotes, if it had sold a comfortably obscure, say, three thousand copies over a couple of years, the response to it from feminism's grimmer tribes would have been much less poisonous. But among those who maintain a victim posture vis à vis the big world, where one can earn an honourable living by writing in a language that the person in the street can understand, nothing is more suspicious than a book which appears to have succeeded.

Crudely, there are two possible attitudes that a hostile feminist might take towards the annoying fact that a lot of people, including feminists of broader sympathy, have defied the girlcott and responded favourably to *The First Stone*. The first one is easy: Garner is a sell-out, a traitor to her sex. She's caved in to the patriarchy and joined the other side. This leaves the grim tribes feeling and looking—to each other, at least— squeaky clean. The other alternative is to wonder whether something might have happened to feminism.

Maybe something's gone wrong.

Maybe something good and important has been hijacked.

Maybe the public debate about women and men has been commandeered by a bullying orthodoxy.

My intention has never been to bash feminism. How could I do that, after what it's meant to me? After what its force and truth make possible? But I hate this disingenuousness, this determination to cling to victimhood at any cost.

Why do the members of this orthodoxy insist that young women are victims? Why do they insist on focusing the debate on only one sort of power—the institutional?

Why do they refuse to acknowledge what experience teaches every girl and woman: that men's unacceptable behaviour towards us extends over a very broad spectrum—that to telescope this and label it all 'violence against women' is to distort both language and experience?

The hysteria that this book has provoked in some quarters reveals clearly and sadly that feminism, once so fresh and full of sparkle, is no different in its habits from any other political theory. Like all belief systems and religions and art forms—like any idea that has the misfortune to have an -ism tacked on to it—feminism has a tendency to calcify, to narrow and harden into fundamentalism. The life spark slips out of it and whisks away, leaving behind it an empty concrete bunker.

To disagree with a fundamentalist feminist, it seems, to question acts carried out in the name of women's rights, is not to challenge her, but to 'betray' her, to turn her into more of a victim than she was already.

One feminist critic in Melbourne put forward the proposition that in telling the Ormond story against the will of the young women involved, I had committed a treachery in the same league as the betrayal of the tribal secrets of the Hindmarsh Island Aboriginal women. The Ormond women, she wrote in the *Australian Book Review*, 'did not want their story told by Helen Garner, writer of fiction making a guest appearance as a journalist. She told their story anyway, has stolen the story that they did not want her to have.'

I find this a piece of the most breathtaking intellectual dishonesty.

In what sense *is* it 'their' story? It is distorting and deeply wrong to bestow on the Ormond complainants the ownership of this story. It could be truthfully called *their* story only if they had decided to keep it to themselves, to hold it to themselves as a private trauma. I don't suggest for a single second that they should have done this. And they didn't. They took their complaints to the police. And the police took them to the courts.

Now the law covering sexual assault may still be seriously skewed against women's interests: it plainly is, and I strongly support the correction of this; but a court in a democratic country like Australia is an open forum. Painful as this might be, a court is open. It is open to the scrutiny of the citizens *in whose names* justice is being aimed at. So, once the complaints reached the courts, the story ceased *of necessity* to belong to the young women, or to the college, or to the man against whom the allegations were made. It stopped being 'their' story, and it became 'our' story—a new chapter in the endless saga of how we, as a community, try to regulate the power struggle between women and men.

I want now to speak briefly about something called eros.

I used the word rather loosely, perhaps, in the book. You could define eros—if it would stay still long enough for you to get a grip on it—as something lofty and mythological, like 'the gods' messenger', or 'the life spirit'. You could call it the need of things to keep changing and moving on. The Jungians call it 'the spark that ignites and connects'. Eros, most famously, comes bounding into the room when two people fall in love at first sight. But it's also in the excitement that flashes through you when a teacher explains an intellectual proposition *and you grasp it*—or when someone tells a joke *and you get it.*

Eros is the quick spirit that moves between people—*quick* as in the distinction between 'the quick and the dead'. It's the moving force that won't be subdued by habit or law. Its function is to keep cracking open what is becoming rigid and closed-off. Eros explodes the forbidden. Great stand-up comics thrill us by trying to ride its surge. It's at the heart of every heresy—and remember that feminism itself is a heresy against a monolith. Eros mocks our fantasy that we can nail life down and control it. It's as far beyond our attempts to regulate it as sunshine is—or a cyclone.

But one feminist, criticising *The First Stone* in the *Australian*, wants us to accept that 'the dynamics of eros', as she puts it, 'are historically produced'. 'We need,' she says, 'to reconstruct eros between men and women *on an equal basis.*'

There will always be these moments, I know, when people who think politically and types like me with a metaphysical bent end up staring at each other in helpless silence, with our mouths hanging open.

It's hubristic to speak of 'reconstructing eros'. The whole point of eros, its very usefulness as a concept, is that it's *not* reconstructable. Eros doesn't give a damn about morals or equality. Though eros moves through the intellect, eros is not intellectual. It moves through politics, but it's not political. It moves between men and women, but it's not in itself sexual. When I talk in the book about eros, I'm trying to talk about that very thing—the thing that's beyond us—the dancing force that we *can't* control or legislate or make fair.

It's an article of faith among some young feminists that a woman 'has the right' to go about the world dressed in any way she pleases. They think that for a man to respond to—and note, please, that I don't mean to threaten or touch or attack—for a man to respond to what he sees as a statement of her sexuality and of her own attitude to it, is some sort of outrage—and an outrage that the law should deal with. I find the talk of rights in this context quite peculiar. What right are you invoking here? You can only talk about rights, in this context, by pretending that it *means nothing at all* to wear, say, a low-necked dress in a bar at two o'clock in the morning, or a pair of shorts that your bum's hanging out of on a public beach. To invoke rights, here, you have to fly in the face of the evidence of the senses—as if they believed that each person moved round the world enclosed in a transparent bubble of rights.

And who's going to protect these notional rights? Which regime will provide a line of armed police to make sure that no bloke looks at a woman's breasts with the wrong expression on his face? I'm inviting these young idealists to get real—to grow up—better still, to *get conscious.* Know what you're doing, what its likely effect is, and decide whether that's what you want. Sexy clothes are part of the wonderful game of life. But to dress to display your body, and then to project all the sexuality of the situation on to men and blame them for it, just so you can continue to feel innocent and put-upon, is dishonest and irresponsible. Worse, it's a relinquishing of power. If a woman dresses to captivate, she'd better learn to keep her wits about her, for when the wrong fish swims into her net.

A woman of my age knows—and it's her responsibility to point this out to younger women—that the world is full of different sorts of men. Many are decent. Some are decent until they start drinking. Many have grown up enough to have learnt manners. Some have taken seriously *their* responsibility to get conscious. Many men like women, and want to be around them. Some men *hate* women, and want to be around them. Many have been taught by imagination, or by reason, or by painful or happy experience, that a woman is a person and not just a clump of sexual characteristics put there for them to plunder.

Some men have learnt to recognise and respect the boundary between their fantasy and what is real. Others, trapped in instinct, have not, and never will—and it's a sad fact that we can't depend on the law to *make* them. Nor will laws alone save us from their depredations, whether trivial or serious. Society makes laws. I am strongly in favour of tough legislation that will give women redress against assault—but around and above and below the laws, for good or ill, there is this fluid element, life. What I'm proposing is that there's a large area for manoeuvre, for the practical exercise of women's individual power, before it's necessary or appropriate to call in the law. And I believe that one of the tasks of feminists should be to expand and develop this area of power.

In the book I describe a photograph. It's a black and white shot of a young woman dressed in an elegant and revealing gown. I wrote, 'It is impossible not be moved by her daring beauty. She is a woman in the full glory of her youth, as joyful as a goddess, elated by her own careless authority and power.' In response to this page of the book there emerged a grotesque distortion of my intent. One feminist critic, for whom perhaps all gods are vengeful, wrote that my admiring description of this lovely, rather wild young woman was in actual fact an invocation, in modern dress, of that monstrous, punitive, man-hating figure of myth—'vagina dentata in her full glory'.

Other feminists have told me severely that by 'sexualising' young women, I had 'disempowered' them. Leaving aside the hideousness of the language, you don't have to be Camille Paglia to see that this is sick, and mad.

There's been a lot of talk, triggered by the book, about symbolic mothers and daughters. Some feminists have a doom-laden approach to giving maternal advice. The young woman in the beautiful dress is not, they insist, in possession of any power whatsoever, potential or actual, and it is wicked of me to suggest that she might be. For them, only one sort of power is admissible to a discussion of events like these, and that is *institutional* power. This splendid young woman, then, so clever and lovely and full of life, is nothing but a sad victim. These traumatic events, they solemnly assure her, 'will blight her life'.

What sort of a mother, literal or symbolic, would insist to her daughter that an early experience in the rough adult world, no matter how painful or public, would blight the rest of her life? That is not good mothering. That is pathetic mothering. That is the kind of mothering that doubles the damage. A decent mother, when the dust has settled, would say to her daughter, 'Right. It's over. Now we can look at what's happened. Let's try to *analyse* what's happened. See how much of what happened was other people's responsibility, and then try to see how much of it, if any, was yours. Take responsibility for your contribution, be it small or large. You are not responsible for men's behaviour towards you, but you *are* responsible for your own. Pick yourself up now. Wipe your tears. Spit out the bitterness and the blame before they poison you. You're young and clever and strong. Shake the dust of this off your feet. Learn from it, and then move on.'

If all I had to go on, as responses to *The First Stone*, were the critiques of these prominent feminists, I'd be feeling pretty sick by now. But I've had letters, hundreds and hundreds of long, frank letters from strangers. The Melbourne critic (male) who chastised me for writing the book 'to please men' may be interested to know that I estimate the male/female ratio of the letters at about 35/65. I was surprised at how few of them were from cranks or nutcases. By no means did all of these letters—and they're still coming—express blanket approval of the book. But almost all of them were from people who had been prepared to respond to the book in the way I'd hoped—with the defences down—with an answering spark. They're prepared to lay out and re-examine examples, from their own lives, of encounters big and small with the opposite sex, which at the time had bewildered them, or hurt them, or made them angry. I lost count of the people who said, 'I'd like to tell you something that happened to me—or something that I did—many years ago; something that until I read the book I had forgotten—that I'd buried.'

Some of the letters were hilarious. I relate in the book an incident about a masseur at a particular Fitzroy gym who kissed me when I was naked on the table. One woman wrote to me, 'I shrieked when I read about that masseur.' She said the same bloke had kissed *her*, and that furthermore *she'd* paid him too, so I wasn't to feel I was the only mug. A man wrote and suggested to me very disapprovingly that I must have led the masseur on. 'Why did you take your clothes off in the massage room,' he sternly asked, 'instead of in the change rooms? What you did was tantamount to striptease.' A masseur who could see as striptease a middle-aged woman scrambling hastily out of a sweaty old tracksuit in a corner gets my prize for sexualising against overwhelming odds.

Some letters, from both men and women, are full of pain, and anger, and shame. Others tell stories of the patient unravelling of interpersonal and institutional knots, and of happy resolutions.

But the word that crops up most frequently is *relief*. Again and again people speak of the relief they feel that it might be possible to acknowledge that the world of daily work and social life isn't as horrible and destructive and ghastly as punitive feminists insist. People are relieved that it might be possible to admit sympathy in human terms with people on the opposite side of a power divide. They're relieved that ambiguity might be re-admitted to the analysis of thought and action. And specially they're relieved that to admit gradations of offence is not to let the side down or to let chaos come flooding in.

A lot of people have asked me if I regret having written this book—and more particularly, if I regret the letter of ignorant sympathy that I wrote to the Master when I first became aware of the case—the letter that got me into so much trouble, and caused so many doors to be slammed in my face. The answer is no, and no.

One thing I do regret, however, is that my publisher's defamation lawyers obliged me to blur the identity of a certain woman who was the young complainants' chief supporter in the college. I did this in quite a simple way: I didn't invent anything, but each time that the words or actions of this woman appeared in the text, I called her by a different name, thus splitting her into half a dozen people. Months after the book came out, the woman identified herself publicly, to my relief, since I had divided her with the greatest reluctance. This is the only ruse I engaged in, but it has given some people the idea that the book is 'fictionalised'—that it's a novel. It is not a novel. Except for this one tactic to avoid defamation action, it is reportage.

I accept that *The First Stone* has caused pain. I know it's no comfort—that it's almost a cheek—for me to say how sad I am about this. But sometimes a set of events erupts that seems to encapsulate, in complex and important ways, the spirit of its time. These are the stories that need to be *told*, not swept away like so much debris, or hidden from sight. My attempt to understand this story was frustrated. My version of it is full of holes. But I hope that these holes might, after all, have a use; that through them might pass air and light; that they might even provide a path for the passage of eros; and that they might leave, for women and men who want to think generously about these things, room to move.

1995

PART FOUR

Cruising

Cruising

AT LUNCHTIME ON the Friday, I buy an anti-seasick patch and stick it behind my ear. By two o'clock my saliva has totally dried up. By half past four, when I present myself at Darling Harbour wharf ten, dressed for a cruise in flowery dress and straw hat, I am so stunned by whatever drug the patch is leaking into me that I can barely stagger along.

The ship is Russian, painted glossy white, and named the *Mikhail Sholokhov*, after the first Russian writer to win the Nobel Prize. At the top of the gangplank, Russia begins: a line of women and men with poor skin and sullen expressions, their hands clasped behind their backs. My solo status and age are noted with a sly, pitying smile by the official ticking off names on a list, and someone whose badge identifies her as Tat'yana guides me in silence down several flights of stairs to my cabin. It's cell-like, narrow, very cold; more Marx Brothers than Fred Astaire. Tat'yana throws open a chipped metal closet and, with a formal flourish, draws the back of her hand along a clump of old, bent wire coat-hangers. She opens a drawer under the bottom bunk, points dramatically to its contents, and utters one word: 'Blenkit.' Handing me a key, she backs out of the cabin, smiling. Little do I know that this is the last smile I will see on Russian lips for quite some time.

I unpack and rush up on deck, my cheeks stinging from the frames of my sunglasses which the ferocious air-conditioning has chilled to below zero. My dream of a restful weekend— wooden deckchairs, gin and tonic tinkling in a glass—shrivels and dies. All the furniture in sight is made of white plastic; and this is not a glass culture. Everywhere I look I see gangs of grinning, tattooed men shambling about in shorts and bare feet, clutching cans of beer. 'Oi don't think y' noid any *sloip* on this boat!' yells a cheerful youth, raising his can for another slurp.

The tannoy crackles and a male voice announces, 'All wisitors and pipple not sailing on the wessel, pliss goink ashore now. *Mikhail Sholokhov* now under sailing orders. Sankyou and good luck.' Mass dash to the rail. With mighty, bone-shattering siren blasts, *Mikhail Sholokhov* eases away from the streamer-less wharf and slides under the bridge, past the Opera House, and down the harbour towards the Heads. 'I've never been on the ocean before,' I confess to a girl next to me. 'I went on a nine-day cruise once, to Fiji,' she tells me. 'I was sick the whole time, but I loved it.' My patch is making my head spin. I retreat to my cabin and lie on the bunk till dinner.

The signal for the meal comes over the tannoy: a sweet and breathy tinkling, as of metal chimes being gently stroked by a brush. How charming! I put on lipstick and step out formally. All along the passageways to the dining room someone has wedged, at strategic intervals between handrail and wall, dozens of crisp white sickbags.

The dining room is severely chilled. People are rubbing their goose-pimpled arms and hunching their shoulders. Two people are already seated at my designated table: Gwen and Shirley, quiet women with short grey hair, no make-up, self-effacing manners. I ask them questions but they are too polite or shy to question me. They are old friends, geographically parted twenty years ago by their marriages, who have kept in touch and occasionally take a holiday together. Each of them runs a small business in a country town. We sit in strained silence till through the door rocks our number four, Lorraine from Lithgow, a machinist. Lorraine is barely five feet tall, a chunky, friendly little dame of fifty-two, with a fresh perm that

suits her and a broad grin that keeps breaking into excited
laughter. In a carrying voice with wildly rising terminals, she
begins, almost before we have exchanged names, to pour out
an account of her life situation, not shrinking from the most
gruelling detail.

'When I first met my ex-husband, he had virtually no
possessions? All he had was a car radio and a tin o' buttons?
Which he wanted *me* to sew on his shirts? He was drunk at
our wedding and I don't think he's been sober since?' Thrilled
by her openness and her natural storyteller's turn of phrase, I
lean forward for more; but the faces of Gwen and Shirley go
blank with embarrassment. They cover their eyes and press
back into their chairs. Lorraine rattles on. She lays out her
illnesses, the moment of realisation that her husband had no
intention of looking after her when she had disabling surgery,
her decision to shake him off: 'So I got a divorce? I fought the
department for ten months? I never told them a single lie? And
they gave me a pension? He still lives in the house—it belongs
to both of us? But we lead completely separate lives?' She scans
the room. 'My boyfriend wouldn't like this atmosphere *at all*?
All this drinkin'?'

Lorraine takes a breath, but is cut short by a card thrust
at her by a Russian waitress, a girl with a pale, grey-shadowed
face who denies us even the briefest eye-contact, and grunts,
'Menu *pliss*,' through clenched teeth. The food, when it comes,
is a shock: meat cooked to death and coated in a glutinous
sauce, with vegetables from hell. Shirley, Gwen and I pick
daintily at the edges of our plates, but Lorraine is determined
to enjoy herself and tucks in with a will. Between mouthfuls
she continues her life saga. She is a born raver, with an almost
poetic instinct for timing and rhythm: 'And so, thinkin' my
own thoughts, I rolled over and went back to sleep?' I could
listen all night, but she is dying to join in the evening's activities in the saloon: cocktails, a disco, a cabaret, not to mention

the casino. Gwen and Shirley keep their eyes on their plates. Lorraine stares at us, puzzled. The meal ends and she dashes off. We three party-poopers scurry away to our cabins. I pass the door of the long, narrow casino. People in shorts are crowding round tables and drinking out of cans. The air is blue with cigarette smoke. I keep walking.

Saturday 7 a.m. A dozen habitual early risers mill about on the aft deck waiting for the dismal Lido Bar to open and sell them a polystyrene cup of tea or coffee. Two women at a white plastic table call me to join them: Norma and Lorna from Hurstville. 'We're merry widows!' they declare. They both have faces whose natural expressions seem to be smiles.

We sit looking out at the churning grey water, sipping disgusting tea with long-life milk and chatting pleasantly about the relative merits of burial and cremation.

'Do you reckon this ship's actually moving?' says Norma.

'It must be,' I say. 'Isn't that a wake?'

'But the shape of the shore doesn't seem to be changing at all,' says Lorna. 'See that hill? It's been in the same spot for fifteen minutes. Maybe it's not a wake. Maybe it's just stuff they're throwing overboard.'

At breakfast, Gwen is pale and quiet. She has felt ill all night. Shirley, however, is rested, and speaks admiringly of John Laws. Lorraine bops in, bright as a button and ready to rave. Last night at the disco, she reports, a man she liked the look of asked her to dance: 'If he hadn't, I wouldn't have been able to stay there, by myself?' Later on, in the casino, another man 'won some money and insisted on giving me half of it? I dunno why—I hadn't put any in, or anything? In the music saloon we had games. You had to pass an orange under your chin to somebody else, or a balloon between your knees—it was great! Why didn't youse go?'

Gwen, paler by the minute, sinks further back in her chair. Shirley's face loses expression. 'We were tired,' I say gamely. 'We went to bed early.'

'Why'dya *come* on the cruise,' says Lorraine challengingly, 'if you're not gonna join in and have fun?' We drop our eyes to the table and fiddle with the cutlery.

A sort of food is slung at us by grim-faced girls and we try to eat it. Shirley tells us the story, while Gwen sits quietly with a gentle smile, of Gwen's husband, 'a lovely man who died of a heart attack at forty'; Gwen has chosen not to remarry. Lorraine listens with eager attention, chin in hand, her generous mouth relaxed. She heaves a sigh. 'Life's cruel,' she says. 'It takes the good ones, and the vagabonds and the no-hopers just keep on going? No harm comes to them? Life *is* cruel.'

Mid-morning. Sun puts a glaze on the thick white paint that covers every visible surface. The pool on the afterdeck has been filled and in its green water frolic half a dozen middle-aged Russian passengers. As couples, the Russians are very relaxed. They flirt mildly with each other. A woman will kiss her husband in conversation; he in turn will place his hand casually on the curve of his wife's shoulder or hip—a sexually tinged affection very pleasant to see. These women are expert in a form of feminine self-presentation rarely seen in modern Australia: they bleach their hair till it screams, draw Cleopatra-lines on their lids with seventies liquid eye-make-up, triss about in flirty pleated skirts and wedgie sandals. They are aware of their femininity and know how to use it: one senses a force in them that is held in reserve. By comparison, the Australian women and men on board show little social ease with each other. Many men ignore their wives, and the women beside them adopt a slightly masculine demeanour, becoming more raucous, standing in mannish ways, walking with wide-swinging arms, sportively. It's as if we Australian women obeyed an unconscious compulsion to be counted as honorary blokes.

Despite the glorious weather (we are ploughing happily north through a sparkling ocean, always within sight of land), a crowd gathers in the music saloon for 'a morning at the races'. Volunteers are requested to bend over and tow, between their legs, little wooden horses on long strings across the dance floor. Rodney the MC, who, Lorraine whispers to me, resembles an ex-boyfriend of hers whom she wishes she had married, carries on a gross patter about fillies and geldings. When not enough fillies step forward, a smart alec calls out hoarsely, 'What about a trans-sexual?' No answer. He adds in a slightly less confident voice, 'What about a faggot?' Everyone ignores him.

I back number five, a tall strong young fellow radiant with good cheer. His horse wins, but he is taken outside 'to test for drugs'. The female MC returns with a brimming schooner of straw-coloured liquid. 'A you-rine test!' cries Rodney, raising the glass to his nose. The audience gasps. He opens his mouth and takes a deep swig. The crowd howls with delight. 'It's clean!' he declares. I have won three bucks.

Out by the Lido Bar, a bunch of boozers behind me are making loud comments about the girls in the pool. 'What's that thing they do,' says one, 'bikini line?' 'Bikini wax!' roars his mate. They bellow with laughter. I glance over my shoulder. To my surprise they are all in their sixties and seventies. One of them is actually on a walking stick.

Over lunch, rudely served and barely edible, Lorraine flashes to us, covertly, the business card of Stefan, the man who asked her to dance last night at the disco. 'Do you think he might be Polish?' she says, musing over his polysyllabic surname. Lorraine has been befriended by the extended family of Stefan's neighbours with whom he is travelling. She seems a bit fluttery, but relieved of the anxiety of drifting around unattached.

I wake from a nap at four, to find that grey has closed in, and that the ship has turned round and is heading south. From inside my metal cupboard I hear a tiny tinny rustling: it's the coathangers whispering among themselves as the sea starts to heave. I stagger up to the saloon. Bingo time. Hundreds of people hunch over tables with their heads down, like children taking dictation. They whistle feebly for 'legs eleven', and to applaud a win they tap their biros on the tabletops: everyone knows the rules.

Walking has become difficult. One minute I feel weightless, the next my legs are made of lead and insist on diagonal movement. I go out on to the afterdeck and lean over the rail. No birds, no fish. I feel dopey from my anti-seasick patch. A man tells me he is sure the patches are 'banned in England'. I would care more if the water in the pool had not begun to tilt on tremendous angles. A poor little green-faced girl is being carried round the ship by her father. She droops off his shoulder, gripping a sickbag, her eyes dull with nausea.

Apart from me, the only solo traveller now is a man in his forties who mooches about smoking Drum and leaning on the rail. He is weather and work-beaten, very thin in his distressed denims; he has a thick moustache to the jawbone, and a dramatic limp. Earlier I have seen him in shorts. One of his legs has had half the thigh muscle gouged off it, as if he had been mauled by a beast. Now, two women spot him as he passes their table at the Lido Bar. They murmur about him with their heads close together. He remains oblivious, breathing smoke and staring out to sea.

At the captain's cocktail party that evening, these two women, neighbours from Bonnyrigg, invite me to sit at their table. They are an unlikely pair. Wiry Bev looks dykey, with very short hair and a hunted, glowering face, but this threatening demeanour turns out to be a mask for severe shyness. 'I've been bringin' up kids for seven years,' she tells me. 'I've forgotten how to be sociable. So *she's* teachin' me how to get on better with people.' She jerks a thumb at Carola, who beams at her pupil with proud affection. Carola, in a tight black dress showing cleavage, has a lazy, sexy, cigaretty voice; her bleached hair is scraped up into a silver scrunchy and falls in locks round her sun-roughened cheeks. Her lipstick is shiny mauve, and her kohl-rimmed eyes, bright with a wild good humour and a readiness to laugh, rove constantly round the packed saloon.

Trays of vodka are brought round by the crabby Russian waitresses. Carola's eyes meet mine, in the cross-class mutual recognition of two clapped-out party girls. We seize a glass each and raise them to one another in a toast. Bev and a young bank manager she has befriended (he wears a red bow tie and she tells me later, solemnly, that he is 'a perfect gentleman') sip at their vodka gingerly, with wrinkled top lips and squinched-up eyes. 'Throw it back!' cries Carola, demonstrating.

'Eewww,' go Bev and the bankman, sipping away.

A huge Australian behind Carola hands me his full shot glass, his mouth curling in contempt for any drink other than beer. I drain it. Carola seizes two more from a passing tray. A Russian band, Kalinka, is playing away dutifully on a small stage. 'What's the thing that front bloke's playing?' says Carola. 'He's cute.'

'Looks like a saxophone,' I say. 'It's got a bend in it.'

'Hyuk hyuk,' says Carola. 'Wonder *what else's* got a bend in it?' Bev turns away from the bankman to hide her laughter.

The lone man with the moustache strolls into the saloon. Carola seizes Bev's arm and hisses, 'There's Ray.'

'Why does he limp?' I ask. 'Was it a shark attack?'

'Nuh. Motorbike,' says Carola. 'He shouted me drinks last night at the disco. He come down to my cabin door with me at 2 a.m. But I sent him away. I go, "You can't come in. Me girlfriend's asleep." He goes, "*I've* got a cabin." I go, "Yeah, and how many people asleep in it?" "Four." "Yeah *right.*" '

Ray turns from shaking hands with the captain and heads in our direction. Carola is beaming up at him, tossing back her hair, but he walks straight past without even a glance at her. Her smile fades. 'He's probably got the shits with me,' she murmurs, 'cause I wouldn't let him in.' She downs another vodka, gives me a crooked grin and says with a shrug, 'Pity. He's a real good kisser. Real nice. *Gentle.*'

Dinner is dried-out slabs of unrecognisable protein, platters of tired old lettuce. People are beginning to lose patience with the Russian service. Looks of mutinous solidarity flash between the tables, behind the backs of the flouncing, scowling waitresses. But Lorraine refuses to criticise anything. She ploughs through three courses, smiling as she chews, and casts reproachful glances at us three ungrateful whingers, who by this time are living on soup and fruit.

Bored and irritable, we let Lorraine drag us back to the saloon, to see the 'Russian welcome show'. The band Kalinka strikes up a folk song, the lights dim and, before our jaded eyes, six glorious Russian maidens float through the door and on to the dance floor. They are wearing long cream frocks with loose sleeves, and above their shining foreheads tower strange, ethereal bishops' mitres, made of palest, dewiest gossamer lace and tied to their heads with sashes. Their beauty draws from us a collective gasp. A man blurts out, 'It's the waitresses!' Another shouts, 'And they're *smiling!*' A roar of applause goes up.

Each holding a lace hanky in her fingertips, the women perform a graceful dance. They sweep grandly, but their feet in white strapped shoes are tiptoeing like mad under the long skirts which brush the floor. We are amazed by the formal sweetness of their expressions. Their smiles are fixed, but there is a soft spark in their eyes and their faces are luminous. One girl mis-steps and is shoved back into place by her partners; they can't help laughing, which brings another cry of joy from the rapt audience. They are joined by handsome young men, some with flashing gold teeth, and launch into a stamping peasant dance that brings the house down.

This marvel is followed by 'one of our very experienced cookers', a stout woman in a long red dress, who seizes the mike like a pro and belts out, in a horribly loud and unmodulated voice, a song about 'a brave captain'. The vibe drops. I sneak on to the deck.

The night is soft with a starless, velvety blackness. I turn this way and that, disoriented, and suddenly, between our ship and the open sea, I notice a small, dense, brilliant mass of light. It surges up in the air, then drops again, then rises. For a mad second I think it's a tiny model ship somehow attached to the radio mast of the *Mikhail Sholokhov*—then I realise we are rolling so voluptuously that the horizon on which the other ship lies is constantly changing position. The ship is like a dazzling brooch, spiked now here, now there, always rising and falling.

Sunday, after a rough night, dawns bright and calm. The sick creep out, blinking and peering about them like souls who doubt their release from purgatory. 'I was stood up last night!' announces Lorraine stoically as she pulls out her breakfast chair. Stefan, it seems, retired to his cabin early and refused to come out. 'We all went down there to try and get him to come up—it was *them* worryin' about him, not me chasin' him—but he was just too sick.' Stefan, meanwhile, is installed at his friends' table, tearing into a cooked breakfast. Lorraine keeps glancing at him uncertainly. The light has gone out of her face, a little.

Last night's mythical Russian princesses have turned back into sullen slaveys, despising those they serve. Lorraine points out that at every meal, when we first take our seats, the teacup handles are pointing to the left instead of to the right. She begins to perceive a meaning in this—'or could it be feng shui?' She wonders aloud whether there might be 'stigma attached to working on this boat: maybe they've been naughty? Maybe it's like our community service?'

'You mean,' I say, impressed, 'that this is some sort of floating gulag?' We stare at the waitresses. We would like to be friendly, but they go on steadfastly ignoring us. Somehow this is painful. We feel rejected and rather glum.

But out on deck, it's a perfect day. The ship is a clean and brilliant white, the sea swarms with shattered fragments of light. Wherever I look there are pleasing shapes, patterns, blocks of white and crimson and dark green against a blue sky. Flags flutter hard, expressing themselves in a language I don't understand. This is how cruising is meant to be. For a couple of hours, tranquillity descends on our ship. All the deckchairs are in use. People stay still, basking, drinking, smiling, talking in soft voices.

Poor Bev, though, is horribly seasick. Carola takes her to the Russian doctor, who charges her fifteen bucks for a hit of Stematil. She huddles in a protected corner of the deck, rugged up in her brand-new, creaking, black leather jacket. Her face is pale green, her forehead beaded with sweat. I squat beside her and try to get her mind off her nausea by asking her whether she is enjoying the book she has with her (the only non-airport book I've seen on board), *For the Term of His Natural Life*.

'To be frank, no,' she says. 'It's too fancy. "The grass was green, the sky was blue, the ocean something or other." I don't care about that. I want to know *facts*.' She smokes fiercely, while she lays out for me her political theories: a GST, instant closing-off of all immigration, then a price freeze, then a wage freeze. I have no views on these topics and my attention keeps drifting away to the dazzling ocean. 'You're a writer. What do *you* think?' says Bev sternly. 'This affects *you*.' She keeps her eyes on me, but I feel her interest in me leaking away.

Lone Ray strolls past. 'I like these blokes on the ship,' says Bev when he's out of earshot. 'But last night one was tryin' to kiss me—they were all around me, pushin' and shovin'—I didn't like it. I didn't like it *at all*. I said to the one with the walking stick, I said, "I like them, but they're goin' about it the wrong way. They make me feel like I'm a bitch on heat."'

·'And what did he say?'

She shrugs. 'He agreed.'

At lunch a rumour whizzes round that last night's fish was off. *Everyone* declined to eat it, even the Russian DJ, who was seen out at the Lido Bar scoffing bought pies. Several people have suffered from both vomiting and diarrhoea. By dinner time there are rumbles of protest about the Russian waitresses' surly manners and the gross food. One passenger, sick of waiting for insulting service, gets up, barges to the sideboard, and fills a plate with her own choices. Two waitresses hurry over and blast her with ferocious looks, but she stands her ground and returns their stares, wordlessly, with knobs on: she is a tall, well-built Australian girl and her face is flushed with rage.

I order minestrone and the waitress slaps down a bowl of watery chicken consomme. 'Excuse me,' I say. 'I ordered minestrone.' She shrugs, picks up the dish and strolls away. Minutes later she returns and places the same thing in front of me. I hear my voice trembling dangerously as I say, 'This is *not* minestrone.'

'Min'stron,' she insists.

I bang the table and yell, 'This is NOT MINESTRONE. Minestrone has *beans*.'

Impassively she removes the plate and replaces it with a bowl of darker, thicker fluid. Our table is frozen in terrible silence. Lorraine is staring at me as if I had used a four-letter word. Flustered, I plunge my spoon into the soup and fish out two dark, kidney-shaped objects. I hold them up. 'See? Beans.' Gwen lets out a yelp, and stifles it.

The waitress comes back with a tilting salad platter. Professionally handling spoon and fork, she slings on to Lorraine's plate one brown stalk off an iceberg lettuce, one quarter of a tomato, and one angled, shrivelling slice of cucumber. She slouches away. For three beats Lorraine looks down at her plate. Then she turns her face up to us, takes a deep breath, and says in a loud, disgusted, incredulous voice, 'Isn't that bloody *miserable?*'

The four of us crack up. Lorraine's face goes dark red with the strain. She mops her eyes with a screwed-up paper napkin. 'I think I've been drinkin' too much?' she gasps. 'I'm gettin' emotional?' At this we throw down our cutlery and shriek. Our heads are bowed among the plates. People at other tables start to crane their necks. Lorraine is possessed by hopeless paroxysms. The napkin is almost stuffed into her mouth. Shirley, flushed and quivering, has to take off her glasses and wipe away tears. 'At last, Lorraine,' chokes Gwen through her clean cotton hanky, 'at last we've got you to *complain* about something.'

When we have composed ourselves, we sit looking right into each other's faces for the first time, without defences. 'I've been thinking?' says Lorraine earnestly. 'It must be because youse have all been travelling before but I haven't? So I've got no idea what it's right for me to expect?'

'Travelling?' says Gwen in her soft voice. 'I've never even been up in a plane.'

In the pause that follows, we hear the huge fat father of a huge fat family, two tables away, heave a contented sigh as he lays down his knife and fork. 'Aaaah,' he says. 'I still reckon Australian food's the best in the world—don't you?' The other members of his family nod happily and go on chewing and swallowing.

'Helen,' says Shirley. 'Can you write about this, in that newspaper you work for?'

'I can,' I reply, 'and I will.'

Lorraine leans forward and lowers her voice. 'Do you think I should ask Stefan to take me out to dinner when the ship docks? 'Cause I'd only be able to see him in Sydney. He keeps saying to me, "Why can't I visit you? You're free, aren't you?" But he couldn't come to where I *live*. It'd be too…complicated.'

'Get rid of your boyfriend,' says Gwen bluntly. 'Then you *will* be free. Because you're divorced.'

Lorraine writhes. 'Yeah but there's something in me that won't let me *do* that. Anyway, I didn't come on this cruise looking for a shipboard romance. Two days ago I didn't even *know* him.' She sits up straight, as if with fresh resolve. But Stefan, on his way to the door, stops five paces from our table and stands there looking at Lorraine. Beaming, she jumps up and dashes over to him.

Gwen, Shirley and I exchange significant glances as they walk out together. We feel protective of Lorraine, with her manoeuvres and her vague fantasies. 'He looks a bit of a tough customer,' says Gwen. 'Don't you think?'

'Yes,' I say, 'Dark. But kind of…interesting.'

'What that girl needs,' says Shirley, pushing back her chair, 'is a property settlement. So she can shake off her no-hoper ex. *And* her boyfriend.'

That evening I make a valiant effort to sit through an Australian cabaret in the saloon. Two scrawny sisters in strapless lamé mini dresses squall a Beatles song, then the MC drags out on to the dance floor a shy man who has proposed, during the cruise, to his much younger Chinese girlfriend, and been accepted. He is ecstatic, she demure. A pav with sparklers is produced and we all sing 'For They Are Jolly Good Fellows'. Some of the Australian women in the saloon cast narrow looks at the new fiancée.

Passing through the casino on my way to bed, I spot Shirley pumping coins into a fruit machine. I stand next to her for five minutes, completely unable to grasp the principles of the game. She is so phlegmatic that I can't tell whether she's winning or losing. Coins start to rattle and slide wildly inside the machine. 'Are you winning, or is it?'

'It's the boat starting to roll,' she says without looking up.

I go to my bunk and read *Moby Dick*. The tannoy in my cabin is leaking an irritating thread of music. I turn the volume down as far as it will go but still the song oozes out. When I look out my porthole in the small hours, the horizon is tilting at a forty-five-degree angle.

It's still dark on Monday morning when *Mikhail Sholokhov* enters Sydney Heads. I hang over the rail, amateurishly angling my camera, and watch the drama of the pilot battling through big seas to reach us. Presently the decks are lined with passengers in raincoats, silently watching the sky turn a murky yellow. We slide past Rose Bay, Double Bay, Rushcutters. The city is going to work all around us; we too are on our way to work.

At breakfast Lorraine agonises about the Stefan problem. 'I can't give him my home phone number, 'cause my ex-husband will be rude to him if he calls.'

At last we dare to give advice. 'Get rid of that creep, Lorraine! Turf him out! You're worth better than that! Get a settlement—get your life together!'

But Lorraine is not listening. 'Anyway,' she murmurs, thinking out loud, 'how could I cook Polish food?'

Stefan strides towards the dining room door, pauses by our table, bends over Lorraine and gives her a kiss on each cheek. 'Goodbye!' they say. He walks away. She turns back to us. Her face is shining.

In the fuss of disembarkation I lose contact with my companions. Passengers shuffle off the ship without ceremony. No one seems to bother with farewells. There is a strange sparseness in the huge empty terminal. People wander away with their bags, looking as lost and shy as they did three days ago when we first came on board. I can't see a single person I know.

I pick up my duffel bag and walk out of the terminal on to Circular Quay. It's a fresh and lovely morning. Fifty metres ahead of me, I see a familiar chunky little figure in sandals with heels, lugging a large bag. She's having trouble with it, she stops and rests it on the sea wall. I run to catch up. 'Lorraine!'

'Hoi! My bag strap's broken? I dunno what's wrong with it?'

We cobble it together and she shoulders it.

'Where are you going now?' I ask. I'd like to invite her for a coffee, but somehow, on land again, our intimacy has evaporated: I'm afraid she'll say no.

'I might as well just take the train home,' she says. 'I could hang around Sydney but what's the point? I was so besotted with Stefan and I...' She looks up at me with her broad, anxious, endearing smile.

I say, 'I've got to go to work. It's been great getting to know you.' I lean forward—she's a good three inches shorter than I am—and we kiss each other and clumsily hug. 'Goodbye! Goodbye!'

Away she staggers with her bag. I want to say goodbye to Carola, to Bev, to Gwen and Shirley. But they have all dematerialised. Did I dream them? Were they figments of the anti-seasick drug? The earth is swaying. I can hardly get my footing.

1995

Aqua Profonda

BILL DECIS IS mad about water. He's got nearly two million litres of it in his care. Every day he filters it, adds chemicals to it, pumps it this way and that through great pipes, takes morning and evening samples of it, and picks small imperfections off its surface with a strainer on a long metal pole. Teaching people how to move through water is the passion of his life.

His baby is Melbourne's Fitzroy baths. He has worked there for eleven years. Thousands of motorists pass the pool every day on their way along Alexandra Parade off the F19 freeway, ignorant of the treasure which lies modestly concealed, rippling faintly in the early morning air, behind an anonymous cream brick wall just east of the Brunswick Street intersection.

The locals know where it is, though. Every summer fifty thousand swimmers and layabouts click through its turnstiles. Bill Decis knows, as do the parents of the area, that the neighbourhood pool is the biggest and cheapest child-minding centre ever invented. Bill's been in the water game so long now that even when he's on holidays or at the beach his eyes can't stop their constant patrolling.

The blokes at the Royal Derby in Fitzroy call him 'Johnny Weismuller'. He's fifty-eight and has the powerful shoulders and tapering torso of the lifelong swimmer and water polo player. He's a moulder by training, and did his apprenticeship at the foundry of H.V. McKay Massey Harris where the basic wage, he says, was created; but he's a swimming coach, a teacher, by inclination and experience. He's lost count years ago of the kids he's taught to swim, of the champions he's coached to victory, though he has a couple of suitcases bulging with memorabilia.

He is as brown as leather; his white shorts are pristine. The wraparound sunglasses he wears when he's on duty have been in and out of fashion several times. He strolls round his pool with hands crossed behind his back, and his manner with those he considers miscreants is direct to the point of giving offence. He doesn't care. He runs a very trim ship.

His is the disembodied voice which barks orders over the PA. 'All right, you fellers, stop your running around. That boy who bombed, report to the manager's office. I saw you. That little lass in the spotted bikini. *You* can't swim. Go back to the shallow end till such time as you learn. Do that once more, that lad in the red togs, and I'll have you out of the water, I'll dress you, I'll send you home.' After each announcement a light hush descends on the mob; then hilarity reasserts itself. Hilarity is OK with Decis, as long as it's *disciplined* hilarity. No one drowns at his pool, and no one gets hurt. If he has to be a child-minder, he'll do the job properly. 'I use the mike as a weapon,' he says, 'I believe we're here to educate people.'

Bill Decis works at Fitzroy but he lives and coaches professionally at Footscray, where he was born, and he still calls Fitzroy 'out here'. When he was a lad, the western suburbs were cut off from the city by the Maribyrnong, at the time spanned by only four bridges. The river was so clear, in those days between the wars, that from the top of a bridge you could see your mate underwater. Young Billy and his gang used to take particular delight in bombing violently beside the cabin cruisers which bore the leisured classes up and down the river on Cup days. 'They used to have pianos going, parasols, the lot—us snotty-nosed kids would be waiting on the bridge, and as they came under we'd do a big honey-pot from forty foot up and drown 'em. Old Commodore Harding used to threaten to kill us.'

The Footscray baths opened in 1929. 'Boys swam naked back then,' says Decis. 'Course, it was segregated. When we got togs we thought we were lucky. They were cotton Speedos, two and six a pair at Forges, and they had to last four years. Our mums were always mending them, sewing cloth badges over the patched parts. They were our pride and joy.

'I taught my first pupils when I was twelve, and I've been in the game ever since. Of course, sport was different back then. It was our social lives, as well as keeping us fit. We went swimming to get better, not just to muck around. I've seen forty furniture vans lined up outside the old Beaurepaire pool near the Yarra there, each one decked out with the banners of a different amateur swimming club, for our annual joint picnic to Mornington. Those things went out, eventually, as sport became more individualistic.

'Another thing that went out was all the illegal things we had to do to raise money to get our athletes out of the country—we sold sly grog, we had raffles, we ran crown-and-anchor games—everything illegal. It was the Australian way of life!

'I got my merit certificate before I was fourteen, so for the last year of school my job was to keep the pool clean, with a mate. Back then there was no chlorine. The pools used to have to be emptied twice a week and scrubbed out with sand soap and ordinary scrubbing brushes. We didn't have heated pools, either. We had to take the temperatures as they were and get used to it. People have changed. Parents send letters to the teachers now, saying the water's too cold for the kids. The Education Department has set a limit of sixty-eight degrees—any colder than that and the kids don't have to go in.'

On his office wall Decis has a wonderful photo of the opening ceremony of the Fitzroy baths in 1908. At the western end, where the brick wall now bears the misspelt sign AQUA

PROFONDA, a throng of bewhiskered gentlemen and gracious
ladies draw back their spats and skirts from the edge of the
pool, upon which float two formally dressed persons in a rowing
boat.

'The Fitzroy Council don't realise what an asset they've
got in this pool,' he says. 'It's the antique pool of Australia.
It's the only full-size open-air pool of Olympic standard within
a two-mile radius of the GPO. Carlton? Small. Collingwood?
Small. With a little bit of updating, this could be the best pool
in the metropolitan area. We need to be able to heat the pool
up to about seventy-five degrees in March and April, when
there's still plenty of sunshine. Many's the Easter we've been
closed during beautiful weather. We could extend the season
by two months.'

Decis was on the barricades in 1977 with Fitzroy residents
who tried to stop the F19 freeway from going through along
Alexandra Parade. The freeway was forced through, and now
Decis and his team have their work cut out to keep the pool in
tip-top condition, for it lies east–west, parallel with the polluting
roadway, 'in the right position to cop all the rubbish that comes
over the wall. We have to hose the decking twice a day.'

But the Fitzroy filter system, installed in 1948, is more
than equal to its job. 'It's a beautiful unit—the Rolls Royce of
filtration,' says Decis with emotion. 'With proper maintenance
it should last a hundred years.' Two-hundred-and-forty-six
thousand litres an hour pass through its six sand filter cells.
Once a month a sample of the pool water is sent up to the
Microbiology Diagnostic Unit at Melbourne University. Proudly
Decis shows sheaves of test results: 'I love to see that water flow
clear and clean.'

He throws the filter system on a backwash and goes outside
to the testing point among the big cream-painted tanks in
their wire enclosure. With alarming force the water from the
system rushes to the outflow pipe a metre below where he is

standing. 'Young lad got sucked out through a pipe like that once,' he remarks casually, yanking a few weeds out of a crack in the pavement as he waits for the moment to test. 'Ended up in the Yarra. He was *extruded* into the Yarra. By the time he got there he was sausage meat. Not a bone left in his body.

'Some more modern filtration systems have a porthole in the side so you can watch what's going on, but we don't need a porthole. We've got the visuals.' He lowers a milk bottle on a string into the turbulence at the pipe entrance, then pulls it out full, holds it up and examines it against the sky. It is slightly greenish and murky with sediment. 'See that? That's all the muck the system's taken out. If you took a bottleful out of the pool itself, I guarantee it'd be as blue and clear as that sky.'

In 1980 the eastern wall near the babies' pool was knocked out and replaced by a cyclone wire fence, thus opening up one end of the baths to the outside world. A small, sunken grassed area was created along this fence, the first concession to comfort and conventional aesthetics in what had always been a Spartan institution with its expanses of bare cement and brisk fir trees.

But surprisingly few regulars lie about on the grass. Most are faithful to the high concrete stands, closer to the water and open to breezes. The tireless kids who swim, cark and swim again until it's time to go home for tea despise the grass over there behind the bubs' pool.

The grass needs no patrolling, for here the intellectuals congregate. A quick survey of poolside reading matter last weekend revealed a high concentration of serious material on the grassy area: Christina Stead, Barry Hill, William Thackeray, Katherine Mansfield, Marge Piercy, Doris Lessing, Charles Perkins, John Fowles, two volumes of an encyclopaedia on UFOs, an advanced French grammar and the RMIT Radiography Clinical Studies guide, while the other eighty-five percent of the pool turned up only one Spanish newspaper, one *Age*, one *Women's Weekly*, one *Time* and one *Dolly*.

'All that has no meaning,' said a non-reader who had come to swim her twenty lengths. 'Everyone's the same down here, even the punks, once they get their clothes off.'

There is no leveller like a public swimming pool, particularly at four-thirty every afternoon when the sun is lowering, and the boss emerges from the store room with a great white hose lashing in his hands and commences his silent, inexorable progress round the concrete edges of the pool and up the high steps, driving before him with the powerful stream of water all grit, paper scraps, dead insects, icy-pole sticks and sundazed people. It's the expulsion from paradise: there is no appeal. People leap to their feet, seize their pathetic belongings, and flee like lost souls before the blast.

The beauty of the Fitzroy baths is of an especially Melburnian kind: not thrusting itself forward, but modest, idiosyncratic, secret almost, needing to be imagined, sought out, discovered through familiarity. Bill Decis's passion for the pool goes deeper than the simple proprietorial loyalty of the bloke in charge. It's water that fascinates him. He has hundreds of Polaroid photographs of the pool in all weathers, at all times of day, undisturbed by bodies: glassy and pale at dawn, criss-crossed at noon by moving strings of light and shadow. The emotion provoked in him by this volume of water and all it signifies is not an indulgent, modern feeling. It is something altogether harsher and more old-fashioned—a bracing, steadfast sort of love.

1981

A Day at the Show

YOU HAVE TO be careful these days at the Royal Melbourne Show. Take a wrong turning, get too far from the animals, and you could start to feel extremely ill, harangued on all sides by sellers of useless plastic rubbish, poisonous food, low-grade toys, tickets for rides that belong at Luna Park, computers which read your palm for two bucks and give you the same result as the person next to you, thousands of stuffed pink panthers hanging by the neck, show bags which cost two dollars ninety and contain a couple of melting chocolate bars and more plastic.

But on a soft morning at the Showgrounds, after one of those dry, mild spring nights when your head has been too light for the pillow, you can still pick up the stabbing sweetness of the blossoming pittosporum trees, sharp enough to pierce the stink of frying fat.

In the great corrugated iron sheds with their green roofs and white woodwork, the light is benign. Human footsteps and voices are muffled by straw. There is a strong but pleasant perfume of excrement and dust. A family sits on camp chairs around a horse's stall, drinking tea and passing from hand to hand a thick album of the horse's photographs. In another stall, harmoniously silent, stand three living creatures: a grey mare and two old men wearing hats. One man is holding the animal's head while the other, balancing on a wooden box at her side, patiently plaits a red ribbon into her mane.

At the end of a row of stalls is a little booth for a human to sleep in. The door is open. The bed takes up most of the space inside. On a table stand a bottle of Worcestershire sauce, a packet of McAlpine's plain flour and a bag of parrot food. The parrot is perched in a cage on the wall outside the booth. All around pours in the gentle, pale light of the spring day.

In this lovely light, the flesh of resting cattle is mighty in the straw. Inanimate objects take on a serene significance: three pairs of boots, worn, polished, soft, lined up on a feed bag; a woman's flowery scarf, with the knot still in it, hung on a stall door.

A young girl squats down with an old towel in her hand and buffs the hooves of her palomino. She leads it into the open air. Sunlight transmogrifies on the horse's perfect hide into a radiant hum of cream and copper.

In the sheep shed, whose occupants are engaged elsewhere, a wall of illuminated glass cases contains mounds of prize-winning wool. Language is not yet dead in a land where these are the criteria for the judging of fleeces: 'Trueness to type. Length. Soundness. Handle. Colour or bloom. Character. Density. Evenness. Yield.'

The Arts and Crafts Hall opens into a pageant of minor horrors: men's khaki cotton fishing hats have been decorated with monstrous embroidery. They are clotted with brightly coloured patterns of stitching which must have made many a husband bite his lip and dream of poison or divorce. People pass briskly in front of the cake decorating, much of which is garish or over-complicated, a form of showing-off.

But at the back of the hall the classic fare is on display: cakes, scones, bread. The flat cases cannot contain their delicate odour. The simplicity of conception and display is breathtaking. Women hover over them, fall into reverie. Their voices grow dreamy. 'How on earth can they judge?' murmurs one, half to her friend, half to herself. 'They're *beautiful*.'

'They look a lovely scone,' says her friend, less given to

ecstasy. 'And they've already been there a week.'

The plain cakes are transcendental in their directness. 'Plain's the hardest thing to do well,' says a woman in gloves. 'You can't hide behind anything.' And the sponges! What is preventing these miracles from levitating? Before them we spontaneously observe a two-minute silence. The woman in gloves draws a long, quivering sigh. 'An old lady from Ballarat,' she whispers, 'once told me that the best sponges are made with swans' eggs. From Lake Wendouree. But it's illegal.'

Years ago there used to be a whole wall of preserves, jams and marmalades at the Show, back-lit like an underwater scene from some weird opera. Gone now, shrunk to a couple of small glass cases. But the bottles and jars inside still have the power to fill the pilgrims' eyes with tears. 'Shred or Exhibition Marmalade,' say the labels, in beautiful old-fashioned hand-writing. 'Shooting Stars.'

In what blissful realm does Miss E. Alexander, does R. G. Pywell dwell? What golden paddocks lie beyond their morning window panes? In what paradise kitchens, on what chopping boards of bewitched timber do they fashion the loose knots and spirals of grapefruit peel which hang suspended so sparing, so exquisitely judged, in the ethereal element of their marmalade? What patience, what intellectual serenity guides these women's hands? In their light-filled jars, craft soars into art. The humble is exalted into the sublime.

1981

Postscript

Everyone at my place thought this piece was hopelessly purple. Several days after it appeared in the *Age*, I received a letter, care of the paper, from one of the marmalade champions. The prize winner was pleased that I had admired the winning works, but wanted to tell me something: 'I don't see paddocks. I live in a flat in Altona, and all I can see out my kitchen window is the gasometer.' The letter was signed Ron G. Pywell. I sent back a squashed but respectful reply.

One evening a week later someone knocked at our front door. On the mat stood a plumpish man in his thirties, with short dark hair and a shy face. It was R. G. Pywell. He was holding in his arms a supermarket carton containing half a dozen jars of his handiwork. He presented the box to me with grave formality, declined an invitation to come in, hopped into his Holden and drove away.

I carried the box into the kitchen. At the sight of what was in it, my family stopped laughing. We arranged the jars on a special shelf. Sometimes we would move them to the windowsill so we could gaze at them against the light while we washed up. Our reverence for the marmalade was such that I don't remember ever doing anything so gross as eating it.

Five Train Trips

The Age once asked me to spend a week taking day-trips by train out of Melbourne. I wrote about what entertained me or made me laugh: mostly people talking, and landscapes.

SPENCER STREET STATION, MONDAY 8.15 A.M. TO BALLARAT AND SOVEREIGN HILL.

It is going to be a very hot day. The train slides out of Spencer Street. Outside in the passageway I hear a child and a woman.

'Here's a toilet.'

'Sit down, Stephen.'

'But I need to go to the toilet.'

'Sit down, Stephen.'

'But I need to go to the *toilet*.'

'Well you just wait until I go, because…'

We travel over flat plains. I see bunches of gums, yellow grass, thistles, the daisy head of a still windmill, cypresses, power pylons in pairs vanishing into a thin mist which the sun has not yet dispersed.

In Ballarat it's already a scorcher. A bus is waiting at the station to take people to Sovereign Hill, the reconstruction of the gold rush days. Everybody but me is in a family. I am attracting suspicious looks.

Sovereign Hill is slick, but the girls who work there wear little white linen caps, and the men high collars, and I see a girl go striding down Main Street in a pink dress with flounces and petticoats, head up and arms swinging. I feel silly going on the horse-drawn carriage by myself, but I go anyway. The sun is so bright that we are all squinting, and the grimace could be taken for a smile.

In the bookshop a woman in a mobcap, who has just sneaked outside and sprinkled herself with water from a hose, sells me Barbara Baynton's *Bush Studies*. I go into the Mechanics' Institute and Free Library to read it. There is a big framed sign on the wall saying SILENCE. People keep tiptoeing in and watching me, as if this lone reader were part of the exhibit. I sit at the long table and read 'Squeaker's Mate', a horrifying story which returns to mind three days later when I go to Bendigo.

On the homeward train I share a compartment with a placid old woman and her three grandchildren. She is telling them about the olden days. 'Life was different before television.'

'What did you used to do, Nan?'

'Talked. Oh…knitted, sewed, listened to the wireless, played cards. *Talked.*' She nods at me. 'This train isn't gonna stop at Sunshine. They're meeting us at Sunshine. I should've asked. It's never not stopped at Sunshine. They're startin' to be all different, now. Well, I'll know next time, won't I. I had a lovely train last time. Man come in, lifted me case down 'n' everything—but this time no one's come near us.'

'It's not your day, Nan, is it,' says one of the girls.

'No, it's not, is it, love. But something will turn up, won't it.'

In West Melbourne, behind Festival Hall, the train stops dead. The air-conditioning goes off with the motor. We sit companionably in the silence and the thickening heat. From the next compartment rings out the piercing voice of a young mother pushed past endurance. 'Shut up, Wayne!'

Nana, the girls and I lower our eyes as if we had witnessed an indiscretion.

'I'll make you cry,' hisses Wayne's mother.

One of the girls slides me a look. We bite our bottom lips.

'Not much patience in there,' says the pacific Nana. 'Are

we movin'?' she calls to the passing conductor.

'Soon as we can get the engine out of the way that's broken down in front of us.'

The girls point out the West Gate Bridge to their little brother, who has just woken up. 'Bridge,' he repeats in a stunned tone. Next door Wayne is getting what's coming to him.

SPENCER STREET STATION, TUESDAY 9.25 A.M. TO WARRNAMBOOL. Hot. There is a train at the platform but we are not to board. A crowd waits. Some surfies are overseeing the loading of their boards into the luggage van. A railway-man approaches them. 'Oi. Take all that stuff out. Not goin' now.'

A woman behind me cackles. 'Typical railways. "Not goin' now!"'

An old man in a brown suit, cloth cap and hearing aid, whose English is poor, tugs shyly at the sleeve of the man driving the luggage trolley. 'Defective train, sir,' shouts the driver. 'Defective train. No good. Bringing another.'

A girl near me squats down against the railing and opens a brand new copy of *Anna Karenina*. There is no formal explanation of the delay. The train simply moves away from the platform and we're left standing like shags on a rock. There are not enough seats on the platform. People start to slow-clap. 'That's giving them more than they deserve, isn't it?' says a man with a beard.

The replacement train, or 'set' as they say nowadays, is new. We pull out exactly half an hour late. Our conductor is a jolly, curly-headed fellow with a faint New Zealand accent. 'If you'll have your seat reservations ready for me please, and we'll move through and chat to you all personally. Thank you.' He is working hard at making the atmosphere in the open-plan carriage like that of a successful party. Without alcohol, of course. Up the front a group of elderly women with Thermos flasks whoops with laughter.

Opposite me sits a blind woman in her late thirties with two girls under ten. They have brought some grapes. I'm starving. The grapes are pale green and sprinkled with tiny drops of water. There are rather a lot of them. The blind woman is sharing them with the children.

I would like to speak to the blind woman. I like the way she deals with the kids. Also she has what looks like a viola in a case on the luggage rack. She is one of those strangers you sometimes see in a public place who have something in their demeanour that makes you want to go up to them and say: 'Please tell me your life story. Tell me what you know that I don't.' She has a long, bony, intelligent-looking face. One of her eyes is ordinary blue; the other is milky. She mustn't be able to see at all: her daughter leads her to the toilet. 'The toilets are very smelly,' I hear her say when she returns.

At Colac people rush the refreshment counter. I get there first. I buy some sandwiches and a Big M, the only drinkable coffee in sight.

'Mum, what does NO SHIRT, NO SERVICE mean?' shouts a boy.

'Well, the men have to wear a shirt.'

'But what does NO SERVICE mean?'

The mother is queuing too hard to answer.

By the time I get up the nerve to intrude on the blind woman with a version of my fantasised request, there is only half an hour left till Warrnambool. She does not seem to find my approach peculiar. She is the kind of person who gets straight to the point. 'I've had a very eventful life,' she begins, and we both burst out laughing. At Warrnambool an old man meets her. She is going to Mt Gambier. We say goodbye, our conversation barely begun, and he leads her away.

Warrnambool is inert under a powerful, dull heat. I walk to the beach, which is lined with a long row of fraying pines like half-eaten fish stood stiffly on their noses. Some are no more than a skeleton with a tail. A great deal of old-fashioned sand-castle building is going on. 'Want me to bury you up to your neck?' says a girl to her brother.

The hot afternoon rolls along slowly. I daren't lie down on my towel lest I fall asleep and miss the train. I keep going into the water to wake myself up.

The train home is on time, but only the first-class air-conditioning is working, so the jolly conductor moves all the economy passengers into first. Good on him. 'It's a bit of a bone of contention with me,' he says, 'that people pay top dollar for seats and don't get proper facilities.'

A dumpy, unhappy-looking girl has a ticket for the window seat I have casually dropped into. I move, but her mother gives me a dirty look as she installs the teenager and kisses her goodbye. All the way to Melbourne the girl reads *True Romance* comics and eats chocolate. She never glances at me or gives the slightest sign that she has noticed my presence. She has two kinds of movements: confident when turning pages or arranging possessions, furtive when breaking off another piece of gummy chocolate and sliding it into her mouth. For some reason I am sure she is going to be a nurse. I hope I never wake up and find her dull, miserable face beside my bed.

On the way home I see into people's backyards. I see a baby in a wooden playpen. Two empty canvas chairs side by side under a laden fruit tree. A woman in a faded apron hosing her vegetables. Three white chooks and a black cat on a carpet of pine needles.

Through the entrance arch of an old railway station I see a fine leafy avenue, a child on a blue bicycle riding away down the dusty road.

The hills, if I can call them that, are very distant and low. The dry grass is so thick as to appear mattress-like; it would hold you up if you rolled on it.

It is getting dark. We come into Melbourne from the west.

The refinery is sprinkled with lights. In the next compartment a woman says to her companion, 'Let's get fish and chips and sit on the beach.'

SPENCER STREET STATION, WEDNESDAY 8.25 A.M. TO BAIRNSDALE.
The best part of each day is the long, fast tram ride along the cemetery in Lygon Street at eight o'clock in the morning. The green blinds are down on the east side of the tram, but sun pours through its open doorways, making it a tube of light and air. Women on their way to work sit in relaxed postures, feet planted apart, their thin cotton skirts fluttering in the wind. Over the cemetery fence the white grass blurs between the flat faces of the headstones.

Heading east today, into Gippsland. I find myself a spot in economy, where the old-fashioned dogboxes are nicely proportioned and lined with timber, and there are curved metal luggage racks and slatted shutters. Today's conductor is very young and anxious, with a new moustache. He settles in for a yarn. Behind him is some graffiti I'm glad he can't see: LEGALISE GUNJA AND SMACK. I look out the window and a hedge slides past, clipped into the legend BUNYIP SCHOOL. A young couple with a baby in a bassinette gets on. The woman has JUNKIE tattooed on her upper arm.

Cattle stand belly-deep in a dam. Two kids on new Lilos float on a creek. A tent is pitched under a bridge.

The trip to Bairnsdale takes four and a half hours. My return booking is on a train that leaves twenty-five minutes after I arrive. There is no cafe at the station. I step out on to the street and look around. I spy the Grand Terminus Hotel a couple of hundred yards along the road. I walk briskly towards it in the battering heat. I order a gin and tonic, and drink half of it in one of those anonymous modernised pub lounges with black shiny chairs and bare brick walls and muzak. Three hippies with backpacks are fooling around in the corner. The boy pops a paper bag. 'Oooh, Rick,' cry the two girls.

'Nerve-rackin', innit,' says the barman to me, out of the corner of his mouth. I haven't got time to finish my drink: if I drink all of it I'll fall asleep on the way home and that would never do. I spank back to the station.

A woman is taking her two small children home to Melbourne. They are colouring in with self-conscious goodness, waiting for the train to start. The boy, who looks about six, is flushed with concentration. He shakes his head. 'Boy, I gotta lotta work to do here!' He sets about it with a will. Without stopping the back and forth movements of his pencil, he launches himself into this conversation with his four-year-old sister, who is also hard at work.

'Did you know there was wee and poo on the railway tracks?'

'Yes,' says the girl.

'How did you know?'

'Uncle Bill told me.'

'Well, do you know how they get there?'

'No. How.'

'Guess.'

Long pause. Colour colour colour.

'I know. Somebody did wee and poo on the railway track.'

'No,' says the boy in triumph, but not raising his eyes from his work, 'because somebody'd *see* the person.'

She does not ask for enlightenment, nor does he offer it. Their mother takes out a Mills and Boon novel called *Tangle in Sunshine* and begins to read.

'I'm trying to do my best colouring,' says the boy, 'but I keep going over the lines.'

An old man with sun scabs on the gristle of his ears taps the arm of another old chap across the aisle. They are both wearing hats.

'Do you play lawn bowls?' says the first one.

'Beppardon?'

'I say, do you play lawn bowls?'

'No. No, I don't.'

'You should. Look at this.' He passes over an article he has just torn carefully out of tonight's *Herald*. The photograph shows women of his age in white bowling hats, wiping sweat out of their eyes. 'THE HEAT BOWLS 'EM OVER. Ha ha ha. Once it gets over ninety degrees, it's too hot. Too hot.'

The temperature in the refreshment car must be well over ninety. The blinds are down tight as a drum, people are stumbling in and out of the hot dimness. I am sitting beside an earbasher from Hobart. She could talk the leg off an iron pot. 'There are hardly any shops in Sale! You just look along one block and that's it! They haven't even got a theatre! They haven't got a Myers or a Fitzgeralds! You should see the size of their Coles! Pfff! What time do the shops close in Melbourne, do you know?'

The mother of the wee and poo expert is saying, at that moment, to her neighbour, 'I like to get in the car and in two minutes be up at the shopping centre. I don't like all this barren land.'

The earbasher has talked herself to sleep. I look out at the land, which is not at all barren.

I get home in time for tea. There has been a weak cool change.

SPENCER STREET STATION, THURSDAY 8.45 A.M. TO BENDIGO.

The train leaves on time. Wind moves steadily over the dry grassy paddocks. The grass swarms, like the backs of living creatures.

Next door a man is talking in Greek to his son, who must be about nine. The father, who sounds like a gentle, quiet man, speaks to the boy in a normal tone. The child responds by screaming. 'Shut up, cunt! Shut up! Shut up! Anyway, I can't even drink my bloody fucking coffee!' The murmur of the father's voice is almost drowned by the boy's manic chanting. 'I don't care! I don't care! I don't care!' He sings it on three notes, G, E, C, over and over again, like a mantra. When he passes the door of my compartment I look up quickly, expecting to see a horned monster with a distorted, grinning face, but he is just an ordinary boy with black hair and slightly over-bright eyes, in shorts and T-shirt.

My ticket to Bendigo includes a visit to Sandhurst Town, a privately owned goldfields reconstruction for tourists—what the bus driver calls a 'historical whatever', as he drives me there in my solitary glory. Thank God several families turn up in their own cars at the 'whatever'. The temperature is hitting forty degrees at 11 a.m. If Sovereign Hill at Ballarat is the sanitised version of the past, Sandhurst Town administers a stiff dose of realism. A rickety train with open-sided carriages trundles the families and me through the bush to 'the diggings', a huddle of miserable tents, brown with dirt and absolutely still in the brutal heat of midday. The sun thunders down out of an empty sky.

The driver and conductor of the little train, dressed up, soldier on. They present an extremely enjoyable historical pageant involving mining licences, guns, sawbone doctors, death in mine shafts, bribery of officials, gold-panning, flogging and the like. The adults laugh shakily, the children stand stupefied in their thongs. One little boy leaps into his father's arms and sobs: 'I wanna go home!' A more stoical lad takes a can of Aerogard out of his mother's bag and sprays himself from head to toe.

After the diggings there is an official visit to a eucalyptus works, from which I sneak away in order to buy some acid drops in one of a row of shops with wooden verandahs, and lace and plough arts in the windows. But it's a ghost town. Everything is open but there's not a living soul around. I call 'Oohoo!' in vain.

Then, in the last shop, I find two little boys of ten and eight or so skulking behind the counter. The younger one volunteers to serve me. The acid drops are three cents each and I ask for twelve. He puts them in a bag and I am about to say 'That'll be thirty-six cents' when it occurs to me that he might like playing shops and working it out for himself. It takes him about five minutes. His eyes take on a distant look, his lips move.

I say, trying to be helpful: 'You just go twelve threes. Tables. Do you learn tables at school?' I should shut up. An ego is at stake here. The little boy gives up on mental, picks up a pencil and begins to work out the sum on a paper bag. He keeps his arm round his work, but I can see that he is drawing twelve groups of three strokes, putting a circle round each group of three, and then counting all the strokes.

He looks up at last. 'Thirty-six cents?'

'Right, thirty-six cents.' I open my purse. Horrors. Only twenty-cent coins. If I give him forty cents he'll have to do subtraction. But I haven't got anything smaller. I hand over the coins. His face goes blank.

'Now you give me four cents change,' I say in a casual tone. Off the hook. He gives me the four cents and beams with pride at a long ordeal brought to a satisfactory end.

Away I go with my bag of acid drops, past two rhesus monkeys sprawled in a cage with their tongues hanging out.

The bus driver is waiting for me in a huge room with a straw ceiling and brick floor. He drives me back to Bendigo and all over town, pointing out the sights, including a huge weatherboard Catholic church. We pause to admire it through the windscreen of the cooled bus.

'You Catholic?' he says.

'No. Are you?'

'Nope.' He laughs and we drive away. I sleep all the way home in an empty compartment.

SPENCER STREET STATION, FRIDAY 9 A.M. TO ALBURY.

You could get excited about going on the Intercapital Daylight, even if you were only getting off at Albury. People cry outside the windows. Luggage is being trundled about and loaded. The carriage I'm in is like a living room. It belongs to the government of New South Wales, and it has framed artworks on its walls. They remind me of Soviet art of the 1950s. One picture is entitled *The State* by Emerson Curtis. It has 'NSW' in curly letters at the top, and railway lines fanning out from colonnades which presumably represent Sydney's Central Station. Then it has stylised sheep, wheat stalks, timber, a rodeo, fruit trees, heavy industry, and across the picture from left to right a symbolic railway track like a zipper on a dress, holding it all together.

I go straight to the buffet car, in which I've spent many an idle hour at crucial times of my life. It is nearly empty. I sit at the counter and feel, for the first time this week, the dizzying power of anonymity which is the reward of the solitary traveller. I order bacon and eggs. The service is quick and courteous, the food good.

A woman with an East London accent leans over my plate and stabs a finger at it. 'Which is that?'

'Bacon and eggs.'

'How much? Four dollars twenty-five.' She calculates. 'That's cheap! In England you'd pay twice, three times as much and get half that amount.'

Just as I finish mopping up the yolk, a waitress comes out of the kitchen and sticks up three hand-printed signs: SCONES RASPBERRY JAM TEA OR COFFEE $1.75.

An American man is in the seat in front of mine. I hear a sharp click. He has taken a photograph. What of? Does anything distinguish this stretch of country from any other we've passed through? It's as flat as a table. Blond grass. Trees. Blue sky with dabs of cloud. Sheep in the shade look like the trees' soiled skirts. Not a human being in sight, nor a truck, nor a car. Click. Oh, a dam. In the air-conditioned carriage you can't tell if it's hot or cold outside.

The hostess comes up to the woman sitting behind me and inserts a slot-in tray across her knees. 'I'm bringing you a nice cup of tea,' she says, as if to a patient.

'I didn't want this, you know,' says the passenger in a querulous tone. 'I was going to have some lunch after Albury.'

'All right,' says the hostess. 'One o'clock, then. I'll tell the cook.'

Tell the cook! Is this a train or an English country house?

In the entrance hall of the Albury station there is a pretty ceiling rose, about a mile high, with green ferns and yellow lilies.

It is very, very hot. I have to find something to do, in a cool place, for four hours. I am not interested in gambling, though we are in NSW where it's legal. I walk down the main street. All the shops are air-conditioned. So is the library. I sit at a table and look up 'travel' in a dictionary of quotations. 'How much a dunce that has been sent to roam/Excells a dunce that has been left at home.' Cowper, 'The Progress of Error'.

I go walking round, staring at people. I cross the street outside the post office and find a ten dollar bill all dry and crackly from lying out in the sun in the middle of the road. The woman who sits behind the desk in the art gallery is of the opinion that there is a cool change every day, in Melbourne. I can't actually remember if there is or not.

On my way back to the station I walk alongside a bloke of sixty or so who is heading for a pub. A wedding car with white ribbons goes past.

'Look at that,' he says with a naughty grimace. 'Some poor bloke just tied the knot.'

'Some poor woman, too,' I snap.

He mimes a jump of fright. 'All right! All right! I'm just

going in here to have a drink!' The pub door flops shut behind him.

Round the corner I run into the two conductors from the train coming out of the Kentucky Fried with parcels in their arms.

'What do *you* do for four hours?' I ask.

'Oh…hang round. Play the pokies.'

'Did you win?'

'Come out ten dollars down, I did,' says the younger one, putting on his tie as we approach the station door.

'I seen an old lady who put in one coin and got the jackpot straight away,' says the older man in his grasshopper green jacket.

'How much?'

'Two hundred bucks.'

'I've never even seen one of those machines,' I say.

'*What? Haven't you?*'

'No. But I found ten bucks on the street.'

'That was mine,' says the young conductor suavely, not missing a beat.

A station attendant hurries along the platform carrying in his bare hands a dripping lump of ice the size of a shoe-box. We slide away to the south. The sky is covered by clouds the colour and texture of a Carr's table water biscuit. So alienated from the world does one become on a train, as afternoon draws into evening, that one is not entirely sure through which window to look for the sunset.

'Mum, are all the trains getting old now?'

'I don't know, dear.'

'Mum, when trains get too old to go, what do they do with them?'

'Shhh. Shhh. Sit down. Shhh.'

1982

Beggars in New York

In 1993, when I worked for a semester at New York University, I was standing one morning at the corner of Seventh and Christopher waiting for the lights, holding in my hand a plastic bag containing a sweater I had just bought. I was dreaming about the word *merino*, how it sounds Spanish but always makes me think happily of the bleached grasslands of Western Victoria. So, when a man's voice murmured something in my ear, I was not prepared.

I jumped and looked around. It was a young black man. He looked me right in the eyes and said again, huskily: 'Can you give me some money so I can buy something to eat?' Before I could even think, I felt my face snap shut and my eyes go blank. I didn't speak. I turned and walked quickly away.

Halfway across the avenue, shame struck. It had a hollowing effect. What had, a moment ago, been me was now an arrangement of warm, newish clothes encasing a me-shaped moral vacuum, just a volume of air in the centre of which floated a shrivelled heart, hard as a nut.

You'd think that the entire housed, fed and employed population of New York would be walking around hollow like this, a host of echoing voids wrapped in impervious skins. But the relationship between the housed and the homeless of the city is much more complex than this. It's a subtle dance of surprise, challenge, demand, seduction; and its fluidity springs from the imaginations and personalities of the beggars, from their various styles of appeal, as well as from the constant fluctuations of guilt in the begged-from.

Mood is everything. Each encounter takes place in a rich context which neither partner can control or predict. Timing, facial expression, tone of voice all matter—also how deep your purse is stowed in your bag, and whether you can be bothered, at that precise moment, dragging it up to the surface.

For example. One lunchtime, I bought a cheese roll at a deli and went for a walk. When I opened the bag, I found that the roll was stuffed with half a dozen slices of cheddar, a week's ration—no way could I gulp down such a quantity. I culled it and ate one piece in the roll. This left me with five slices of perfectly good cheddar in a paper bag. What to do?

Along Sixth Avenue I trotted, carrying my little burden. The fact of having something to give away, something I *wanted* to give away, paralysed me with shame and awkwardness. What if I misread somebody's signals? What if I copped a scornful knock-back? What if a black person laughed at me?

As it happened, the first beggar I came to was white. He was a young man with long, tangled hair, sitting in lotus position against a building with his hands resting lightly on his knees, and he was chanting, with his head thrown back in histrionic ecstasy, 'Jee-sus! Jee-sus! Jee-sus!' In front of him, he had propped a cardboard sign that said, 'I'm hungry.' I stopped. He kept on chanting. I waited. After a few moments, he became aware of my presence and opened his eyes. I held out my paper bag to him and said, 'Would you like this?'

An irritable look crossed his face. He clicked his tongue, reached out one hand for the bag, and peered into it with his neck on the aggrieved angle of a child expecting a boring birthday present. He dropped the bag on to the pavement beside him and, without another glance at me, resumed his posture and his chant.

I slunk away in a ferment. Had I expected *gratitude*? How

grotesque. But still, I felt cheated of something. The encounter was unresolved.

One night, as I was travelling uptown to a concert, a black man in bedraggled clothes and broken shoes worked my subway car. People heard him coming, and became intensely interested in the patch of floor between their feet. The woman beside me addressed a very intellectual question to her companion, and he answered with gusto: this manoeuvre gave them somewhere to look other than at the beggar, who came sidling along the carriage, pouring out his accusing monologue: 'Can't anybody gimme some money? I ain't eaten.'

No response.

'How can I get a job and become a member of society if I ain't got no money to eat?'

Good question but no one moved.

'Well,' he said with a heavy sigh. 'I guess this must be my day to *die*.'

'Jesus,' muttered the woman next to me. 'This is a bit over the top.'

It had worked on somebody, though: I heard a jingle of coin. A ripple of relief ran through the carriage. No one looked up to see who had cracked. Our feelings towards that person would have been too complicated to express in one glance: thankfulness, for having been let off the hook, but also a tinge of contempt. Soft touch. Mug. This is ethically appalling but psychologically fascinating. The beggar's style was wrong. All he provoked was irritation and boredom. He could not make us like him. Something about him soured what little selflessness we still had. The very sound of his voice filled people with resentful aggression.

When I came out of the concert, it was raining. I walked down Lexington to the subway. On the concrete steps to the station, a black woman was sitting, without an umbrella, on a folded sheet of cardboard, fully exposed to the drizzle. She heard me coming and held up a cupped hand to me, with a smile of quiet, charming sweetness, and murmured a plea. Perhaps it was her manner, or the music I had just heard, or the rain: without a thought, I pulled out a note and pushed it into her cup.

I jumped on to the first carriage whose door opened and sat down. My Gahd! It was like a party. The car was full of people talking loudly in different languages. Everybody seemed to have been drinking. A white man who hadn't shaved for days borrowed my pencil to write down his phone number for someone. A moment later, he plonked down beside me, reeking of beer. 'Don't be scared,' he said. 'Who's the ex-cop on the subway?—the guy sitting next to you! I'm a member of the Merchant Marines. I'm a devout Catholic! So don't be scared.'

The door at the end of the carriage flew open and a beggar strode in. He was black, with dreadlocks and in rags, but his face was shining. Talk stopped. Instead of hiding their eyes, though, people looked up at him. He struck a pose, beamed round the carriage and began to sing. Close to his waist he was holding not a dirty paper cup, the traditional New York begging receptacle, but a little, brown, round, woven, African-looking basket: the shape of it gave you an urge to put something into it.

He moved along the carriage between the passengers' outstretched legs, not proffering the little basket, just carrying it near his waist with both hands. He was surfing down the car on the wave of his own voice. People gazed up at him while they burrowed in their pockets and bags. When he broke into 'Hooked on a Feeling', a white boy sprang up and joined in; the beggar beamed and hi-fived him. The whole motley crowd of us burst out laughing. Any minute now, we would all get to our feet and start dancing and twirling and clapping our hands. Money flew through the air.

It seems so unfair. What does it mean? That even so low on the ladder of fortune, charm and sweetness of nature are rewarded? Or does it illustrate that unbearable remark from the Bible, which preachers have such a hard time explaining: 'To him that hath it shall be given, and from him that hath not it shall be taken away'?

1994

Marriage

At the old Royal Mint in Melbourne, where civil marriages are celebrated, it is hard to be an inconspicuous observer, for many of the wedding parties are small, some no bigger than four all told, and although I take my place at the very back of the huge Victorian room, wearing what I hope is an unobtrusive black suit, I can't help worrying that my spectre will show up in the background of the photos, a small grim figure with a notebook and a cold. Who was that woman? I feel I have turned into the Fairy Blackstick herself: sceptical, ironic, but still I hope, benevolent.

There's a cold wind and a weak sun on this Saturday morning. The Mint car park has savage little square speed-humps, and the building is still shut tight at nine o'clock. The pretty garden at the back has a sign that says, 'No confetti to be thrown in or outside this building'. The plane trees do not observe man-made rules and are letting their big claw-like leaves lie about all over the grass. Round and round the building I roam, keeping my hands inside my cuffs, looking for an open door. One has an unfortunate sign, which must have occasioned its share of manly jocularity: 'Please enter: Sentencing Committee'. I peep through a window into an office. Some wag has tacked up a poster saying, 'Cows may come and cows may go but the BULL in this place goes on forever!'

Nobody around. I lean over the stone wall and find myself looking down on Little Lonsdale Street. I see a couple emerge from the front door of the Peter MacCallum Cancer Institute opposite. The young woman has a white dressing over one eye. Her husband is leading her by the hand. She is wearing a parka: her arms are not in the sleeves but the hood is on her head. She is weakened, stepping feebly. Her mouth is set in a line. Soberly he opens the back door of the car and helps her in. All this is done without a word or a glance passing between them: they have been here before. *In sickness and in health.* They drive away. Two parking officers chalk the tyre of the Alsco Linen van parked in front of the hospital.

The Mint doors have opened. The first wedding party has arrived, and is gathering its forces in the lobby. A little boy cranes his neck at the ceiling. 'How hoi is it?' he asks. His mother doesn't answer. She is a beefy woman in a synthetic dress and high-heeled ankle-strap sandals. She is getting her camera ready for the bride. The boy, bored, trots off to the splendid staircase and scales the ornate banister. 'Giddown off there,' says his mother without looking up, 'or I'll smack you down.'

Ah! the bride. Her tender face. Her name is Kerry and she is marrying a man called Sergio. She and her attendants are carrying ethereal little bouquets. She gives instructions in a quiet, pleasant voice. They are waiting for the men. A few children cluster round the bride, getting in the way of the photographers of both families. 'Now can we have this little devil out of the way?' says another strapping member of the sylph-like Kerry's family, smiling through clenched teeth.

How short a civil ceremony is! The celebrant, a Maltese Australian with serious eyes, a sweet expression, and the faint remnants of an accent, does his best to make it warm: he manages to utter formal phrases like 'solemn and binding nature' and 'by being in a prohibited relationship' as if they were drawn from the vernacular.

Australians are not much good at ceremonial behaviour. We have no public graces. An event seems to be that which a camera may record. There must be half a dozen of the big photographers now, galumphing about in their unsafe shoes, snapping from this angle and that, bridling and whinnying.

Sergio's grandparents sit quietly on their chairs.

The best man has a plain, naughty face: he is curly-headed and cheerful, with a mobile mouth and lively eyes, the kind of man who has looked like a grown-up since he was ten. He keeps wanting to laugh out of sheer high spirits. He grins and nods at everyone, including the Fairy Blackstick, who mentally crosses him off her hit list.

The high room echoes, even to the shy voices of Kerry and Sergio as they make each other vows which, on paper, are so breathtaking in their solemnity and import that if any of those present should turn their full attention to what is being so lightly promised, they might be unable to hold back a cry of warning.

But it's done, and now the kissing starts. Kerry has been around Italians long enough to pick up the habit of kissing on both cheeks. She is flushed and charming. Sergio wipes a cousin's lipstick off his face, turns to one of his large female in-laws and asks, 'What' appened to Kev's van?'

There is nothing worse than a wedding for bringing witnesses out in a rash of sentimentality. Even crabby old Fairy Blackstick in the back row gets a lump in her throat, ten times for the ten marriages. What struggles have the protagonists gone through to arrive at this point? And what further battles lie ahead of them?

Some have made the booking and don't turn up. Today it's a real estate agent and a boutique manageress, both divorced and living at the same address. Was it a whim half acted upon? 'Looks like a no-show,' says the celebrant. 'Actually you'd be surprised at the number of couples who put the same address on the documents.' This is the way the world is going—at least for people who marry at the registry office.

Some couples (though none today) shock even the celebrant with the inappropriateness of their union. 'I remember one couple,' he says, 'or rather, I'll never forget them. The lady was beautiful, but the man was an absolute pig.'

'On Saturdays,' says the official Mint photographer, 'they're usually pretty good. But during the week you get all kinds. No shoes. One goes this way afterwards, the other goes that way. All kinds. But it's improving.'

Once the thrill of watching strangers sign their lives away has worn off, there remains the feast of tiny human dramas available to any idler in a public place.

A divorced woman remarries, with her small daughters behind her. The woman's face is as stiff as a schoolgirl's with shyness and nerves. She is wearing a really chic suit; pinned in her hair is a piece of pink fluff like what comes in a box with an Easter egg, and she has fixed to her lapel a dashing little twist of net, as if to symbolise the veil she wore the first time round. When she turns and smiles at her girls, she screws up her face and sticks out her tongue as embarrassed children do. The girls, in tartan and pearls, try to sing 'Here Comes the Bride', but nobody joins in and they fade out after the first few notes. A relative takes a picture. The girls stand cheerfully in front: 'Bob down! Bob down!' cries the photographer.

The drama of the exchange of rings is often dissolved in the comedy of having to push hard to get them over the knuckle.

Two Uruguayans. Their names are fabulously, polysyllabically, mythologically beautiful. The room is suddenly warm and noisy, overflowing with handsome women in jewellery and furs and heartbreaking young men in bomber jackets, one of whom sidles up to the celebrant and says to him in a stage whisper, 'Listen—lock the door, or he'll run away.'

Two Australian divorcees, both getting on for forty. The man keeps looking round with a goofy grin. He gets through his statement with difficulty, then turns to his friends and says, 'Phew!'

Equality of the sexes has entered even the wording of the marriage vow: 'man and wife' has become 'husband and wife', and there is no talk of anyone having to obey anyone else. But a peculiar rite persists: the institution of The Kiss. 'John, you may now kiss the bride.' It is usually the signal (among Australians, anyway) for a burst of awkward merriment, of adolescent guffaws and even of risque comments *sotto voce*. I'm sorry, but it's the men who show this extraordinary reaction. When you think about it, though, to kiss in public, to join mouths, is an astonishingly intimate thing to do. And to do it again, at the request of the inevitable slow-thinking photographer—oh là là!

A young German, tall, broad-shouldered, dressed in a subtly coloured jacket and leather trousers, repeats the statement after the celebrant: his accent does something strange to the words, and as he says 'to be my luffly wedded wife' he stares at her as if he can't really believe that this is what he is required to say. They kiss. 'That's enough,' says a man's voice from the crowd.

A bloke with a stud in one ear marries a woman in a crown of flowers. When he kisses her there is a laugh then one or two claps…a pause…then a boy in the back row, wearing ripple-soled suede shoes, calls out, 'Yay!' and they all applaud. The groom turns round and opens his arms to his friends. 'OK, folks!' he cries. 'Let's pardy!'

And now two Asian students approach the desk. They look alarmingly young. Can this be wise? They have no wedding party, only an Australian couple in their sixties, the woman in a great deal of pancake and blusher and a lairy fur jacket. Is she his landlady? She seems fond of the young man, who says to the celebrant as he stumbles over the pronunciations, 'I use Shane as my Christian name.'

'Just marry them,' says the landlady, 'before they change their minds.'

Shane's knees are making fast little rhythmic jerks inside his neat trousers. From my angle I can see the bride's chubby cheekbones go up and out, again and again, as she smiles and giggles. Shane kisses her enthusiastically, before he is told he may. Everyone laughs. While the landlady and her friend sign the papers, the new couple compare their rings and giggle.

The landlady's friend, a punter in a snap-brim hat, does his level best to make conversation in the awkward pause that follows the formalities. 'You're from Sarawak, are you?' he says.

Shane nods, looking eager.

'It's on the other side—of—um—Borneo, isn't it. I was at Labuan. During the war. It's off the coast of Borneo. Near Brunei.'

'Course,' says the landlady, wanting to keep the conversation on marriage, 'during the war a lot of Australian girls wanted to marry American soldiers. Before they could leave the country.' She gives a shrill laugh.

Shane and the bride, puzzled, nod and nod, never losing their eager smiles. They all shuffle towards the door, with the celebrant in attendance. The jollifications of the next wedding party can be heard in the hall outside. The Fairy Blackstick can't bear the tension. I step forward to open the heavy door for them, but they see me coming and think I work here, that I'm part of the deal: they welcome my approach with beaming smiles, and put out their hands to shake mine. The celebrant, a *really nice man*, is grinning at me from behind the ill-assorted four. We shake hands all round and I say, keeping my notebook behind my back, 'Congratulations! I hope you'll be very happy!'

'Thank you!' they say.

I open the door, I wave goodbye, I wish them luck, and I mean it!—I do! I do!

1986

Death

WITH A BURIAL, what you see is what you get. Body in box, box in hole, earth on top. Jews understand the worth of a real burial—not just a few symbolic clods and walk away, but mourners pass the shovel from hand to hand, fill the hole right to the top, cry out loud while the job is done slowly and with physical effort; and who can fail then to feel the grave as a bed, a fine and private place, into which the dead one has been tenderly laid, then covered as a child is tucked in under blankets, and left to sleep?

With a cremation you get a curtain drawn between the weeping and the fate of the body. People must have wanted this at some stage, or it wouldn't be the industry it is. But isn't there a curiosity we feel is morbid, a longing to know what happens to the coffin after it clunks down and out of sight? What weird ideas do we brood on? I told a friend of mine—in her forties, intelligent, worldly, witty, who's held my hand at more than one funeral—that I'd spent a day at Melbourne's Springvale crematorium.

'Oh, don't tell me,' she said with a shiver. 'They cut the body up into pieces, don't they.'

'Oh no!' I said, astonished. I told her what I'd seen. She listened. When I'd finished she gave a sigh.

'What you said makes me feel better,' she said.

The funny thing is that anyone could go out there and find out what they want to know.

'You can look at anything you like here,' says the manager.

'Otherwise you get the hidden mysteries.'

'The what?'

'The mysteries. The unknown.'

He shows me the layout of the place—the huge garden, the four chapels, the furnace room—then goes back to his office and leaves me to my own devices. This surprises me: I'd expected to be kept under surveillance and given a laundered view of events. I feel like a kid suddenly given more freedom that it knows what to do with. I know what I really want to see, but I am embarrassed by my curiosity which I still cannot help feeling is *morbid*, so I go for a long walk round the garden, through the enormous cemetery.

It is a cool, sparkling morning. A couple of the gardeners, full-blown eccentrics with unidentifiable European accents, corner me and bash my ear. One of them tells me a long and comical story with actions.

'One day I was raking,' he says. 'Like this. And I saw on the ground, just near the tap, a black handbag. It had an address, a hundred and seventy-five dollars and a pension cheque. I took it to the boss. Other blokes they say, Eddy, why didn't you take the money and dig the bag into the garden? No one will know. I say, No, honesty is the best thing in this world. There *is* no honesty in this world.

'Some time later she comes out, a lady, she says to me, Are you Eddy? I say, Lady, I am Eddy but I don't know you. She says, You found my handbag. She gives me an envelope. I start to walk away, I say, Lady, I don't need anything. I don't need your envelope. But she runs after me—and she's not young—fifty-eight or sixty—and she sticks the envelope in my back pocket, here, this one—I didn't even feel it go in, I was walking away. But later I find it in my pocket, and there's five dollars in it.'

His colleague, a freckled man in a towelling hat, wheeling a barrow and whistling with expert trills, shows me a little area where the gravestones are decorated with artistic and fanciful sculptures. He is content to draw my attention to them but Eddy hurries up to interpret them for me.

'Some people spend seventeen thousand dollars on a memorial. See? This is all bronze. They come out and put a kind of wox—a yelly—on it. See this? This is the *Mona Lisa*. See the little dove on her hand? And what do you reckon this means? A river? Course it's not a river! It means—the ocean! Crossing the ocean.

'And these? Yes! It's a choir of angels! You look at it from over there. Makes a nice effect, don't you think? One day someone came out and put a lighted cigarette in their mouths. It dropped—see these marks? Tsk tsk. Oh, she was wild.'

This is highly entertaining but not what I have come for. I find myself drawn back towards the chapels and to the furnaces: where the action is. The first funerals have begun and I stand at the back of one of the chapels listening to the limp-backed tributes that are being paid by a minister to a man he never met. We have to get paid functionaries to do even our speaking for us. What a pathetic, stiff, frightened lot we are.

I go outside and loiter between the chapels in the sun. I am longing to go back to the furnace room but I'm scared. Scared of what? Not of what I'll see, but of *what people will think*. What people? *I* don't know. Anyone who sees me. They'll think I've got a sick mind. They'll think…

I am saved from this nonsense by a man from the furnace room, to whom the manager introduced me an hour ago before the fires had been lit. He's wearing his uniform of maroon blazer and grey trousers, but on his feet are Frye boots and his hands are tattooed. He sees me dawdling with intent, strides up to me and gets straight to the point. 'Do you want to come and have another look?'

He takes me through a little door marked 'Private'.

Oddly, this is the most shocking moment of the day, this

one quick step from the outside world of colour—sun and leaves—into the monochrome of the furnace room. I panic, my legs go weak, I think, *It's the gas chambers, it's the underworld, I can't write this, only a photographer could show this place as it is, it's made of dust, there's no blood, everything's a shade of pale grey, the huge ovens are grey, the walls and floor are grey, the workers are grey, the air is grey. I'm not going to faint but I'm going to lose control of my bowels.*

This does not happen. The shock lasts two seconds and passes, and I see I am in a long cement-coloured area that must link the business ends of the four chapels which are built in pairs, back to back. Men are walking about. There is a low roaring sound.

My guide gives me a sharp look. 'You don't mind seeing the actual…umm…'

'No! That's what I'm here for.'

He nods, and leads me to the end furnace. I think they call them cremators in the official brochures, but a furnace is what it is, huge, wide and tall, like a giant pizza oven.

My guide opens a door, like the door of an old fuel stove, only bigger, and I bend over to look in. First, with relief, I see colour, the only colour in the place—orange flames—and then the small end of a coffin. The heat is so tremendous that everything wavers: the coffin is covered with a network of fine cracks, its surface reminds me of an old porcelain jug in an op shop, with a glaze that's covered in lines while the china's still in one piece underneath.

I've never been so curious in my life. I want to stare and stare. As I look, squinting against the heat (they burn at between eight hundred and a thousand degrees Celsius) the end of the coffin goes *pouf!* and disintegrates. I can see two burning lumps. I gape. What I am looking at is *a man's feet*. In the heat of their consumption they turn slightly, almost gracefully, as if he were moving to a more comfortable position in bed.

I don't see them as pink human *feet*, you understand, with skin and heels and toes, but as two shimmering dark-centred objects of flame, which the context instructs me can only be feet. This is not the slightest bit horrible or disgusting. I am not aware of any smell.

Perhaps this wonder I am feeling is a very exaggerated version of that dreamy hypnosis that comes over us when we stare into a fire of wood, or coal. Why are we so drawn to fire? It's the spectacle of matter being transformed. And that's what I'm seeing here.

My guide glances at me. I'm struck dumb. All I can think to say is 'Wow'. He nods again. The rest of the coffin loses form and collapses. What I can see now is a sort of humped, curved lump: it is his torso, the line of his spine, the bulky part of his body. 'The feet take only a few minutes,' says my guide. 'The head goes last. The oil burner's aimed at the head and the torso. They're the hardest parts of the body to burn.'

He closes the door and leads me to the next furnace. Here a body has been consumed and a man is about to rake out the top section of the burning chamber to allow what they call the CRs, the cremated remains, to fall through a grille into a lower part, for collection. I can see a long bone, a femur, pale and dry-looking. 'The thigh-bone's connected to the kneebone,' I foolishly think, but nothing's connected to anything any more, all the links have been burned away and the furnace floor is covered with ordinary-looking ash in which the few bones, fragile and ready to be crushed, lie about as naturally as if they had been bleached not by fire but by a pure desert sun.

The man is raking and raking and the crumbly ash tumbles down into the under chamber.

Like a lot of people, I used to think that when the coffin disappeared behind the curtain in the chapel it was devoured instantly by flames, as if the chapel were built astride a hell where fire forever raged.

Of course, it's not like that at all. My guide takes me up some steps to a concrete area like a garage, open at one end to the garden. Here we stand and wait. A red light on the wall goes off. This means that a service is over and a coffin is on its way out of the chapel. It heaves into view, thickly encrusted with flowers. A young man in jeans and runners tips the bouquets off into a wheelbarrow and briskly takes hold of the coffin. He straps it to a metal arrangement of rails, a kind of overhead conveyor belt. We go down the stairs again and I see the coffin go sliding smoothly above our heads on its elevated track. Down and round it goes to the furnace room, where it is unstrapped and put to wait its turn outside one of the furnace doors.

The burning goes on all day. Each one takes about two hours. One at a time they are consigned, burnt, raked and collected. It is possible that by the time you have driven home across town after the funeral, the coffin is already in the fire.

This is not, after all, the underworld. In one sense it is simply a place where people work. In the storage room behind the furnace section the radio is going softly on 3KZ. Someone has pinned to the bulletin board a caricature of a workmate, complete with rude message. The men in charge are obsessed with labelling, checking and checking again.

The walls are covered with shelves and on them are ranged scores of black plastic containers, each one about the size of a shoe box. These contain CRs waiting to be collected by their relatives.

'Some people never collect,' says my guide. 'We scatter them by default. Oh, after three to six months.'

A young man is working at a bench with a big electric magnet shaped like a goose's beak, or the mouth of a small dog. He plunges it into the container of CRs, works it round and round, and draws it out bristling with nails, screws and staples. 'If we didn't use the magnet,' he says, 'the metal'd break the blades of the grinder when we put the CRs through.'

My guide hands me a shallow metal container, like a tray with sides. 'That's what's left of a person,' he says. 'Not much there, is there.'

No, there is not. About the equivalent of one and a half stale hi-top loaves if you crumbled them up. It's a mixture of ash, bone and a honeycomb-like substance which I suppose is also bone, or its insides. It is a pale, greyish-fawnish-whitish colour. It looks dry, delicate, purified. 'It's completely sterile,' says my guide. I put out one finger and lightly touch the honeycomb. It's sharp. Good luck, spirit of these ashes, wherever you're travelling.

One of the men gets a box like an old-fashioned biscuit tin down of a shelf and shows it to me. It is full of metal things, all the same dull burnt brown colour, and with the same crumbled surface, like a jam tin after a bonfire. I don't know what they are, in their jumbled pile. My guide picks them up one by one and names them. 'A horse shoe. A watch. A woman's neck-chain. A war medal. The metal parts of a pocket knife. Toe caps off an old man's boots. A bottle opener. A pacemaker out of somebody's heart. A hip joint.' These objects have come though the fire. He lays each one down with care.

On a special shelf by themselves are treasures which have survived the cremation of children: a metal piggy bank with the coins still in it; a little porcelain dish with a decorative knot of china flowers on its fitted lid, the kind of thing a young girl might have on her dressing table.

'We get babies here too,' says my guide. He reaches up to a high shelf and brings down one of the plastic containers, but a very small one. He opens it and draws out a sealed plastic bag, which he shakes so that its contents slide down to one end. He holds it out to me in his palm.

'See? Hardly even a handful. The babies are stillbirths, mostly. We call 'em billies. I don't know why. That's what they called 'em when I first came to work here, and that's what

I call 'em too.' We stand in silence looking at the tiny quantity of ash in the plastic bag. He handles it gently, and nothing he says about it is sentimental.

On our way to the door he says, 'I reckon they ought to bring the gardeners in here, after they've been working here a while, and show 'em exactly what goes on. Because often you get people who come out here a few months later, when they've got over it a bit, and they ask the gardener to tell 'em what goes on and the gardener doesn't know.'

I didn't start shaking and crying till two days later.

And on my way home I had, for the first time in my life, a conviction—I mean not a thought but knowledge—that life can't possibly end at death. I had the punctuation wrong. I thought it was a full stop, but it's only a comma, or a dash—or better still, a colon: I don't believe in heaven or hell, or punishment or reward, or the survival of the ego; but what about energy, spirit, soul, imagination, love? The force for which we have no word? How preposterous, to think that it could die!

> Dry bones! Dry bones! I find my loving heart,
> Illumination brought to such a pitch
> I see the rubblestones begin to stretch
> As if reality had split apart
> And the whole motion of the soul lay bare:
> I find that love, and I am everywhere.

'The Renewal', Theodore Roethke

1986

Labour Ward, Penrith

THE LOOK, ROUND the corridors of the maternity unit at Nepean Hospital, Penrith, in Sydney's far west, is a perm on long hair. It's tights or leggings, chunky white socks, boots or running shoes, a big loose cotton top. It's a toddler plus a baby in a stroller before you're out of your teens—and often before you're married. It's *The Bold and the Beautiful*, a packet of smokes, some chips, the odd bruise. Women out here are called 'ladies'. So what? Only a fool would go to a maternity unit looking for sociology. What goes on here is elemental. Even time, behind these doors, is a different substance. A story in maternity has no beginning and no end.

Mala isn't in labour, but apparently she should be. Her blood pressure's up, and she's a fortnight overdue. It's her first baby. She's from Madras: dainty and dark and scared. Her husband is with her, backed into the curtain that's drawn around her bed. The PA is pumping out easy-listening music and frequent reports of torrential, drought-breaking rains, strong winds, a bad smash on the motorway. The labour-room wall is papered with a huge colour blow-up, peeling at the corners, of a river rushing down its rocky bed.

A young woman doctor comes streaming in, a registrar in obstetrics and gynaecology. At twenty-nine, with fine cheekbones and bobbed fair hair, Linda wouldn't look out of place in a Bloomsbury movie, but her accent and her directness are broad Australian. She whips back the sheet. Mala's brown belly gleams in the dim light. 'What did you grow such a big baby for?' says Linda cheerfully. 'Little people can hide big babies. Flop your knees. Loosen the muscles. Good.' Her gaze, while she internally examines Mala, gets lost between bed and wall: her fingers are connecting directly with her mind.

Mala lets out a grunt and her husband steps in closer. Her tiny feet with their pale soles stretch and go crisp with pain. 'Good girl,' says Linda, stripping off her blood-specked glove out of sight. 'We'll put cream in to start your labour slowly. I'll see you in six hours.' Mala's husband takes her hand. You can tell from the look they exchange that he's a stayer.

Linda's offsider is Nik, twenty-six, a freckled and bearded young resident with a strong Liverpool accent. They forge out together along the halls to theatre, where another first-time mother, Sharon, is booked for a caesarean.

'Are you gonna cut or am I?' says Nik.

'You,' says Linda. 'You said you would.'

Nik looks nervous but resolute. 'As long as you're not hoping for any kind of *speed*.'

Sharon on her trolley sweeps in through the milky plastic door-flaps. The theatre hums with fanatical cleanliness and order. Faces vanish behind masks, leaving only eyes to carry expression and signals. A midwife stands ready by the table, her arms and hands swathed in green sterile cloth. Linda and Nik, scrubbed up and gloved in translucent rubber, step in and face each other across Sharon's great belly, which is laid bare and swabbed with brown fluid.

'Make it *bold*,' says Linda.

Nik leans forward with the scalpel, obscuring Sharon's body with his green-clad back. Five minutes of intense, working silence. 'OK,' announces Nik loudly. 'I'm roopturing the membranes. Stand back.' Everybody flinches and leans away. A ropy stream of cloudy yellow fluid shoots into the air on an angle and splatters the floor.

Again, the absorbed silence. 'The cord's round its neck,'

says someone. From the ruck of backs round Sharon the baby soars up in a pair of gloved hands: a tiny, lavender-tinged, cream-blotched, clenched-up boxer. The midwife seizes it in her draped hands and arms, and steps fast and smooth across the room to the resuscitation trolley, a breast-high, tilted little shrine, indented at its lower end to take the baby's head.

The room has split in two.

They are clearing the baby's airways. 'Come on, kiddo,' says a woman's urgent voice. There's a faint, muffled squall, a choke, a gurgle. Someone polishes the creature with a soft cloth. Deftly it is swaddled into an intricate white parcel, so stiff that the midwife can hold it up vertical. The baby's minute face, eyes squinched shut, shows in the top corner of the triangle like that of a wee buddha. 'See you later, guys,' says the midwife in a squeaky baby's voice. The plastic door flops shut behind her.

Meanwhile, Nik is suturing the cut in Sharon's uterus, under the fiercely watchful eye of his teacher, Linda. Their faces are damp inside the perspex masks; Nik's is fogged like a windscreen, large drops trickle down inside. He is wielding, with forceps, a mean-looking curved needle, forcing it into springy tissue and drawing it through, tying off and snipping each stitch separately. Linda guides his hand. Once she takes the needle from him and demonstrates, tugging a stitch firmly into a beautiful knot. Soon the interior incision looks as neat and tight as a shark's mouth.

Between it and the outer cut there's a layer of fat in globules; it looks like small creamy grapes, or corn on a cob. Linda checks the ovaries: two pale, glossy beans. 'Let's get up speed now, Nik,' she says. He works his needle carefully along the border of the wound. Linda keeps pressing and steering his gloved, bloody hand with hers, teaching by touch. He's got the knack of it now, though his hand still trembles slightly as he works. Two nurses count the swabs aloud in unison. Sharon's body is already closed.

A nurse presses down on Sharon's flaccid belly. Out between her legs oozes a little stream of bloody fluid. She twitches. She is coming to. They run a sucker round inside her mouth, clap an oxygen mask over her face, and wheel her away.

'Linda's a *gweat* teacher,' says Nik earnestly, climbing out of his theatre gear. Linda laughs: 'It's hard to keep my hands off.' Nik's still a bit shaky, but by the time they get to the lobby where Sharon's husband and extended family are gathered, he's beaming. 'It's my twelfth grandchild!' cries a grey-haired woman, grabbing his hand. The lift door opens and an old man in a pale-blue cardigan and battered bush hat joins the group. His brown face is alive with feeling, but restrained with a sort of irony. He doesn't speak, but stands just outside the excited circle, chin on one fist, head cocked and eyebrows raised.

In neonatal intensive you can spot Sharon's daughter without needing to read the label. She already looks like a person: her squarish head, her hair growing in flat curls. Her name is Zoe, and apart from low blood sugar, she's doing fine.

Nik fills in forms as they walk to the kiosk for a coffee. Someone passes them, heading for the kids' ward, carrying a wire cage with a great big fruit bat in it. 'Must be a new way of taking blood,' quips Nik, recovering his bounce.

Linda sprawls at the cafe table in her white gown, one foot up on a chair. 'Phew,' she says, 'I'm slowing down. Trouble is, once you stop, you settle.' Outside, the wind has dropped. The sky has cleared. Linda heaves a sigh. 'You work these incredible hours,' she says, 'with the threat hanging over you that you'll make a mistake. It's such an intense world, in here. And then you stop and look out the window and see this…calm.'

Her beeper goes off. She drags herself to her feet. A young woman in casualty is miscarrying. Linda is on her way. The pace at which doctors travel! Not haste so much as a surging, forward motion, without pause or hesitation: on, on, on.

Mala is leaning back in an armchair now, her head tilted to one side, her eyes closed, one arm raised over her head in a dramatic gesture of abandon. Her husband is right by her. 'She's got the look,' murmurs Linda. The PA is still raving, some terrible seventies guitar solo. Mala moans. Her voice is very soft and mild, even when it's high with pain. 'Good,' says Linda. 'Good strong pains. That's what we want.' Even from outside the labour room, from the nurses' station, Mala's voice can be heard, rising and falling, light, rapt, strained.

On the front porch of the maternity unit, half a dozen young women in hospital nighties are fagging away. One of them has a black eye. A sign listing the hospital's interpreter services has been defaced: the languages most savagely scratched out are Macedonian, Serbian and Croat. Someone has sticky-taped to the glass door a message: PIZZA MAN WE WILL BE HERE AT 2.40 OK. WAIT FOR US WE ARE HUNGARY THANX. An old woman is tenderly helped down the steps by a scrawny, wild-looking girl with multiple skin-piercings. The old woman is saying to her, 'It gets worse. It gets worse. The grief gets worse.'

In the canteen the doctors sit together. They eat sandwiches, fruit, yoghurt. Nik recites from memory a long comic poem he has composed, in severe classical metre and rhyme, about a hungover doctor trying to deliver a baby. Between stanzas his face adopts a special expression that discourages interruption. Linda and three male doctors laugh and applaud. At a nearby table, a nurse opens up her sandwich and stuffs it with hot chips. Linda speaks with longing about her two-year-old son at home: her face, a striking mixture of delicacy and toughness, turns soft when she mentions her husband and her child. The others stare blankly out the window at the eucalypts while they chew. A beeper goes off. Five doctors dive for their belts, in curved, two-handed plunging gestures, as graceful as if they were dancing.

Midwives are the sort of people you'd be glad to see come striding through the door in an emergency. Doctors too, of course—but while doctors can seem driven and head-tripping, midwives have the relaxed physical confidence of sportswomen. With their slow, wide-swinging gait, they radiate capable calm. Their professional mode is unflappability.

In delivery suite they mill about their big station with its desks and computer and filing cabinets. They are forever drawing up rosters and equipment order lists: 'Can we please please please please *please* get some smaller cannulas? I've rung and rung and *rung*.' The fluorescent light is harsh and wearing. At times the foetal monitor in one of the rooms is turned up so loud, to reassure a labouring woman, that it thuds through the nurses' station like a funky bass-line. Otherwise, the PA faithfully seeps out tired old hits. After a couple of days in here, you not only get used to the radio but start to like it—even to depend on it. It's better than muzak. It's an infusion of the outside world, which is in danger of being forgotten, in all this intensity. Day and night lose meaning, here. What land is this? You could be anywhere.

Midwife Sandy, square-set, short-haired, ironic, does a boppy dance-step between desk and shelf. Listening to an account of Nik's triumphant caesar, she remarks dryly, 'I was pleased to learn, in general training, that *even thin women* have globules of fat.'

From labour room number six comes a low, strangled cry. Everyone looks up. Sandy walks steadily and without haste towards the room. The woman's cries intensify, breaking as they go up the scale, the way Ricki Lee Jones sings. The other midwives go on talking and joking, grumbling as nurses will about people who *don't put things back.*

A harsh rising howl bursts from room six. Tremendous grunts of effort and strain. A pause. Then—so quick!—the choking, protesting, stuttering squall of a new-born baby. What amazes and moves a stranger is all in a day's work, round here.

And outside, it turns out, there *is* still an ordinary world. As the sun goes down over the immense, rain-puddled carparks of Penrith, the air fills with the aroma of grilling meat. In the 6 p.m. queue at the Sizzler, the madly excited small son of two recent Polish immigrants clambers up the barricade and peers over it at the scores of tables. 'Ai caramba!' he shouts to his embarrassed parents in perfect Bart Simpsonese, 'this place is packed!' The waitress offers a choice of seats: near the salad bar, or the window. 'Lots of people,' she says helpfully, 'prefer to sit near the window. To keep an eye on their car.' Coaches roar up to the Penrith Panthers Leagues Club and disgorge troops of touring Japanese. The pokies whirr late into the night. At breakfast time a solitary gambler is still slumped on a stool, confronting his fate in the machine.

At eight in the morning Linda, too, is sitting alone, with her bare arms resting on the cold formica in the delivery suite tearoom. She's been on call all night. One of her socks is twisted, its heel poking out over the top of her shoe. She is coughing, her skin is pearly with exhaustion, a cold sore on her lip is daubed with cream. But her eyes are lively and she's smiling.

'I sectioned Mala at three-thirty,' she croaks. 'We bailed out. She got too tired. She'd had enough. We were a well-oiled team. Got baby out in two minutes. Twenty-seven minutes go to whoa. The midwives were fantastic. They gave me a hot pack and I went to sleep curled round it.'

Mala, upstairs in a ward, is tired and weak. Her husband is still at her side. Their baby son, in a crib near her bed, writhes in his sleep. His long nails scrape the pillow. The change, the deepening in Mala's face is sobering. Yesterday a girl, today a woman. Her face, as Patrick White once put it, has 'received the fist'. She is sorry, her husband courteously explains, but she can't eat the hospital food. Linda is gentle with her: 'the first day is the worst day'. She checks the wound. No problem there. The husband is concerned because at home they've got too many steps.

Out in the hall, Linda says, 'I'm anxious about Mala. She seems flat. No sense of pleasure in the baby. Hope it's not post-natal depression coming on—the signs of it are so subtle. And her community sees itself as a very closed one. With Hindus, the caste problem makes it kind of delicate even to choose an interpreter, when we need one. We'd like to help, but we feel we can't intrude into their lives.' Later that afternoon Mala's husband, head bowed, carrying an airways bag, trudges down the hospital drive, going home alone.

Downstairs in delivery suite, a box of special new protective glasses has arrived. Midwives and doctors jostle for the coolest styles and model them, to each other's mockery. 'Vanity, thy name is Nik,' says another resident crossly. The big doors from the hall burst open and a wheelchair zooms in. Everyone stands up. They know her. It's Melissa. She's having twins. Her waters broke four days ago, seven weeks prematurely, and she's been in a ward, waiting. Her husband and two girlfriends follow her chair into the labour room.

Inside, the room is breathless with surprise. The two friends, very bright-eyed, keep doubling over with excited laughter. 'Youse have had kids,' Melissa tells them solemnly. 'Youse know what's gonna happen.'

Linda examines her: fully dilated, but with no urge to push. Her husband, in the peaked cap, old boots and deep reddish tan of an outdoor worker, can't find a spot in the room where he's at ease. Under his tan he's pale. He keeps smiling but his lips are pressed together. They've already got two girls at home: oh, how they want a boy.

Melissa's bare feet knot in a contraction. She starts to breathe and blow, like a swimmer. 'Action stations!' calls Linda. Two resuscitation trolleys glide into the room. Linda and Nik put on their new protective glasses. The room is filling up with people. The midwives stand still with folded arms: they are used to waiting.

'Ow,' says Melissa. 'Ow ow ow *ow.*' Her husband gives a histrionic shudder and turns his back. The foetal monitor is turned up. The babies' heartbeats sound feathery and yet deep: an intimate, steady, authoritative throbbing.

'I can't lay on this side,' says Melissa. 'Sorry.'

'Beanbag!' calls Linda. Melissa leans back on it, belly bare, legs apart, an awkward, powerless posture. Her face ripples with expressions of comical self-deprecation. She looks focused on something that no one else can see or hear. Her hair lies flat against her head. She's stripped down for action. She's not scared, but she's respectful—preparing herself for what's about to go rampaging through her. A gust of stifled chatter and laughter breaks out among the midwives: it's like being at a party, or an outing to watch the sun rise.

'Shhh,' says Linda. 'Bend your legs, Melissa, and give us a push.'

Melissa's face is white. The skin around her eyes darkens, her gaze gets blanker. Between her contractions, a watchful quietness fills the room. A green flourish as the doctors robe up and the sterile tray is opened. One of Melissa's girlfriends holds her hand and tickles her inner arm with her fingertips. 'I'm uncomfortable?' says Melissa. 'On m' back? I need to lay differently?' She turns on to her right side and lies with her bent legs open like scissors, in running position. She's giving little rhythmic sighs with a touch of voice in them: ah, ha, ah, ah.

The composition of figures in this room might have been

arranged by a mediaeval painter. There must be a dozen witnesses gathered round the labouring woman, in attitudes of alert waiting, all turned inward to her, focused on her and the immense power she's host to. And yet at the same time it's all completely casual: it's work.

Linda, in sterile gown, gloves and glasses, sits half-stunned with fatigue on a chair beside Melissa's bed; the tip of her nose is pink, her eyes are glazed with waiting. With each contraction Melissa starts to breathe deeper. Each breath becomes a groan. Between groans, though, she is calm, almost conversational. 'Give a little push,' says Linda. 'Does that feel better?'

'Yes.'

'Means you're ready to push. Put your legs up, Melissa, and give us a bit of a push.'

Her husband leans against the wall. His booted foot taps in a fast, nervous rhythm. Melissa's on her back now, with her legs sharply bent up and her chin right down on her chest. With each contraction she strains downwards. Her face screws itself up, she bares her teeth with the force of it.

'Keep it coming,' says Linda. 'Make those pushes last about ten seconds.'

'OK,' says Melissa, in a voice faint with the desire to co-operate—but she is in control here, it's her team, she is the star. Her single-mindedness is awe-inspiring.

Another push. 'Chin on chest, Melissa. *Hold* it, Melissa. *Use* it all. Fantastic, Melissa. Well done.' They are urging her to the best of her strength, calling to her loudly, as if she were somewhere else, far away, needing to be shouted to across some divide. A small dark hole between her bent-up legs starts to expand and broaden. Her husband clutches at himself and giggles anxiously. 'Hold your breath like you're taking a dive,' says a midwife. Melissa's friend strokes the hair back off her sweating face. Melissa calls out her husband's name.

'I'm here!' he shouts, pressed against the wall.

'Get angry,' says Linda. 'You're backing away from the pain. Get mad. *Fight.*' Melissa shoves tremendously, silent, resolute, efficient. The dark hole between her legs keeps getting bigger. Surely it can never be big enough—can there be room? But yes—it's the top of the baby's head, you can see the curve of it, and someone grabs a mirror and holds it out so Melissa can watch as her baby crowns. She shouts, 'It's coming! I've got the urge to push!' The whole room explodes in laughter.

Two more shoves and a purplish silvery blunt-headed thing shoots out of her, face down. Faster than the eye can follow, the baby is freed from her and whisked across the room to its high trolley. A pale grey twisted tube hangs out between Melissa's legs.

'Is it the cord?' she gasps. 'It feels slimy.'

'Like an eel,' says her husband. With his arms folded, he walks to the baby's trolley and looks at it as they work on it—it's a girl. Without expression he returns to his place by the wall, then approaches the baby again. 'Netball team's lookin' good,' he says in a low voice.

A midwife brings the wrapped baby to Melissa who's still in the thick of it but keen to see. 'Oh, look how *small* she is—hang on—can I just get rid of this cramp?' She is incredibly composed and well-mannered. She is almost professional.

A quick internal tells Linda that twin two is in breach position. The tension has slackened in the room—and in the uterus, which must build up again its expulsive force.

'Any pain?'

'Not pain,' says Melissa, 'just—'

'A horrible sensation?' says a midwife sympathetically.

Soon Melissa is back on the job, good-tempered, determined, utterly focused. She's on her back, with her legs bent, heaving away. This is how it got to be called *labour*. It's slog, it's the laborious completion of something.

'Don't let the pains go, Melissa,' says Linda. '*Use* them. Big long strong pushes. Good girl. And another one. Hold it there! Don't let it slip! This is *brilliant*, Melissa. One more, if you've got it. The baby's coming down bum-first.'

'Gonna hurt more, isn't it,' gasps Melissa.

'Nup,' says Linda, 'gonna hurt less.'

Melissa's pelvic floor, with each push, is absolutely bulging. 'I want to do a wee,' she says faintly.

'Go right ahead,' says Linda, 'it's part of labour. No one cares.'

'I care,' grunts Melissa.

'*Do* it!' cries her girlfriend, 'just *do* it!'

In a sudden hush, piss gushes out and runs down in a clear stream over the swollen dark hole, making a tiny musical rilling sound.

'Good,' says Linda. 'I was worried about your bladder. Now—*show* us something, Melissa. Come on—*show* us the baby.'

'My legs are getting tired,' says Melissa. Her friends, one on each side, rush to lift up her legs: they bend her knees up to her shoulders, and give her their hands to brace her feet against.

'That's better,' says Melissa, faint but business-like. 'Ohhhhh kay—here comes another one.' Her face is clenched tight with concentration. Linda leans over, slides the white plastic amnihook into her, and ruptures the second twin's membranes. 'Are you right?' Melissa calls to her husband.

'Am *I* right?' he answers, incredulous, almost laughing. 'Yeah, *I'm* right—are *you*?'

Melissa doesn't speak. She draws a breath and utters a long, slow groan.

In a flash the midwives uncouple the lower section of the bed and whip it out of the way. One kicks the discarded half-mattress right across the room, while others draw Melissa down what's left of the bed so her bottom is level with its end. She's yelling at them: 'Hurry up! Hurry up!' They lock the stirrups into place, and raise her legs on to them. In a green blur, blond bob flying, Linda leaps between her legs—and out bursts a bum, feet, torso, shoulder-tip. Linda grabs the baby with a cloth, twists it once, twice, flips it up and over onto Melissa's belly, and draws out the head—and Melissa's husband, craning forward, sees that it's a boy. Oh—a *boy*. He didn't know there was a boy in there. Melissa knew but hadn't told him. She wanted to give him this surprise. His lips clamp into a hard line. He turns his wind-reddened face away and folds his arms across his, chest. His eyes are full of tears.

Next morning, in a ward where the sun lies in squares on the shiny floor, a teenage single mother is learning to bathe her baby. The girl is hollow-cheeked, with long dark hair, and a row of silver sleepers in each ear. But her face is full of surprised tenderness, as she gingerly cradles her baby's head in one palm, following the nurse's example. The baby cackles, it gives gasping, quivering cries. The nurse murmurs something to the girl, who shivers and says in a loud, cracked voice, 'Eeeeww *no*. I don't *want* to breastfeed. No *way*. Eeeewww *yuk*. I don't feel good about it.' Water sloshes gently in the pale plastic bath. The nurse's soft voice soothes and soothes.

In a bed screened by blue curtains, a woman lies peacefully on her back reading *Name Your Baby*. Another is ready to take her baby home; as Linda and Nik approach, she thrusts her bare legs out from under the sheet and flashes her feet at them: 'Look! I've got *ankles* again!' The room next door is empty: everyone's sneaked out on to the sunny balcony for a smoke. They are herded back in, giggling guiltily. Sharon, Nik's caesar and Zoe's mother, shows the doctors her abdominal wound. Its excellent neatness and speedy healing are universally admired. She lies back, passive and content.

Melissa of the premature twins is sitting up against her pillows, in fine fettle. Hard to recognise in her the pale, determined labourer of—was it only yesterday? Her hair is washed and fluffed out in a big cloud. She is cheerfully expressing milk for her babies who are still in neo-natal intensive. She has photos of them wedged cleverly into inverted polystyrene cups so she can see them from her pillow.

She talks only of the boy twin. His name is now the issue. Melissa and her husband have disagreed. The name he wants is 'from another generation,' says Melissa firmly. 'I'm not budging.'

Mala today looks livelier. She smiles at Linda and whispers a shy greeting. Linda examines her and pronounces her 'medically fit—ready to go home'. Her husband nods, hesitates, then points to the baby in the crib and says something in his soft voice. Linda mishears him and thinks he's telling her the baby's name. 'Does it mean something?' she asks.

The father clicks his tongue in frustration. 'Not name. *Skin.*' He urges her to note that the baby's skin is much lighter in colour than his or Mala's.

Nik stands stock still at the foot of the bed. Linda steps forward to the cot and leans over it. A beat. 'His skin,' she says clearly and carefully, 'will darken in four to six months. As soon as the sun hits him—boom. All babies are born with light skin.' She hovers over the baby. She looks up at Mala's husband. Something more needs to be said. Linda swallows and takes the plunge. 'He bears a very strong resemblance to you,' she says. 'Oh, *very* strong. Doesn't he. Yes—the father's the winner, with this one.'

A pause; then everyone breathes, moves, smiles. The doctors leave the bedside. Passing the baby's cot, Linda flutters her fingers above his fragile little skull, barely holding back a desire to touch. The baby has a pensive expression, as if he's just had an important thought but can't quite remember what it was. The feeling in the air is complex beyond words.

1995